Marker

A true story of misery

and misinformation

with an Appendix of Lies

by

Mel Green

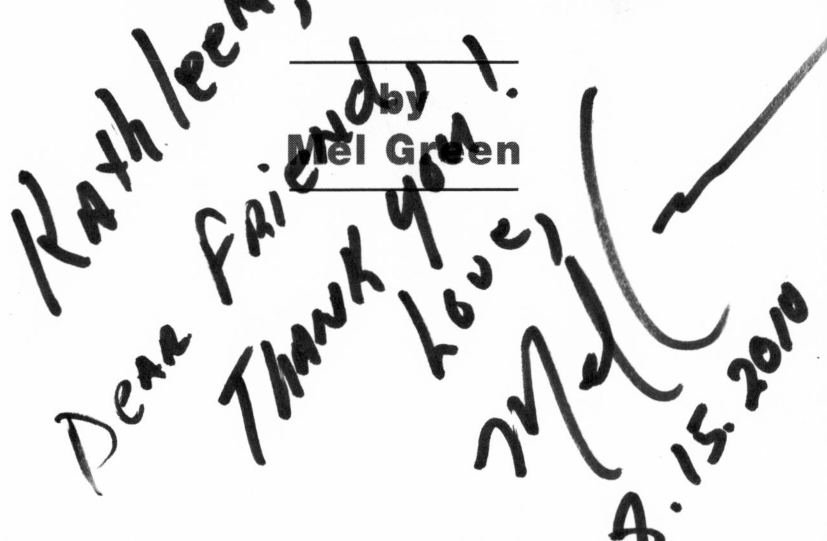

Marker

Contact:
Mel Green
info@melgreen.net

Cover photo by Gracie Harrison
Book design by Chris Yeseta

There's the person you are told you are.

There's the person you discover you are,

and then there's what you do after.

Marker

TIME THICKENED AND SLOWED THE WAY it does when disaster strikes: the burning wick rolled into the fuel puddled at my feet; a circle of blue flame opened around me like a mouth drawing a breath and *whoosh*—rose up to swallow me. There was a dry hiss as my beard turned to foul smoke ...

Attempted suicide? That's what they thought at the party. Had I intended to set myself on fire, on my thirtieth birthday—the one I was *never* supposed to have? With a fucking Tiki torch?

Chapter 1

Odessa, Texas

I'M NOT SAYING IT WAS ALL ROSES UP UNTIL the day my father told me, at fifteen years old, that I would likely be dead from a disease in just as many years. But after that day, things sure as hell took a turn for the worse.

No doubt it also had something to do with stealing Mom's station wagon, driving over to Turdy's and throwing rocks at his window. I won't go into the origin of his nickname except to say he was aptly tagged and it would likely stick. Which often led me to wonder why I hung with a lanky-boned cackler who extracted such glee from the suffering of others. But it seems both youth and crime crave company, and I was guilty of both. So there we were, on the fresh side of fifteen, in Mom's Delta 88 with the power windows; her golf clubs rattling in the back, hell-bent for the Fish Ranch. Scared mostly.

It was a warm west Texas night. The wind flapped around our heads like a loosed bolt of dark cloth. Turdy polished off our first pint of Southern Comfort and flung the empty out the window. The bottle glinted a farewell in the headlights before it shattered against the sign for the Fish Ranch. It occurred to me then how easily things are broken, how little thought or effort is required—just a sort of carelessness would get the job done; that and what an asshole my best friend was.

"Moody!" Turdy crowed as he steered into the turn. I'd let Turdy drive to feel less responsible. That and I couldn't get Dad out my head.

Dead by thirty was his estimation, and that would be after a good chunk spent flailing around like a broken sail, babbling nonsense. Being a doctor and all, I had to take him seriously. Dad didn't tell jokes or sing ditties; no bedside manner.

"Cheer up, Moody!" Turdy hollered. Turdy's not really the sort you tell things to.

"Don't be throwing shit at Bohner's sign," I hollered back, not just for the flung bottle, but for his long history of abuses. "It's disrespectful."

Not that the sign was any big deal: a hand-painted hieroglyph of a bow-legged cowboy, his fishing-pole lasso snugged tight around a buxom blue-eyed girl-fish, all curly lashes and lipstick grin—happy to be caught was the point.

But my call for respect had not been for the sign so much as for Sam Bohner and his daughter who lived out there without the benefit of wife or mother. It was also my opinion that Kaydeen Bohner was caught just like that girl-fish on the sign, but it was no fisherman's line or cowboy's lasso that held her—Kaydeen Bohner was a teenage girl caught inside a woman's body.

Like anyone with eyes, I'd seen her bolt between classes, jouncing down the halls at school: shock of red hair, equal parts Aqua-Net and bed-tangle; the hip sway—the high bounce and shiver. Books clutched to her chest did little to rein it in; it surged at gussets, peeked and spilled over here and there—a Whac-A-Mole of female maturity.

Head down, she maneuvered past the male teachers adjusting their glasses, the gabbling leer of pimple-faced boys, the narrow-lidded smirk of jealous girls—it all threatened to throw Kaydeen into a panic before she could duck into the next classroom, scurry to the back row and get that body folded-up behind a desk.

Outside the room, the locker-lined halls shrank back into quiet, but her passing lingered in the mind; her silhouette etched on book covers. Poor girl-fish, not only had she just entered the ninth grade, but Kaydeen Bohner was a new kid at school finding her own body to be the greatest obstacle to fitting in.

And I, in my own way, had done little to help her situation. Made it worse in fact. During the Sock Hop—girls' choice at the gym dance—Kaydeen had just walked that body over, put it squarely before me and asked me to dance. With her bouffant hair she seemed a full head taller than me.

And though I cannot recall the song, I do remember she landed solid in my arms, the iridescent green skin of her dress moist and heated as if just pulled from an ironing board. The scent of a female body unmasked by deodorants took hold—a cat-like scent I'd noticed venting off Mother some mornings when I brought her coffee in bed (spoon and a half of sugar, no milk). None of the other girls at school smelled like that; don't think it was allowed.

At first, I'd tried to smile, but dancing with Kaydeen was like being taken-up into something larger than myself; she moved me around the dance floor—stuck to her like one of those stuffed dolls with the stirrups you attach to your feet and dance around with.

And then I got embarrassed, aware the other kids were watching—laughing at me dancing with the new girl; the trashy one with the big boobs. Had I joined in that? Smirked behind her back? All the while the smell of her, like camphor rose up in my nose, up in my head.

When the song ended, Kaydeen seemed to set me down as a passing tornado might drop a chair out in a field. And move on.

And Turdy, of course, quick on my heels as I retreated to the bathroom, cackling and drooling with his cruel hilarity. *Why* was he my friend?

"Kaydeen Bohner," he whistled through the V gap chipped in his front tooth. "I felt sorry for you, Bert. Did you hear her mom went to the pen for kiting checks? You shoulda seen your face."

I nodded and maintained my pose: body bowed-in towards the back of the urinal, attempting to pee, but couldn't. I still had a hard-on.

When I returned to the dance, she was gone; nowhere to be found. Too much for the place she was. Too much for all of us. And I had let her leave like that, with the mark of humiliation on her.

"This it?" Turdy asked as the car tires thrummed over a cattle guard. The road veered toward a cluster of red roof tops that winked through the mesquite.

"Cut the lights," I said and Turdy fumbled for the switch. The car rolled to a stop in the sudden darkness. A backwash of dust whirled through the windows and settled as we sat listening to the ticking engine cool. The silence became louder, broke itself up into the chirr of crickets and frog croaks—the lush ripple of the creek out there in the dark. The light from the Coke machine came filtered through a lattice of clinging bugs. The moon glowed orange as a hot plate set on the tar-black sheen of the swimming pool. We had arrived.

Ranch house, whorehouse, bootleg liquor outlet, the Fish Ranch had been all that before Sam Bohner took it over. And each incarnation had left its mark upon the premises—a ramshackle history of notorious intents and purposes.

At least Bohner's had been a legitimate if impractical vision: fishing in the middle of West Texas, a semi-arid region that requires at least ten acres just to keep one scrawny steer standing. Undaunted by nay-sayers or the climate, Bohner packed his cheek with Beechnut, bent the bill of his CAT gimme cap sharp as a garden spade and set to work with a military surplus D-9 bulldozer and a crew of "wetback Mescans." They gouged out an old stock tank fed by a creaky windmill, expanded and deepened it. Berms were piled-up, and then another, second hole was purchased with sweat and diesel from the dry dirt. Now he had what amounted to two small lake beds—one higher, the other lower. Marking the ground with loping spurts of tobacco juice, he dug a network of irrigation ditches connecting the 'lakes' to a spring-fed creek that bubbled up out of the ground and flowed on south to join up with the Pecos River.

Bohner may not have parted the waters, but he certainly made it flow where it had never been before; fish swam where sand burrs and goat heads once festered. The 'lakes' were regularly stocked with perch, bass, catfish and crappie. And he made a killing selling all manner of bait: night crawlers, red wrigglers, shiners caught in the creek, blood bait, stink bait, cut bait, chicken innards and an assortment of frozen candy bars.

"Some of them fish got a sweet tooth," Sam was known to

say as he slipped a coin in the juke box and crooned along with the Everly Brothers. *Dre-e-e-am Dream Dream Dreeeam ...*

When the fish weren't biting, he'd blame the heat and invite people to the rec room to drink Big Red and shoot pool while he kept the juke box spinning. And the people came, stayed in the creaky little cabins with their duet rattle of swamp cooler and refrigerator. Some were greeted by the occasional rat stranded in the toilet bowl clawing for dear life; or a daddy-long-legs spider caught napping in a bath tub drain. It was that kind of place; funky, a little bit dangerous, like Sam Bohner. That night I caught myself wishing he was my father.

"Shiii-ut, goddamn, water's cold!" Turdy shivered as he eased into Bohner's mossy, homemade pool. It had acquired a fame all its own. Unlike the turquoise beauty shimmering out at the Odessa Country Club, Bohner's pool was filled with spring water, untreated with a soft feel and fragrance. And scary deep it was, with a four-foot shelf called the 'shallow end' that extended out about ten steps before dropping down somewhere around the Marianna's Trench.

On the bottom he'd dumped several tons of round boulders. Moss had grown over giving them the appearance of an underwater patch of fuzzy watermelons. The pool's concrete side walls were slick with the moss making it impossible to crawl out without use of the rebar ladder. It was less a swimming pool than it was a very deep man-made swimming hole—a perfect place for drowning.

"I wanna go down the slide," burbled Turdy.

"You'll make too much noise," I warned, but he ignored me just like I wanted him to.

That was the other thing—the slide—bolted together in sections, it resembled an industrial sluice more suited for pouring concrete than slamming people into the water at a forty-five degree angle. It must have been three stories tall and painted rattle-can silver. From its top rung you could look out over the whole spread: the roofs of the six little cabins and the two old trailers where the Mexicans camped—a ramshackle paradise.

I peeled off my jeans and tried to ease in, but slipped

and was up to my neck in cold water. Then the slimy bottom dropped away beneath and I was treading out over the deep end. Turdy had emerged from the depths and was paddling for the ladder when a flood-light banged on and we froze in the blinding glare.

Turdy shivered in the shadows. I hugged the moss-slick side. Listened to the incriminating slap of pool water.

"You gotta be a registered guest to swim here."

Her voice came out of the dark in a creepy, unexpected way. She already had a kind of a low voice resonating in that ample chest of hers. And I think she was just plain fucking with us. Then I saw her, watching from behind the slide, her eyes big and glassy like those stuffed deer heads in the rec room.

"Hey, no problem, we're outta here," Turdy warbled and heaved himself out, his boney ass dribbling water. Kaydeen couldn't help herself, she gave an amused snort and stepped from behind the slide—barefoot, sweatshirt and cut-offs ripped up the sides, white pockets dangling down over the swell of tanned thighs.

"What's so goddamn funny?" Turdy sputtered as he grabbed his pants. Kaydeen shook her head, "Jus wonderin' what happened to the rest of yer ass?"

"Well, whatever I got you can kiss it goodbye."

She giggled as he struggled to get his pants pulled up, and then she switched her eyes on me hanging on the pool's edge.

"... And what brings you out so late?"

I'd practiced what to say, but that went to hell under her look. I doubted it all—stealing the car, driving to the Fish Ranch—the sum total of my life up to then. Everything.

"Uh, just couldn't sleep I guess."

She reached and doused the floodlight. The moon danced orange again on the water; crickets and frogs resumed their pulse.

"Good thing Daddy's not back from Pecos," she said looking away. "He'd have you boys begging for yer mama 'bout now."

"Water's too damn cold anyway," Turdy piped-up. "Come on, Bert, let's git."

"Yawl drinking?" Kaydeen asked with a shift in tone.

"Southern Comfort," Turdy said. "Already finished a pint, got another in the car."

"Bull."

"Out in the car. Want some?"

"Something to do while I'm waiting."

"What you waitin' for?" Turdy asked.

"Waitin' on your skinny butt to go git the liquor."

Turdy cackled and trotted off towards the car while Kaydeen worked a mashed pack of Marlboros from her cut-offs, dug one out with her chipped nails and struck a match.

"Whose car?" she asked.

"Uh, it's mine."

"You drive a station wagon?"

"It's mostly my mom's."

"Bet she don't know you got it."

"You might be right about that."

'Must've wanted to git some place pretty bad steal your mama's car."

"Yeah … I guess maybe. I just did. Dunno why I do most things."

She considered my words, then tapped the ash off her cigarette, took another puff and looked at me.

"How come you never came back to school?" I asked.

"Buncha stuck-up people. Cowboys are better dancers anyways. Drive their own cars too."

She had a right to punish me some. It was time to make a move. I scrabbled up the moss-slick side of the pool, dragged myself on land, belly-down like a crocodile to obscure my scrotum shrunk-up tight as a dove's breast; penis backed-up in a pucker of skin.

Got to my feet with my back to her, grabbed my jeans and made to stick a leg in, but it got stuck. I hopped around all my goods flopping, struggling for balance until I fell over smack on the concrete. This merited a laugh from Kaydeen.

"To hell with it," I groaned and rolled onto my back, naked, shriveled, goose flesh coming up. It got quiet.

"You all right?" she asked.

"Not really," I said. "But there's not much I can do about it." I began to squirm back into my jeans inch by inch, the opposite of a snake shedding its skin. She smoked and watched my progress. I didn't much care anymore or at least that's what I wanted to start believing.

Turdy reappeared, whiskey bottle held like the only trophy he'd ever won. He unscrewed the cap, turned it up and after a couple of he-man glugs, he beat his chest as it burned down.

"Whoo-eeee!"

Kaydeen pulled three cold bottles from the Coke machine. We drained them half-empty and topped them with the Southern Comfort so sweet and strong it made your head swim when you swallowed it. Turdy let out one of his extended musical burps that never failed to win applause in the cafeteria. Kaydeen rolled her eyes and looked out into the darkness.

"The creek's warmer at night," she said as if recalling a far-off land. "Warmer than the pool. It's the rocks under all that shallow water—like a magnifying glass, it heats them up during the day."

She stood and walked away a few steps. We just sat there watching her, waiting to hear some more about those warm rocks, and then she stopped and turned as if just remembering us, "Yawl coming?"

The black surface of the creek chewed the moon into a thousand pieces. Turdy kicked off his pants and charged in. Kaydeen took a swallow from her bottle, set it on the ground and waded in wearing her clothes. I followed. The water was warmer; the small smooth rocks shifting under your weight, would reform and pocket your feet with each step.

"Hey, I thought we was skinny dipping," Turdy called out.

"You're skinny dipping so shut up," I said.

Kaydeen demonstrated how to lie down in the creek maneuvering feet first, so you could bump gently over the smooth rocks until you were swept all the way into the slower, deeper water of the lower lake. Then we'd climb up the muddy bank, flop in the creek and do it again. The repeated rhythm quieted the swarm in my head. I was simply there in my skin feeling one of the last warm nights before autumn closed in.

Hair dripping, Kaydeen and I lay back on the bank of the lower lake. We gazed up at the stars to the music of Turdy heaving his guts up over in a bush.

The night sky removed of all horizon and edges became a vastness I was hurtling through; like a hood ornament on a really big car. And when I closed my eyes, the acceleration became a light that pulsed through my body, building in brightness and intensity until, afraid I might get sick, I opened my eyes, and spread my hands out wide to stop the momentum. That's when I touched her hand.

I turned to find her gazing in a still, settled-in way like she'd been staring for a while. Usually people look away when you catch them staring. This was not the kind of look you could easily turn away from—it was the kind of look that makes you do something.

Her lips were plump, dry as caterpillars, and then her tongue peeked out, thick like a third lip between the other two, and with it came moisture. Together, our mouths opened upon each other and sealed into a tunnel of shared breath passed back and forth.

When she pulled her mouth away, it was as if a window had been thrown open and I was back in the cold world. She sat up, looked around. Then with one motion pulled her wet shirt up over her head. As she lifted her arms, I saw the dark patches in her armpits, dense and pubic.

My eyes got caught on her breasts. Refused to let go—fixed like a starving infant's as she laid back, arms folded behind her head, face luminous, the dark tufts, her scent mingled with the smell of lake water, the damp earth beneath us.

"I only done it one time," she said. "He come into my room, one of the Mescans, but different. More like an Indian he was. Come through the window. I knew it was him. Seen him looking at me."

"He lay down on top of me. Next day he was gone. Probably thought I'd tell Daddy. That's the only time."

Her gaze fell upon me. Settled. "And what about you?"

I mumbled something about a girl at summer camp, but the story grew flimsy as I talked so I just let it drift off with, "… anyway, we had some fun …"

There was the glint of amusement in her eyes; a slight smile teased at her lips.

"Show me," she said a hint of challenge in her voice. "Show me what you done with that girl."

Turdy heaved again in the bushes. My water-puckered fingers trembled at the button of her wet cut-offs; the impossible angle of attack, the unyielding denim button hole. Finally, she took mercy, reached down and with a twist of her fingers released the top button. She waited, patiently amused, while I struggled with the zipper.

Her hips lifted and, with a side-shimmy, she helped me wrench the wet shorts down while I did my best to pretend I wasn't having a severe wrist cramp. By that time we were both half-covered in mud, and still there were my jeans to deal with. With one mucky hand, I worked them halfway off while maintaining a prolonged kiss for fear if I stopped she might get a good breath of fresh oxygen, come to her senses and call a time out.

My arms shook as I slid up on top of her, a paste of grit mortared between us—I was shaking—afraid that she would stop me or maybe that she wouldn't.

Then I couldn't find it. The place. *Where* was the place? There was the abundant muff diving down to parted thighs. It was in *there* somewhere. As if in answer, she levered her pelvis up into my ignorant hand and to my surprise I found it somewhat further south than expected. *Were they all like that?*

My penis bumped along, caught like a blind man's cane. She reached down between us and took me in hand; pumped her hips up and I pressed through a fine grit, resisting folds gave way triggering an "Oh," to come out of her like someone just dropped something that's about to break. Muddy arms reached around me. Another adjustment of her hips and I docked firmly against pubic bone.

"Don't move," she instructed and urgently pressed the palms of her hands flat against my shoulders.

"Okay, I won't," which sounded not only unnecessary, but amplified in the moment—ridiculous.

We lay still, coupled in the mire; oozing as if she were the earth itself—mud become animated, given arms to pull me into this softest entrance, and as water rippled and frogs croaked, I felt all my different parts and feverish thoughts organize themselves around an invisible and growing force, like iron filings around a magnet; they were all lining up, flexing into place with a rapidly building precision.

"Pull out!" she hissed. "Now!"

And that was the absolute last thing my body wanted to do—stop the perfect internal organization that was occurring—unplug myself from this original warmth—pull out into the cold confusion of the world.

She arched against me, muscular, slaked in clay. A short cry, her lips peeled up into a smile all her own, gapped teeth caught in moonlight.

And out I pulled myself with a wheezing sound never made before, pressed against her belly, all my molecules now organized into a singular looming pressure, like a charlie-horse that once it gets started you know it's not going to stop only this felt much better. A hot rope of pleasure loped out of me with such force that I felt my physical self turning inside out, shooting right out of me: hair, toes, jelly eyes and liquid bone all being bumped out through the pin hole in my penis—insides emptied out into a wetness glistening there on her stomach.

And in the wake of this severe pleasure, before it had hardly subsided, came Dad's voice: *Did you get out in time? Well?*

Oh, had I gotten her pregnant? What a grievous sin against humanity—the bad gene passed on! To have done it with the knowledge, the very thing I had been warned against.

And it all came flooding back to fill the vacuum where urgency had been—the whole bad news scene from that afternoon: Dad coming into my room, the letter in his hand—"regarding your natural father," he had said.

Never knew my natural father. I had been adopted at two. So I thought maybe I'd inherited something. And I was right though not in a way I might have hoped.

Dad sat on the bed. He never sat on the bed. He was not a sit-on-the-bed kind of dad. The letter, sent by the neurologist treating my biological father, dying somewhere it said, dying from Huntington's disease, a hereditary disease, or they wouldn't have gone to all the trouble of finding me.

The floor had gone mushy. A Tilt-A-Whirl reeled in my stomach as my dad (the adopted one), being a doctor, laid it all out: it was a disease of the brain you see. My brain. And as my brain deteriorated, things would start to lose control like walking and talking, and then a gradual, but complete breakdown of the system. Me.

Then you die? I asked.

"Yes, you die." He answered. "There is no known cure," he said taking off his glasses.

This is no dream. You are wide awake; those are your hands moist and clenched in your lap. Those are you father's eyes unblinking.

"So you think I have it," I asked. "This thing?"

"What makes your case unusual," Dad continued with a hint of scientific appreciation which quickly shifted into a dead serious look into my eyes. "The disease has been manifested on both sides of your natural father's parents. It seems both carried the gene ..."

I started to realize nothing would be the same after this.

"... But until you show symptoms we don't know whether you are carrying the Huntington's gene or not. But if you are carrying the gene, you will get the disease."

"Symptoms?"

"Loss of coordination, diminished mental acuity, concentration, confusion, difficulty with speech. A flailing of the appendages ..."

But I had them already! All the symptoms were up and operating!

Follow me through my teenage day of dropped books, stair stumbles, forgotten homework, lost library books, complete and total inability to listen in class, garbled responses. Not to mention an all around stooginess exampled by hanging with the likes of Turdy—all sound evidence of a deteriorating brain.

"Well," I stammered (another symptom), "How long have I got? I mean if I have it *now*?"

"In the case of juvenile onset, survival would be unlikely beyond thirty."

There was some talk regarding propagation, the risk of passing the disease on. When I asked about children, the answer was a grim shake of his head—*no.* A vasectomy at some future date was advised. He could arrange it.

Later that night, lying in bed, I made an inventory of my body. My feeble teenage circle of reasoning moved something like: if I was using the same brain to think with that might already be deteriorating, meaning I could be getting bad messages from an already damaged brain; and if my entire thinking process was in fact a part of that very deterioration—well, then *what* could I know for any certainty?

Nothing.

My entire point of view had been altered. Everything was now seen through the filter of this disease—on the lookout for symptoms I had previously never considered. It was as if doom, garbed in a lab coat, had stepped in and begun to whisper in my ear—a perpetual babble of threat and mortality.

That's when I noticed the foot. My right foot twitching. Then it stopped. Then it started. Then I tried to make it stop. It wouldn't. The disease was down there in my foot, signaling to me: *Here I am, pretty soon I'll get up in your arms and then your mouth and we'll have a good ol' time.*

Turdy showed me a book once; torture and execution was the subject. It said a hanged man ejaculates just before he dies. There it is then, the last effort as one expires, a final blind toss for some procreative landing zone—reflex of the ever-chugging gene train. Damn the torpedoes! Into the breech!

The brain is capable of deluding even itself: imagining things where there are none, refusing to see things when there clearly are things; tweaking the perspective to see what it wants to see: like the devils *or* the angels in the Escher drawing—all depends on what you're looking for.

Mom had reached the bottom of her third bourbon and didn't have much to say regarding this news from Dad—something about her missing breast and what she had suffered. And I knew she had suffered, but I found little comfort in that. I also found I couldn't just lie there in bed twitching. Like that hanged man, I had to do something. So I waited until they were asleep and sawing the big logs—then I took the car.

"Hey, can I get in on the party?" Turdy was looking down on Kaydeen and me, slack-jawed, a greedy gleam in his eyes.

"Don't be a jerk, Turdy," I reached over and handed Kaydeen her shirt to cover herself. But she didn't take it. Just laid there fully exposed, exuding a confidence not generally found in naked teenage girls.

"Whadda ya say, Kaydeen?" Turdy leered.

"… Maybe if you ask me just right," she purred.

Was she serious? She had just done *it* with me. Now she was going to do *it* with him? With Turdy?

Or was she just teasing him? Had she finally taken control of that body and decided to see what would happen if she stopped cowering under the attention it brought her and instead turned it back on people and let it intimidate them?

While Turdy and I labored to sort her intentions, the sound of an approaching truck was heard. Kaydeen sprang to action—all composure evaporated as she grabbed her shorts. We could see headlights bounce along the road. Then it veered off the road and turned in our direction; beams wiped across the cedars above us, gears downshifted—there was no mistaking it—the truck was headed right towards us.

"Fuck, it's her old man!" Turdy dropped to the ground. Kaydeen wriggled into her wet shorts. Naked was suddenly a terrible thing to be. Her smell was all over me as I wrenched my jeans up. Sam Bohner would smell that smell right before he broke my neck.

"Hide!" she hissed, "In the water!" We belly crawled, slid into the lake; our heads low down below the bank. The truck kept coming.

Lying in the shallows, diesel fumes burned my nose. The weight of the truck resonated in the water as it lunged and humped over ground. Another downshift, and just as it seemed about to drive right in on top of us, it wheeled and turned—the twin beams slashing across the surface of the lake. Gears shifted, the truck reversed idling up to the bank where we hid. Sam Bohner was seriously fucking with us.

Turdy lifted his arms up into the air as if to surrender. The cowardly wheedle of his face drained of color, mouth shaped into a plea for mercy just as it disappeared behind a wall of water. Like a rogue wave, it knocked Turdy down; landed on us so heavy I couldn't get my breath, lost footing and then it was all wiggling and alive—thick with fish!

The fish stocking truck, making a delivery, had dumped several tons of water and fish on top of us. They bounced off our heads, slapped against our bodies: bass, trout, perch, catfish croaked as they banged against our chests and shoulders, churned the water with their numbers; fins and tails brushed against my belly and thighs.

Turdy held his arms cringed against his chest. And Kaydeen, standing waist deep, caught her breath and looked at me, her mouth open in wonder and relief; eyes bright she began to laugh, shoulders thrown back, bare-breasted like a seanymph cavorting with her minions. Laughing, she scooped up a wriggling fish and flung it at me like a souvenir thrown from a float—queen of her own parade.

Chapter 2

Sewanee Military Academy

THE BUS SHUDDERED TO A STOP. OUTSIDE THE window, darkness had come all at once. The driver hocked-up a chest rattle and commenced to waxing the floor with it when the doors flapped open and, in a burst of cold air, a short blonde cadet stomped on board in a pair of shiny black jump boots that appeared to be laced-up to his chin and proceeded to have a psychotic fit.

"WHAT KIND OF PIECE OF SHIT ARE YOU!?" He yelled, red-cheeked from the cold. Dressed in a blue-gray uniform: black stripe down the pant legs, Ike jacket, chevrons laddered up the sleeve, saber rattling in a shiny metal scabbard—he was full to bursting of himself—all four feet.

"OPEN YER FUCKIN' MOUTH, NUMB NUTS!"

I looked around to see whom he might be hollering at, saw that skid-mark of greased hair I'd been staring at for the past hour and remembered that, besides the driver, I was the only one on the stinking bus.

It was an old school bus, purple and white with Sewanee Military Academy stenciled on either side, sent to haul me, like so much reluctant cargo, up the mountain from Monteagle, Tennessee—a place that appeared to be little more than an intersection with a couple of weathered motels and a sad-as-hell gas station. The Greyhound from Nashville, reeking of disinfectant and baby vomit, had dropped me there to stare at a pinup posed on a greasy wall calendar from two-years ago—Miss Snap-on Tools didn't seem too happy to be there either.

"IS YER NAME KELLY?" The blonde cadet mouthed in an exaggerated way as if I were mentally impaired which was not entirely out of the question. A clipboard appeared clenched in one fist while he pointed at me with the other.

I began to nod my head not so much in answer to his queries, as in bafflement at his performance. He barked with such a total exertion of his being that he appeared to lift momentarily off the ground—bouncing forwards and back like a miniature, hyper-active dog.

"STOP NODDING YOUR HEAD LIKE YER GIVING A TWO DOLLAR BLOW JOB AND SAY *YES, SIR*!"

"Yes, sir."

"LOUDER!"

"Yes, sir."

"OPEN UP, PUSSY LIPS! SING IT!"

"YES SIR!" I managed to shout though I could not help but wonder if my lips actually brought this to mind and immediately tried to make my lips harder and less pussy-like.

"STAND THE FUCK UP!"

I sprang to my feet which promptly drove my skull into the metal luggage rack overhead.

"Watch yer head, dumbshit! I hope that knocked some goddamn sense into you. But then you are from Tex-Ass. I'M SORRY WE DON'T HAVE ANY GOATS HERE FOR YOU TO FUCK, COWBOY!"

Things hadn't gone well since that night back at the Fish Ranch. On the way home, to demonstrate a 'doughnut,' I floored the station wagon and turned the wheel to make it spin on the dirt road. But I lost control and took out a five-foot mesquite bush before coming to a sickening stop against a fence post. I'd wrecked Mother's car.

"LOOK AT ME WHEN I AM TALKING TO YOU, GOAT FUCKER!"

A caustic blue poured from his eyes and ran over my features. It got disturbingly quiet as he scrutinized my longish hair, the thin black trench coat, my scotch grain penny loafers with the kiltie fringe. His voice dropped to an intimate register.

"Uh, you queer, Kelly?"

"Sir?"

"Knob gobbler? Lance the raisin? Which is it?"

"I ... "

He slid in next to me on the seat; snugged up close and removed his officer's hat: admired the gold strap above the jut of shiny black bill; flipped it around and seemed to contemplate for a moment the eagle-crested insignia of the Sewanee Military Academy, and then, as if suddenly weary of all the bluster, he let out a sigh.

"See, Kelly, once upon a time we had us a queer up here at the academy. Didn't do well—hung himself from a tree out there in the woods. Pissed his pants they say. Quitter is what I say. Goddamn quitter. Wanna see the tree? You and me can take a little walk in the woods and find it. Take some rope along, if you get scared you can hold my hand. You scared, Kelly? I'd be scared. Because if you don't do what I say, when I say it, the way I say—I'll shove this saber up your ass. Am I getting through, goatfucker?"

Turdy's old man had come and bailed him out. But when it came my turn, all I could do was stare at the black phone on the detective's desk while he tapped his pencil on the report. Couldn't bring myself to ring Dad up at 4:00 AM and tell him his son was in jail. The same son he had adopted twelve years earlier, had welcomed into his successful life.

"You decline your phone call?" the detective asked through a yawn. "Well, you might feel differently in a few hours," he added with a bleary wink.

"YOU FUCKED-UP! THEY YANKED YOUR ASS OUTTA GOAT-FUCKER HIGH SCHOOL AT MID-TERM!"

The screaming blonde cadet had a name tag that said: 'Nagle'.

"They couldn't wait until next year to get rid of you!"

Probably right about that one. It got him up again, like a wolf browsing for a place to park his teeth. Then he went quiet, turned away and paced thoughtfully towards the rear of the bus.

"And if you fuck-up here, well, what's next, Goatfucker? Reeform School? Juvie Prep with the rest of the trash 'till you move on up to da Big House."

His head pivoted back to consider me, "Is that what you're all about, Kelly—gettin' sent to prison so you can have your corn hole decorated on Christmas Eve? IS THAT WHAT'S GOING ON HERE, SISTER!? I'M JUST ASKIN'!"

There had been this kid in the cell next to mine, must have been asleep when they first locked me up. All of a sudden—out of nowhere—he piped-up and nearly scared me off the metal slab where I had been contemplating the mental and physical insult of incarceration: the cold metal, no mattress, the burning bulb that never went off, the crude cross scratched into the green paint with the caption *Save Me Jesus.*

"I'm sixteen," the kid said, a year older than me. "I been in jail for fourteen days. My goddamn teeth are fuzzy," he complained with a frazzled intensity.

Seems after a week, his dad had shown up to bail him out. But they arrested him right on the spot for an outstanding warrant. "Now my old man's in jail, I'm in jail and Mom is too goddamn drunk to bail either of us out. Fuckinhell man, I sure could use a tooth brush."

"DO YOU UNDERSTAND ANYTHING THAT I AM SAYING?!" Cadet Nagle, wheeled around at the back of the bus, seized the grip of his saber and unsheathed it with such an impressive ringing of metal that I found myself marveling that it was actually a real sword, double-edged and gleaming as it welted through the air and came down with a TWHACK broadside on a bus seat.

"YOU BETTER MOVE WHILE YOU STILL CAN!" Nagle sang as he stalked down the aisle, moving towards me, slashing the saber down in a repetition of fierce whacks. WHIP CRACK! WHIP CRACK! He laid the broadside across the bus seats, scaring up dust motes in the wan yellow light.

Instinctively, I fled before him, harried by the slapping blade. Down the aisle, toward the bus door I scrambled. Lost my footing on the steps and slipped in a puddle from the snow he'd tramped in—landed sprawled on my back—legs hanging half way out of the bus.

"Gawdamn, they didn't tell me you were handicapped too! Shit let me get that door for you."

The operating handle was stationed by the driver who sat puffing a damp hand-rolled. He stared out the window as if nothing unusual was taking place while Nagle snaffled the handle and closed the doors, clamping my leg just below the knee in its hard rubber mouth.

"GET THE FUCK UP!"

Then just as quickly he opened the door releasing me. I attempted to roll over and pull myself up, but he closed the door, knocking me back down.

"I can't tell if you are trying to get on the bus or off. Which is it, Kelly, ON or OFF?" The door opened and closed in quick succession—three times it chewed at my legs.

Finally, I yanked my right leg free, lost my loafer, but rose shakily to my feet, one sock soaked from the frigid puddle of snow melt. Panting, I glared at him with what could only be interpreted as homicidal rage, and he returned my glare, unblinking with a rosy-cheeked smirk on his smooth face.

Dad was waiting in the lobby when they released me from my cell. The grim set of his face said it all—eyes dark with anger, unbearable to look at. Come to bail his son out of jail. The offense of it was entirely outside the realm of his behavior, of who he was and where he found himself at this insulting hour. And as I looked at him, heart in a tumult: overwhelming gratitude for getting me out of that cell, and boundless shame for having made him do it. Oh, it was clear there in his face; clear as a bleeding wound—I had disappointed him. Or was this just the high-water mark; the finale? The latest and largest of many disappointments?

Mother was a deafening silence that occupied the car. I skulked into the back seat and closed the door on the smoke-filled interior. As we pulled onto the highway, no longer able to contain herself, she stubbed out her Salem and with a half-turn of her head fired into the back seat, "Your father has never even seen the inside of a jail! He is a pillar in the community. Why don't you just kill us!"

I sat engulfed in shame.

Kill them? Like an enemy. Tarnish their standing in the community. Humiliate them to death, further evidence that I was not one of them. I was someone else—certainly not the two year-old child they had met in the park that day. That day the lady came to visit. She had worn serious brown clothes with an authority that registered in the faces and sounds made by the other people in the room, the people I considered at the time to be my mother and father. I got the feeling something was up about me.

One of the problems with being a kid is no one bothers to explain anything even though you'd have to be dead not to have an inkling. For instance, when they said, "Let's go for a walk in the park," there was something in the sound of it that told me to skip that walk.

This was followed up with, "It will be fun." Always suspect. But any protests were hushed. My jacket appeared; the door was opened, my hand firmly grasped.

At the park, a man and a woman waited—Hillard and Arlene—the 'very nice people' the lady who came to visit had spoken of as she tugged me along. Together we sat on a bench. Coded small talk swirled over my head, and then the lady rose and said goodbye. When I stood to follow, it was made clear that I'd be staying.

Lured inside their car with gifts, we drove into the night, Hillard and Arlene and I. In the back seat, I scribbled with crayons until the colors could no longer be seen; only the waxy smell. All colors, I discovered that night, smelled and tasted the same.

They sat in the front and smoked a lot. It was as if Hillard and Arlene had a small, damp fire going up there in the front seat, and with the windows up it became difficult to breathe. So I slid down on the floor board and found a pocket of air. I lay curled there, and as I breathed the clear air, memory seemed to dissolve in the warm thrum of the road passing under us.

"...You gonna hit me, Kelly? Is that what you're thinking?" Cadet Nagle seemed like a quivering, highly volatile gelatin that had temporarily taken the shape of a young man. His face, inches away, a drop of his spittle cooled on my cheek as he rasped, "Go on, Kelly. Let's get things settled right up top."

He had eaten roast beef for lunch.

"Well, since you lack the cojones to hit me what is it? ON OR OFF!"

"Off," I barely choked out, so angry I banked tears in my eyes; anything to make him shut up and find my goddamn shoe.

"Then get the fuck off the bus NOW!" I turned towards the door, but saw it was only half-opened and hesitated.

"GO BOY!" He shouted. I lurched down the steps CLUMP SQUISH, wet sock slapping. The saber whistled through the air as I pressed myself into the door's rubber cleft. It fell stinging across my backside, followed by a boot, then the abrupt release through the breach and I was delivered out into a world that I was in no way dressed for.

Chapter 3

How's the Cow

KERN (SHORT FOR COLONEL) WAS IN HIS seventies, uniformed in Army khaki, bald head daubed with liver spots. Like a gentle old grandfather, he surveyed my form through a pair of blurry horn rims. A limp measuring tape hung from his neck, the numbers faded to a series of smudges. Then, with little more than a grunt, he rose from his desk, looped the tape around my neck and began to strangle me, stopping only when he had determined my exact collar size.

A wall of cubbied stacks rose up behind him, easily sixteen feet from floor to ceiling. Kern kicked a ladder that slid on tracks, mounted it and climbed up several rungs, reached some boxes and called out like an auctioneer:

"Twelve uniform shirts grey."

The boxes of the shirts, three to a box tumbled towards me. These would be sent out weekly to be boiled and passed through a button crunching device before being shellacked and pressed to a nipple-rasping stiffness.

Next, Kern attacked my inseam, running the tape from my instep up the inside of my leg until the back of his hand smacked into my balls. Again, he consulted the smudges on his tape while I bent over and groaned.

"Two trousers winter grey. You'll grow into these," he muttered and flung a couple pair of wool pants the thickness of a saddle blanket. In addition to providing warmth, the coarse wool was a natural depilatory, worked like a slow moving belt sander to daily grind away the hair from thighs and calves. Clothing should hurt seemed the guiding principle; uncomfortable garments kept the mind sharp, better able to decipher what infraction was currently being screamed into your face.

Done with the formality of measuring, Kern 'eyeballed' the rest of my parts as he tossed various items of clothing, calling out their official designation as they tumbled towards me.

"Two trousers summer grey. One Ike jacket." (Way too big.)

"One dress blouse. Two trousers dress white."

Occasionally, he would pause, consider me, then turn away grumbling.

"One pair jump boots leather black." (A size too large.)

"Two pair gloves dress white. One pair gloves wool grey." (I immediately put them on).

One garrison cap.

One dress hat.

One hat cover dress white.

One hat cover rain.

One rain coat.

One over coat. (In the West Point style with scarlet under the shoulder cape. It would eventually be bought by some hippie at a second-hand clothing store.)

I tottered off to my assigned room beneath the forehead-high stack of issued goods. The room, illuminated by a naked hundred watt bulb in the ceiling, was furnished with a dented metal wardrobe locker, a two-man desk that looked to have been hewn by forest dwarves wielding flint tools (the surface was gouged with the initials of those that had come before me). A paint-chipped metal bunk with folded mattress was shoved against one wall. A pair of bare windows and a cast iron radiator occupied the back wall. Not quite jail, but a solid reminder—it could only get worse.

I began shoving my pile of stuff into the wardrobe locker:

Twelve socks nylon black (foot-rotting).

Eight T-shirts white (embossed with itchy SMA purple felt letters).

One pair fatigue overalls green (self-wedgie inducing).

Two shirts dress white.

Two ties (four in hand) black.

One brass button board.

One tin Brasso to keep shiny bright all pieces of metal attached to my uniform.

I had crammed most of the stuff into the locker and turned to make-up the bunk so I could crawl into it and hide when Nagle strode into the room with his nose in the air like something smelled dead.

"STAND AT ATTENTION WHEN AN OFFICER ENTERS YOUR ROOM!"

I complied.

"PULL YOUR FUCKING CHIN IN!"

I did so. Nagle walked over, reached up as high as he could, grabbed the wardrobe locker, tilted it forwards until it crashed to the floor spilling the contents.

"LEARN HOW TO FOLD YOUR SHIT, KELLY!"

He executed a snappy pivot and was out the door. I had no idea how to fold my shit. There was no seasoned roommate waiting to impart knowledge, warnings, or guidance of any sort through this arcane outpost. How was I supposed learn to fold my shit? Having no idea how to behave promised to be as humiliating as being dressed in the unfamiliar and ill-fitting clothes: the hat was held up by my ears, the scratchy wool pants were four inches too long. Not only did I feel stupid, but a glance at my reflection in the bare window confirmed that, in fact, I looked stupid. And so I began to crumble into, not a post, but a pre-traumatic stress disorder—that would be the anticipation of the imminent disaster ahead of me.

As I heaved the metal locker upright, two bursts sounded from a high-powered electronic bell system that could be felt in your molars. Then the rumble of feet as the corps of three-hundred cadets moved out into the hallways and down the stairs. They wore:

One Ike jacket with name tag.

One tie black.

One cap garrison.

I stepped out of my room and merged with the swarm; allowed myself to be carried along down the stairs, out the doors and back out into the stupefyingly cold night.

The yard was lit up like a gulag under the glare of floodlights; the power lines swagged with icicle snots, the surface of the quadrangle iced like a sheet cake.

Hoping to escape notice, I shambled along within the gray mass of uniformed boys. But they began to spontaneously organize themselves, forming a pattern around the quadrangle as if each man had been assigned a square on an invisible chess board. And wherever I happened to be standing, it seemed I was always on somebody else's square.

Guidance came with a series of anonymous nudges, kicks and bumps. I caromed along like a played-out pinball until I rattled into a slot at the end of a line in back of three other lines—the four squads that made up my platoon, one of six platoons that made up the three companies of a—BATTALION TEN-HUT!

Three hundred cadets came to attention facing Quintard Hall and its big silver dick of a flag pole. Erected from tumbled blocks of sandstone a foot thick, Quintard rose five stories tall. Twin turrets ran up the front and crested in gothic battlements. Flood lights mounted in the crenels, tilted down like cannon to blast a glare over the cadets assembled below. It was a medieval keep, impervious and drear, anchored to a cold mountain top in Tennessee. I was fucked.

Ice cracked from its rope as the flag was lowered and folded while all shivered at attention; each of us chuffing fog, leached of color by the floodlights' glare. Any sensible soul could see it was ludicrous to be outdoors dressed in anything less than One Parka Inuit. Someone dearly needed to break ranks and holler out, "Fuck this shit!" But I was cold and scared and my clothes didn't fit.

RIGHHHT FACE!

Everyone turned except me. The one cog out of sync. I quietly eased myself around until I faced in the same direction as the other three hundred.

FORWARD HARCH!

Into the basement of Quintard we marched. I followed those in front of me to a table set for ten and like the others, I came to a stop behind a chair.

"SEATS!"

If it had been the Arctic Circle outside, inside it was a moldering swamp thick with a haze of seared grease. The farty reek of boiled cabbage with an unidentifiable base note of foulness lurking beneath it all—burnt hair?

In contrast to the glare of the prison lights outside, within the basement a crypt-like yellow glow seemed to suppurate from the bug-house globes that hung from the ceiling.

The room was bathed in a spectrum of light that was neither dark enough nor light enough—the eyes constantly worked to focus—a canny maneuver to camouflage the condition of the cuisine strewn before us. It looked like chicken. There was a familiar shape to the pieces, but unusual lengths of bone protruded from flesh that appeared eerily flattened as if run over by heavy equipment prior to being, not so much fried as *stewed* in grease.

There was a stainless steel pot of what appeared to be mashed potatoes, but of a grayish tint and loose consistency. They did not heap on the plate so much as puddle and disperse. Another industrial platter offered a pile of thinly sliced meat with an iridescent sheen near the center and dry curled edges as if it had been both freeze-dried and boiled. And something somewhere on the table just plain stank.

My eyes darted about the gathered faces seeking signs of scurvy. Yet, few appetites seemed dampened for at the command of "SEATS!" a din erupted as three hundred boys pulled chairs out, sat and seized cutlery to joust for their portion.

There were four first-year cadets or 'new guys' on either side of the table; a platoon sergeant at one end and Nagle, of course, sat like a tiny despot at the head. He ignored the scramble for victuals, poured himself a glass of murky iced-tea and then stared at me until I felt compelled to look his way.

"Kelly, how's the cow?" he asked as if making a pleasant inquiry about the weather on my side of the table. The clatter of cutlery dropped a note; the passing and getting of food slowed, became more cautious.

"Sir?" I stammered in confusion.

"How's the cow?" He repeated.

Was it slang? Did he want me to pass the milk? Should I give it a taste and report whether or not it was sour? Something was certainly ripe on the table.

"We are waiting, Kelly. Everyone will stop eating until Kelly tells us. How's the Cow?" Motion around the table ground to a grudging halt.

"Sir, I don't know anything about the cow," my face glowed with the shame of keeping my table mates from their offal.

"Then you will sit at attention, Kelly," Nagle said and turned towards a big-eared, skinny guy seated across from me whose parts jangled with the looseness of a dropped marionette.

"Ween?" Nagle called out.

"Sir!" Cadet Ween wound-up the slack in his limbs, pulled himself to attention in his chair. But his name tag said FORREST. Not Ween.

"Ween, How's the Cow?"

"Sir, she walks, she talks, she's full of chalk, I squeeze her tit she never balks!" barked Ween, a trifle too loudly judging from the expression on Nagle's face.

"Very good, Ween. Now let's enjoy our supper."

Still at attention, I watched as a plate was passed from man to man, each dished up a serving of one item until it had made the round and was set before Nagle. He studied it with visible disdain.

"Ween, do I eat peas?" He simpered.

"Sir, I guess not, sir." Ween responded.

"You *guess*? I hate fucking peas, Ween. And *they* are on my plate. I want them gone."

The plate was lifted by the boy next to Nagle and passed back to Ween who took it and scraped the offending peas off onto his plate. The corrected plate was then passed back where it settled once again before Nagle.

"I want all the peas gone, Ween. I don't want to see any peas on this table unless they are on your plate. Unless someone else would care for peas?"

No one spoke as Ween emptied the remaining contents of the serving bowl into a pale green heap on his plate. The peas had the appearance of puckered pellets, rations left over from the last war or possibly the one before. I watched Ween dig in with a spoon, and without a moment's hesitation, shovel them into his mouth.

"I'll have some peas," I said without thinking. Ween stopped in mid-chew as did everyone else at the table.

Nagle put his fork down and smiled at me; he wiped his lips with his napkin, took a sip of his murky tea.

"You are at attention, Kelly. Even an ignorant goat-fucking spic like you can see the peas are all gone. But go ahead and help yourself to the—what is it there next to you, Drew the Jew?"

"Turds, sir," answered the boy in the John Lennon glasses with Isaacs on his name tag.

"What?"

"Turnips, I believe they are, sir," answered Drew the Jew.

"Well, pass them to Spic here and let him have at 'em."

As I took the pot, I detected a gleam, a thin vein of subterfuge that ran through the eyes of the low ones around the table.

"Good peas, sir," Ween said chomping through the peas with an overly earnest gusto.

"You're a tool, Ween. Shut up. How's the Cow, Spic?" Nagle stared at me.

I sat up at attention. "Sir, she walks, she talks, she's full of chalk, I squeeze her tit she never balks, Sir!"

"And how's the turnips?"

Was this another trick question? A nonsense rhyme regarding a root vegetable? Nagle must have gotten his quota of amusement from my befuddled lost expression.

"Eat 'em up, Spic. You'll need your strength."

Drew the Jew piped-up, "Permission to ask a question, Sir."

"Ask your stupid fucking question."

"Is cadet Kelly of Latin heritage, Sir?"

"He's a Spic and you're a Jew, now shut the fuck up before I make you eat this goddamn table down to the legs."

"Yes, Sir!"

"And get my laundry after dinner, I want it folded and in my locker by CQ."

"Yes, sir!" Isaacs answered as if he couldn't wait for dinner to be over so he could relish the assigned task.

Nagle's composure slipped into irritation. He pushed his

plate away; his fingers flew unconsciously to his face and appraised the stumps of the three golden hairs that comprised the sum total of his whiskers. From the corner of my eye I could see his finger nails were gnawed to the bleeding quick. He caught me looking before I could turn away.

After we were dismissed from dinner, I negotiated my way up the stairs, through clusters of cadets as they loitered in dimly lit halls; leaned in doorways amid clouds of cigarette smoke. Others raced by with paper-wrapped bundles of laundry balanced on their heads. Laughter, taunts and loud talk erupted from the rooms; rolled through the halls.

Eyes kept low, I hoped to escape notice until I could duck into the refuge of my room. But a wrong turn led me down a hallway populated with older boys; they had the beard-stubble and heft of grown men. I had just reversed, wheeled about and taken a step in the opposite direction when I noticed my feet were no longer on the floor. All the wind left my chest. My back slammed against the wall. Like a well-timed linebacker's hit, my head whipped back and cracked against the plaster. Bright stars burst in my skull, full-color and cartoon-like.

"BRACE, KELLY!" I heard the hit man growl as he swaggered on down the hall past me.

What would be considered a felonious assault anywhere off a playing field was acceptable here—a brute reminder—they had that kind of power over you. As far as custom was concerned, I had failed to 'brace' or hit the wall when an old man passes by a new man.

Shaken, I wobbled away down the hall; doubting my ability to distinguish an 'old' man from a 'new' one, (some 'old men' had no rank on their sleeves). I decided to cover all bets and keep my back against the wall—just slide along, sidestepping, folding myself around corners, eliciting smirks and cackles, until finally, I found my room and turned in head still sputtering.

Crouched on my bunk, mind awash with the vision of what lay before me: a bad cartoon scheduled to run for over 3 years, that was 42 months, around 1, 277 days and nights; 3,832 grisly meals down in the crypt, along with countless trips through the gauntlet of the halls. I looked at the items scattered on the floor where Nagle had spilled them.

One web belt black.

One web belt dress white (brass buckle interlocking).

One blanket grey.

One leather belt black heavy brass buckle embossed with SEWANEE (suitable for hanging self from tree).

And I hadn't even learned to fold my shit yet. It all rolled out before me—a vast wasteland of time, seemingly endless in the mind of a fifteen-year old. My foot began the twitch, and then my body shivered all over. As my stomach convulsed and I reached for—

One trash can metal grey.

Chapter 4

Infirmary

THE CLANG OF METAL JOLTED THE BLOOD; the eyelids fluttered—the brain awakened to a white room. The infirmary, a double-room reserved for the sick and infirm at the Academy, and I, depleted of firmness, had qualified for a bunk, a lower one against one of the four white walls.

Again the sound of metal clanging from the cast iron radiator stationed beneath the bare windows, as if someone were pounding it with various hammers; spits of steam hissed and gurgled—the iron chambers expanded, flexed—gonged to life.

A diffused winter light pressed against the bare windows; hoarfrost trees stood outside in silhouette. On stiff white sheets I lay, hair shorn to the scalp, breath visible in the cold. The unspeakable sadness of bare windows in a cold room, a naked scalp on a winter's morn.

Glass cases set with brown bottles, swab sticks bloomed in jars—the medicinal smell of a hospital released a bat flight of memories. I rolled over to burrow back into the oblivion of sleep, but the door creaked wide and, with a squeak of rubber soles, Nurse Lyme entered.

Over the starched white cotton of her uniform hung the effigy of a once beige sweater now so pilled and smudge-ugly it brought to mind the ass-end of a sheep long in need of shearing.

A soft sigh as she unclamped her nurse's cap; a lock of dark hair twined with gray fell in wisps about her ears. She bent down towards me, her moist brown eyes magnified by a pair of surprisingly nerdy glasses with a constellation of rhinestones (some missing) in the cat's eye curl of the frames. The glasses were totally incongruous with the dour set of her face as if someone had played a practical joke switching her usual glasses with this gag pair and Nurse Lyme had yet to make the discovery.

"Let's have a look," she said jaws clamped tight around a Tennessee accent. She clicked a penlight, hunched like a mechanic over a faulty engine, and lanced each of my pupils with its beam. Done, she doused the light and left me blinking at a riot of yellow orbs.

Upon my forehead, she laid a warm hand and the yellow orbs melted away. Peace settled over me. Unexpected comfort. A simple gesture. Human touch. And I found myself unable to recall, in that easeful moment, the last time someone had touched me for a second longer than required by social custom or personal vindictive: the perfunctory pat on the back, shake of the hand, push, shove, punch in the arm, boot in the rear, lash with the broadside of a saber. Good morning, world.

Nurse Lyme's touch was clearly professional in purpose—dry hand, blunt sturdy nails. It illuminated the motives of those who reportedly checked themselves into hospitals, not because of sickness, but for just this very thing: the warm hand at rest on the skin. It was a reminder—a scratch for the itch forgotten that brings the itch so brightly to life and the joy of scratching it! Tail wagging, happy salivation—*touch me again please!* And as if reading my thoughts, Nurse Lyme promptly withdrew her hand.

"Not feeling well," I mumbled in hopes of calling back the warm hand; produced a series of dry coughs to support my statement. She seized the opportunity to jab a thermometer under my tongue. In my forced silence, I noticed Nurse Lyme also sported a wispy mustache set-off by an asymmetrical chin wart.

So what? She had the Warm Hand. And the starched white uniform; the clean crisp sound of professional care—something I felt deserving of after having had my head introduced to a very hard wall. My belief being that the incident—hazing—had given the Huntington's disease a boost: knocked a few frayed wires loose in my deteriorating brain pan.

In a play for additional sympathy, I was tempted to reveal

to Nurse Lyme the real source of my suffering: *progressive neurological disease—hereditary—doomed!*

But lacking documentation, it might be a lot for her to take-in all at once. And, since I liked being in the infirmary, felt a little safer there, I stuck with the lesser complaints of a mild concussion (slipped on the stairs) and a virulent chest cold. I was infirm by any standards and deserving of her care.

She plucked the thermometer from my mouth, gave it a frown and grasped my wrist for a pulse check.

Why did she frown?

Was it that bad?

Or was it *not* bad enough?

I performed another coughing seizure just in case. She released my wrist, the orbit of skin cooling where the warm hand had been. There was the squeak of hinged metal. She opened the glass door to a cabinet, removed two bottles the size of airplane liquors from a shelf stocked with rows of them—a platoon of bottles—each hand labeled with a strip of adhesive tape and filled with a viscous, red liquid.

"Drink it down," she instructed with a twist of the black cap; then lifted my head with the warm hand and brought the bottle to my lips—a moment of grace.

There it was—true religion—she doth give me succor. And there came upon the innards a spreading glow as the cherry-flavored elixir fluoresced within, smoothed the kinks and quieted the sparking tangle in the brain. Thank you, Nurse Lyme—a kindness remembered.

"Use this one later as needed," she set a second bottle within reach. Duty done, a quick tidy at the desk, she clamped the nurse's cap helmet-like back upon her head, tugged the dirty sheep's wool around her and, accompanied by the squeak of rubber soles, pivoted towards the door. There she paused and cast her gaze above me. With a resigned shake of the head, she opened the door and squeaked out.

Steam chuckled in the radiator, warmed the room. Or was it the red elixir easing through my system? My eyes turned to the bottle left behind. Encouraged by the effects of the first, I reasoned downing the second bottle could only be a further improvement.

I unscrewed the cap and just as I had it raised to my lips—from out of nowhere or actually, from right inside the very room, came a voice. A guy's voice spoke to me!

"Did you see where she put the key?" The voice asked with a detective's intensity. I was frozen, the bottle poised before my lips and startled in that way you can only be when caught in the midst of a guilty act.

"Helloooo down there?"

The voice originated from the bunk above me; a bulbous sag in the mattress overhead shifted and an inordinately large head dropped into view—upside down. He squinted at me there on the lower bunk: bottle raised—deer in his headlights—poised as if for a toast.

"Mother's milk," he cracked. "Four does the trick. Nice buzz. Like a couple of Teddy Bears." Squint, squint, he peered at me.

"Teddy Bears?" I mouthed still baffled by the sudden appearance of his upside down head and squinty eyes.

"Valium. The blue ones, Teddy Bears I calls 'em," he explained with a crane of his neck as he looked around. "She nicked my specs. See my glasses anywheres?"

"Why would she take your glasses?" I asked more to find a subtle way to break out of the ridiculous pose with the bottle.

"She hides my glasses to inhibit my reading. We're supposed to be resting," he tossed an almost fresh Playboy onto my bed. January—she was on skis.

"Enjoy," he grumbled, "Personally, I find little pleasure in jerking-off to blurry tits. Where did she put my glasses?"

Having only my newly opened bottle of cough syrup, I offered it up in gratitude for the magazine. Then made what I hoped was perceived as a nonchalant shuffle through the magazine's glossy pages: roaring fire, bear skin rug, winking through splayed legs.

"Delightful," I heard from above followed by a smacking of lips as he returned the half-drained bottle and added, "But it only whets the appetite. We need to tap the source."

I wasn't sure if he was referring to more Playboy magazines—a collection hidden somewhere. But after much shifting and groaning of bed springs, he bounded from his bunk and landed with a resounding thump, his bare feet square on the concrete floor.

Attired in a night shirt of dark flannel covered in tawny leopard spots, trimmed in white piping and embroidered with script over the breast pocket the words "*I Am Hunter*". Something a child would pick out to wear, ludicrous on this figure akimbo in the center of the white room, eyes furrowed in a squint as he scanned about. It was the guy from dinner, Isaacs—Drew the Jew, sans glasses.

"And what has that vixen done with the key?" He murmured.

"Key?"

"To this," he tapped the white metal cabinet filled with the platoon of little red bottles. "Le Cookie Jar."

I shrugged ignorance.

"What were her movements after dispensing your bottles?"

"Uh, she closed the cabinet."

"And she locked it. And she removed the key, because as we can see, zee key is not in zee lock," he spoke with a first-rate Inspector Clouseau impersonation. "So whot she do wid zis key, hmmm …? It would behoove us to know, n'est pas?"

"She straightened some stuff on her desk," I offered wanting to be helpful.

"Did she open the drawer?"

"Uh, not sure," I said reluctantly setting aside the Playboy as I dropped my legs over the edge of the bed. The floor was astonishingly cold, but I stood anyway. For some reason I wanted this guy in the ridiculous leopard night shirt to like me.

"First, she opened one of the bottles, held it up for me to drink," I recounted.

"Sweet communion, the dear angel. And did you gaze into her eyes as she suckled you?"

Caught off guard, I was embarrassed by the tender feelings Nurse Lyme's ministrations had stirred in me.

"It's okay," Drew said with a mischievous wink. "We can share her, but as you can see—she both giveth and she taketh away," he jiggled the locked door of the metal cabinet.

"She is Queen of the Nectar. And the Nectar is desired by all who taste it. That's why she locks the shit up."

"Probably takes the key home with her," I guessed.

"Yes, but if the good Doctor happened to sober up enough to make an actual appearance here, then he would surely need access to this very cabinet. The key is here somewhere. Hidden. And we must find it ..."

I joined him in the middle of the room while a cooling draft in my posterior reminded me that I was outfitted in one of those humiliating ties-in-the back ass-baring hospital gowns. In an effort to recover some dignity, I reached around with one hand and twisted it closed. Still I felt ridiculous, exposed. Not wearing something as brilliant as a leopard skin night shirt. It was the one wardrobe item you were allowed to bring from home—your own pajamas.

Mother had shipped me off with two pairs of those clingy, slithery nylon crap pajamas she and Dad wore in those mad Christmas candy colors. I'd be beaten to a fine pulp for wearing those around here. But the sheer *fuck-you* of a leopard print night shirt! A deck of Camel non-filters tucked in the pocket. That and the spot-on Inspector Clouseau impersonation—Drew the Jew had won me over.

Eyes asquint, he stood over Nurse Lyme's desk, his fingers played lightly over everything, pausing here and there, tickling for a clue. He bent over, his eye practically against the lock on the metal cabinet.

"Pick it, my dear? Why, I can't even see it?" He sighed to himself and straightened up. But for the impaired vision, he seemed in good health, not the least bit infirm.

"Why are you in here?" I asked wiping sweat from my forehead.

"Self-induced narcoleptic state," he casually replied.

"Sleeping pills?"

"Very good."

"My father's a doctor," I offered.

"There are worse things. Tell him you need Ritalin to keep your grades up, Valium so you can sleep and, of course, food of any kind. Where the fuck did she stash my eyes! This total disregard of my basic human rights," He whined. "And she calls herself a nurse. I tell you never trust a uniform."

"Yeah, it's a little weird to take your glasses. What if there was a fire or something?"

"Or if I wanted to *start* one or something."

Once again, I cast my eyes around the room to demonstrate solidarity, to extend our little bridge of friendship. By the door, I noticed a coat rack with several hooks fixed to the wall and over this, just above eye level, was a shelf. I reached up and felt along its surface.

"Are these yours?" I said and held out his tinted John Lennon glasses.

Gleefully, he plucked them from my hand and eased them in place. Face illuminated by a broad smile, he held out his hand for me to shake.

"Drew Isaacs," he said eyeing me through the thick rosy lenses. "You're the new guy—Spic."

"Actually, I'm Hawaiian."

"Hawaiian? Aloha. But, looks like you've been tagged 'spic'. Wear it with pride, amigo. Now, let's see what I can do with that cabinet," he said with a rub of his hands.

After the fourth bottle any troubling thoughts had vanished. My body floated, suspended like a bather in the Dead Sea—adrift on the warm red tide of cherry flavored codeine. A sense of well-being permeated everything. I drifted along until I came upon myself or rather I emerged up into a vision of myself: found my feet beneath me on a promontory, an escarpment of rock where I stood erect, clad in a brilliant yellow outfit the thickness and cut of an Eskimo parka and pants. The yellow color graduated into a fiery red halfway up my head which culminated in a top knot of black hair standing straight and fully red at the very tip.

I did not feel encumbered, but powerful and protected. And though I knew I was strange looking, I also knew that no one had ever looked like me and it was important that I accept my strange beauty. Strong and confident as I walked, though I had no idea where I was going. But it didn't matter. I was doing exactly what I was supposed to be doing.

I became aware that there were others like me; they didn't look like me, but each was equally striking in his own unique way. And we were headed in the same direction. We were gathering. At some point, and with no word spoken, I knew that we were a tribe. And the tribe had a name: we were the Makau. One of us was blue, another purple, each shaped differently. The purple one had a baby's skeleton attached and suspended by a flexible stem protruding from his navel—not a horrific baby skeleton, but a delicate thing that floated in gyroscopic harmony with his movements.

We were to journey to a place where there were more of us. And after some tough decisions regarding the appropriate luggage to complement our outfits, we continued on. I had no idea what was in my metallic suitcase. But I knew it was all I would ever need.

We arrived at the meeting place—a large, well-furnished Victorian house. There we met others, fantastic variations of color and shape. And just as I began to relish belonging to such a magnificent tribe, there arose a murmur: a low, troubling sound that grew louder and more insistent until panic was in the air. We were being hunted! The impulse was to hide immediately.

I watched the pathetic scramble for cover within the house—one tried to blend into pieces of furniture, another under a pile of quilts, but it was hopeless—we were too obvious to blend in. And all the while you could hear the terrible sound as It, whatever it was, sped towards us ... I awoke to an amazing headache, an empty bottle sticky in my hand. Drew was gone.

Chapter 5

Five Painful Things Learned

1: A 'NEW MAN,' WAS A FIRST YEAR CADET: a 'tool', a lackey, traditionally a target for scorn and derision or as Nagle took the time to constantly remind me—*a piece of dog shit*. You were a 'new man' until you returned for a second year when you became an 'old man' and could begin to exact your revenge on the new men below you. Since I'd come in at mid-term, I had the added distinction of being a semester cadet—a 'new' new man—the lowest of the low; one who hadn't even been able to share the bonding experience that all the other new men had gone through together.

2: Bracing: brutality masquerading as tradition. 'Bracing' required that whenever an "old man" passed a "new man" in the hallways and corridors, the new man must "brace," that is stop and slam his back against the wall, and remain frozen at attention, chin pulled in tight against his throat until the old man had passed him by. Failure to brace could result in being physically slammed against the wall as a reminder—*getting your bell rung*.

3: Showers! You had to yell "showers!" before you flushed the toilet or the sudden diverting of cold water in the plumbing system would scald whomever was standing in the showers—most likely an old man since there had to be some hot water left (it went fast) to actually scald someone. Retaliation was swift and merciless. Bells were rung.

4: Never ever say anything against the senior class. Lords of the campus, they would seek their vengeance. It had resulted in more than one ticket home for the convalescence and continued safety of the victim.

5: 'Sticks' were formal demerits written up for infractions. Three sticks bought you a PT or Penalty Tour—one hour of marching at 5:00 AM around the quadrangle in front of Quintard Hall, rifle raised over your head at arms length—rain or shine (there was never shine—too fucking early).

I made desperate calls to Texas; aired my grievances over the phone. Attempted to drive the wedge of my recent illness into my parent's firm resolve: "I'm still weak, dizzy spells … it was a brain concussion ... brutal hazing incident—happens all the time here!"

It was a naked plea to return home, no more shenanigans or back talk— "… the food poses a health hazard as well …" and the final, pathetic: "… I don't know how long I've got—the Huntington's has set in!"

For this maximum effort, I was rewarded with a slight pause on the other end of the line, and then Mother spoke: "Your tuition has been paid. It's a prestigious Episcopal school—you don't know how lucky you are."

I played the adolescent trump card: "Then I'll run away!"

But she was an expert hand at bridge and coolly rolled her cards: "If you run away then you will go to another military school. One in Texas, how about Allen?"

My blood ran cold. Allen!? Prior to my exodus from the nest, she had littered the coffee table with private school brochures all chocked-full of soft-focus lies: horses leaping fences, crisp cadets beaming over test tubes. Then there was the brochure from Allen Military Academy—they didn't even try to lie: grainy sepia shots of a barren outpost scraped out of the desert, nothing but rocks and dirt that seemed to radiate a relentless heat, all the amenities of a cattle stockade—the Foreign Legion for boys.

No, not Allen!

"And if that doesn't work we'll find you another one," she added for good measure.

The folks were done. My room back home already converted to a hobby nook: Dad's photography, Mom's ceramics. I hung up after spitting out a hollow threat: "We'll just see ..." But, in fact, I already did see.

It was your military basic training movie: sweating, grunting, running, crawling, panting—yelling. Lots of yelling. It was Nagle's preferred tone.

"Give me twenty push-ups now, Kelly! That's not a push-up! That's not a push up! NOT A PUSH UP! … THAT'S *ONE* … "

Or, you having to yell something back, usually self deprecating:

"I'M A GOAT FUCKING CRETIN, SIR!"

Only it wasn't a movie. It was my very real life. The Commandant, a Major in the 3rd Army named Crane, occasionally made a glowering appearance; stood before the corps, swagger stick in hand, oozing a physical lethality; his dark teeth barely visible as he chewed and spit warnings—issued pronouncements:

"Men, just a little reminder—the penalty for drinking is immediate expulsion from the Academy. Some of you may have noticed we are located in an isolated area of the Cumberland Mountains. In addition to the poisonous snakes found in the surrounding woods, you might happen upon a still—an illegal batch of squirrel whiskey being made by the local Covites. Should you find yourself in this situation you will execute an immediate about face and clear your ass from the area. I repeat—remove ass from area. Report any such encounters to my office. Do not fuck with the Covites, gentlemen. Or their moonshine. Dis-missed."

The daily grind began at 6:00 AM not with the traditional bugle call to reveille, but with Al Hirt's hideously perky trumpet ditty, "Fancy Pants" played at full volume over the P.A. system—twice. Evoking such an immediate and physical hatred for Al it literally drove you from your bunk, got you dressed and out the door with the thinnest hope that you might possibly encounter Al, rip that trumpet from his pudgy hands and beat the breath out of him.

All cadets not on bed confinement were required to stand in ranks at attention for four formations a day: reveille, breakfast, lunch and dinner. And there was drill three days a week; you formed for that too, you and your issued weapon.

"Men, this is the .30 caliber M1 Garand rifle. The firing pins have been removed in case you had any thoughts of sticking it up your ass and pulling the trigger."

Lot's of talk in the military of stuff going up-the-ass: guns, thumbs, boots, heads. Eventually, most everyday objects were threatened to be lodged there.

Sunday we marched to All Saints Chapel, a neo-gothic spire in the middle of the village. We paraded, brass gleaming, in full dress uniform, to the accompaniment of a draggy, off-key "Onward Christian Soldiers" tootled by the sparse school band. Townspeople lined the streets to watch, university students pelted us with snowballs. To my surprise, I found it oddly stirring marching in step with 300 boys to "Onward Christian Soldiers"; to be, for a moment, part of something larger than myself. And I felt stupid for liking it. For I really did hate the military; saw the whole chain-of-command thing as a shit-runs-downhill-factory with the lowest ranking grunt standing knee deep in the careless whims of others.

But the march to church, the martial cadence of the drums, the synchronized swing of all those white-gloved hands. Maybe I just wanted to put on a good show for the folks. I never told anybody. Especially not Drew who railed against the gung-ho pricks like Nagle, even saying once to his face, "This is not fucking Saigon. Okay? We're in high school!" He got two hundred push-ups and four hours of PTs for that one.

Endless bitch sessions were held in Drew's room. He would go on a rant, pacing in his slippers and leopard night shirt, puffing a perpetual Camel.

"... And no matter how much they yell and toss our rooms, saber up the ass, all that homoerotic shit, let's not forget who owns this bug house—the Episcopal Diocese! That's right, the fucking church! It's their ball. Hey, this is a business, okay. And our parents are the paying customers. Point being—they are not allowed to kill us! It's bad for enrollment, okay. So let's maintain perspective here."

It was Drew who clued me in. Drew who pointed out the rats. Drew who showed me how to fold my shit; introduced me to marijuana; to "The Jimi Hendrix Experience" roaring inside a set of Koss headphones. To the *"…purple haze all in my brain…"*

Drew Isaacs' entrance to the Academy had been accompanied by a doctor's letter detailing his "nervous condition" (ADHD with a manic/narcoleptic bi-polar cycling) "… all of which can be controlled …" with the box full of mostly prescription pills tucked under his bunk. The school wasn't sure how to deal with him, but it looked good to have a tuition paying Jew on the roster.

And it was Drew who introduced me to the crew: his roommate, The Ween, had the biggest dick any of us had ever seen, hence, The Ween. When he first introduced us, Drew insisted Ween pull The Ween out.

"Come on, Ween—air the beast."

Accustomed to this ritualized self-exposure, Ween nonchalantly unzipped and hauled The Ween out.

"It's *alive*!" Drew screamed like a frightened school girl and hopped onto his bunk. "Batten down yer knickers girls—it looks peckish!"

And though he was skinny, Ween ate huge amounts; the running joke being that he was eating for two.

Babu was from India. And for that alone he was awarded a steady stream of abuse. Cadets would pass him in the halls and start chanting his name "… *Babu Babu Babu* …", then someone else would pick it up "… *Babu Babu Babu* …"

In groups, boys are prone to cruelty and when they smell blood it can turn into an ugly, predatory thing. Even faculty members had resigned after being tormented by the pack. It was enough to send most new guys over the edge, but not Babu. He possessed an unflappable superiority. His family probably owned a good portion of India. So with a disdainful roll of his dark eyes, he dismissed the jibes and taunts—waved them away with his hand as if passing through a cloud of annoying gnats.

And me, they just called "Spic". They didn't yell my name or anything; they just said Spic like they would have said Tom or Bob. It did no good to resist, it would only get worse. So I was Spic. Spic Kelly if you wanted to get formal.

Sunday nights were the dreariest. What ever there was that could be missed about home was most missed then. A cold supper: platters of sliced bologna gone stiff around the edges, logs of Velveeta, a consommé with congealed skin scabbing the surface, half-thawed wedges of frozen Boston cream pie hacked with a cleaver. And then there was the dread of Monday staring you in the face—the inescapable knowledge that the cycle would all begin again.

The snow turned into rain. It rained for years. For decades the Uniform of the Day was black raincoats and plastic hat covers. Ween, so bitterly bored with the monotony of rain, appeared at formation standing at attention with his dick dangling out of his raincoat like the arm of a sleeping infant.

"Stow the dick, Ween!" Nagle yelled.

"Request assistance, sir!" That got him two hundred pushups on the wet asphalt and a week of penalty tours. Well worth it we all concurred back in Drew's room.

So it was the four of us: Drew, Ween, Babu and Spic together on many early mornings, in the dark, marching around the perimeter of the quadrangle. It was a cruel hour, at times so cold it made you want to cry. It was on one such occasion when Drew called out a limerick as we tramped around:

There was a young lassie from Morton,
With one long tit and one short one.
There was still more to come
From her great hairy bum
Shot farts like a six fifty Norton.

Quality stuff. We took it up in unison chanting as we tramped in the shivering dark, useless rifles resting on our shoulders. In the mornings that followed, new limericks were hatched.

We marched, made up filth and cackled; did them in different accents. We started looking forward to the morning PTs. Of course, no one would admit they actually enjoyed it because that would ruin it. But if, by some miracle, you happened to have a week where you didn't get PTs—you felt a little left out, like something was missing until you fucked-up enough to get invited back.

Something else started on one of those drizzling, piss-on-your-head mornings. As we tramped around wet and profoundly miserable, Ween came up with this one:

There's a girl I know at St. Mary's.
With friends whose looks she says varies.
Friday night we could sneak out.
Toss rocks till they peek out.
And set about popping their cherries.

St. Mary's was a legendary girls' school located somewhere on the mountain; a cloister of nubile femininity fiercely guarded by a gang of nuns. The limerick referred to a girl Ween happened to know from his home town—"a nymphomaniac," according to Ween, "... she did so many guys on the football team they gave her a fucking jersey." Hence her current incarceration with the nuns. St. Mary's became an obsessive topic of conversation. Ween related reports from his contact the 'nympho' about nude midnight forays at St. Mary's, out into the woods to get 'moon tans.'

"They're all nymphos, hell that's why they're sent there," claimed Ween to his rapt audience of three. "They never serve hot dogs out there. The nuns won't allow it. Or bananas. And broomsticks are kept locked in closets after one girl was sent to the hospital with a three inch splinter in her twat"

"No."

"Yes."

"Three inches?"

"Yep. They're all mad for it. The nuns make some of them wear this thing, sort of like a baseball cup for girls, locks in place with a belt. So they can't touch themselves or insert stuff."

"No."

"Yes."

"A cup?"

"Yep. The girl I know, Marla, she said she knew two of the girls who put rubbers on the grip-end of lacrosse rackets and did each other in the locker room."

"But that is ridiculous," said Babu. "A condom? Do they fear getting pregnant from a lacrosse racket?"

"It's so they can lube it up at night and still play field hockey with it the next day. Popular sport there. All the girls go out for it."

"No."

"Yep."

"How far is it?"

"About eight miles," Ween said looking around and then pointed, "That way."

"Eight miles?" echoed our other three voices, weighing the distance in our minds, visualizing the path.

"We probably walk eight fucking miles right here marching PTs," said Drew.

"How many girls?" asked Babu.

"Why? You thinking of going there?" said Ween.

"Maybe to view a lacrosse match."

"We can't just *go* there," said Ween.

"Why not?"

"First of all it's fuckofa long way and second of all … they might be in their periods."

"Ahh …" came the collective response.

"You know, I heard somewhere that women in groups synchronize their periods," Drew mused.

"There is that time of the month when my sister, would get very "sensitive" and did not like being touched," said Babu.

"Well, maybe your sister doesn't want you touching her Babu because you are her fucking brother," Ween sniped. "Maybe you haven't heard, but incest is frowned upon in this country?"

"Even in Tennessee?" Babu quipped.

We had stopped marching and stood huddled in a clump, all thinking about the same thing—the nymphomaniacs of St. Mary's.

"When do we go?" I said.

"Ween," said Drew. "If your friend, and I use that term loosely—if your nymphomaniac friend Marla is in her menses then it might be likely that all the other girls would also be in their time."

Ween shrugged his shoulders. "Maybe."

"You've simply got to find out when she is in her 'woman's time' before we risk our asses getting there just to find a bunch of touchy girls who don't want to do anything but talk," Drew said. "Lads, this requires timing."

We all nodded our heads. Then slowly, without thinking, we ambled back in line and resumed marching. But now, with eyes lowered as a light rain fell upon us, we were no longer merely tracing the parameters of our assigned punishment, we had each of us embarked on a path to St. Mary's school for girls.

Chapter 6

Sherwood Road

THE NIGHT WAS INKY DARK. A PALE SLIVER of moon leaned on its zenith. We were crouched in the brush just off the road, sweating like crazy from Benzedrine and fear. After crunching along on the gravel road for over an hour, we had just crested a rise when Drew thought he saw lights from an oncoming car, that's when we dove into the kudzu.

"I twisted my fucking ankle," groaned Drew.

"I told you guys it's too fucking dark out here," Ween whined.

After several minutes of hearing nothing but our sweat splatting on dead leaves, we periscoped our heads up: the road gradually dropped down away from us for about a mile—a luminous gray ribbon that cut through the black mass of woods before it curved left and disappeared into the trees. It was empty.

"We've lost too much time," Ween carped.

"We're lost period," said Babu.

"Fuck you, Babu."

"Fuck you, Ween."

The expedition to St. Mary's School for Girls was not going to plan. In the preceding weeks, Drew had imersed himself in research at the university's library: perusing medical texts and journals related to menstrual cycles, fertility, ovulation—hormonal stuff. From his calculations, he determined it would be about three weeks after Ween got the 'word' from his nympho friend that we should plan to make our midnight raid on St. Mary's.

Getting the 'word' was Ween's job, to find out when Marla the Nympho was having her period. The general assumption being, if she was, then they all were. And if she wasn't—well, it follows. Ween took pains to let us know this would require some finessing on his part: very delicate round-about questioning, casual inquiries into her health and well-being, sly use of the double entendre.

And so, it was a series of veiled questions we listened in on down at the guardhouse where the two pay phones were bolted to the wall. We gathered in a hushed semi-circle around Ween as he talked to Marla the Nympho on the other end of the phone.

"How's the Lacrosse team doing? Swimming much?" We listened intently as he repeated the descriptions of Debra, Annie and Dara. At the end of each call there would be a flurry of high-fives, and then we would stride down the hall like a winning team. Until we passed an Old Man, and then, of course, we would brace against the wall—the usual humiliations, but it didn't seem to matter as much—we had a goal, a focus larger than the immediate and de-humanizing details of our incarceration. We were a separate and independent clan. A tribe.

A month passed and Ween still hadn't gotten the word. Enthusiasm for the mission threatened to wane.

"But I thought she was a nymphomaniac," Babu said, "Why don't you just ask her?"

"Because maybe nymphos don't like to be called nymphos," countered Ween. "Always treat a slut like a lady and vice versa. Or didn't you know that?"

No one seemed to have any immediate evidence to refute Ween's logic. But the grumblings continued that Ween might not be able to pull it off. Then one day after lunch, we were hanging out in Drew's room passing a Camel around after skipping chapel when Ween showed up with a sly smile making it obvious something was up. He offered nothing until we threatened to fart on his pillow (a common abuse). Building the suspense, Ween told Babu to close the door.

"Boys," he said, "She's riding the red pony."

Drew grabbed his calendar and began counting off the days. Twenty-one he thought would be the best, even if cutting it a little close, it promised to be, "Maximum potential for arousal or PFA: the time that the girls will be the most susceptible to our charms is around ... Thursday the 15th," Drew declared and tapped the date with his finger.

"Kiss her neck."

"Blow in her ear."

"Rub her like Aladdin's lamp, the genie will appear."

Again we gathered in a semi-circle while Ween held the receiver cupped with his hand. He looked over at us, winked and gave the thumbs up. It was on! Preparations moved into high gear. We'd wear dark sweat suits with hoods, equipped with flashlights, bandoliers of condoms, cigarettes, canteens and one bottle of Jade East cologne to freshen-up on arrival.

Under Drew's pharmacological guidance, we had each broken open the plastic tube from a Benzedrine nasal inhaler, the solid kind that you stick up your nose for a snort of mentholated fumes. Once the tube was broken, the Benzedrine soaked cotton wad was removed, folded once and down the hatch with a Coke chaser. Drew claimed it would buzz us for hours providing the stamina to get to St. Mary's and back before reveille formation the next morning.

Two hours after slipping out of the barracks we were buzzed all right. But we also kept bringing forth these mentholated belches; fumes would roll out of our mouths and noses. And when I pissed, a wave of rushes spread up from my clenched scrotum to the top of my scalp. My senses were all keyed-up. I was on an adventure with my friends. It was a cool feeling except for belching the vapors. At least my breath would be minty fresh.

"Sorry about the ankle, boys," Drew said. "Unfortunately, it is one I use to walk." He hobbled a few steps, and then crumpled back to the ground. "I don't think I'm going to make it to pussy heaven. Just leave me with some smokes and a hand grenade—I'll wait here for any Nazis."

"St. Mary's has got to be over there somewhere," I said without knowing why. Just to make something happen. Keep us going. "If we cut through the woods we could make up time."

"Yes, we can cut through woods. We have flashlights," said

Babu. "They are expecting us. It would be rude not to show."

"I'm done, boys," Drew said tearing open the foil wrap on a condom. He took a deep breath and blew it up and touched it with his cigarette. POP!

"Goddammit, Drew! What if somebody heard that?" Ween screeched.

"Just testing the prophylactics, Ween. I think the Benzedrine has made you jumpy. You know, Babu, you should have gotten Ween some XLs. These might be a tad snug for the Ween."

Babu spit onto the ground, "Did anyone bring gum? This inhaler taste is terrible. My breath has a smell much like my grandmother."

We left Drew with a donation of additional smokes. He said he'd rest for a while, and then start back. Babu, Ween and I stepped off the road into the woods and it got spooky dark. We walked single file so we could all trip over the same branch, same root, same rock. We heard a muffled POP in the distance as Drew dispensed with another condom. I chuckled.

"Shut up, Spic," Ween hissed. "Anymore noise and I'm outta here."

"What's your fucking problem, Ween?"

"Why don't we just tell the whole fucking world we're coming?"

"Shut your mouths both of you and look there," said Babu.

In the woods off to our left, there was a glow of light reflected up in the canopy of trees.

"Is it St. Mary's?"

"Must be."

We quietly moved towards the light, listening to nothing but our mentholated breathing and the amplified snap of each twig under foot. Twenty steps more and we could see—it was a fire. A camp fire. We watched the figure of a man pass back and forth in front of it, feeding the fire.

"Fuck, it's a goddamn still! They're making whiskey," hissed Ween. We froze in our tracks.

"I think this is where we are supposed to about face and

remove ourselves from the area," said Babu. And without another word, we began to clear the area, moving back in the direction we had just come. We were picking up speed when Babu tripped and fell. It sounded like a single engine airplane crash landing. Then everything got very quiet: Babu on his back on the ground, Ween and I crouched motionless, waiting to see if they had heard.

Nothing. No sound from the camp.

We were easing Babu up off the ground when it happened—the terrible thrashing sound of people charging heavy-footed and fast through the woods. Coming from different directions. My feet slipped from the sudden acceleration, and then I found traction—branches whipped me in the face, roots grabbed at my feet. I slipped and slid as I tore through the woods.

Was there something still behind me?

Yes, there was.

It was gaining on me. Something slammed me in the back and I fell forward.

Babu yelled from somewhere behind me. I tried to get up, but was knocked back down. There was a knee in my back. He yanked me over, with a hand hard as a shoe, slapped me across the face.

"Git them others!" he called out. The metallic taste of blood in my mouth.

"Lookin' for my whiskey, boy?" He globbered his foul breath into my face. "Thinking yew can come up here maybe steal yoreself some?"

He smelled like a wet dog—an old dog with bad teeth that had singed its fur in a fire.

"I'm gonna learn you sumpin', boy."

He reached around his back and pulled out a nasty looking curved blade. I felt the flashlight in the pouch of my hooded sweatshirt.

"We were looking for the girl's school, that's all," I whimpered.

"Yer lyin! Yer lookin' fer whiskey."

"No, sir, I goes up to tha Academy," I said trying to sound a little more country.

"The Academy? Hell, yew goin' to school, right here, boy!" He wrenched me over so I faced him. Inside the sweatshirt's pouch, my hand tightened on the flashlight. I figured if I missed, he'd kill me for sure. With my left hand I reached out along the ground, grasped at some leaves, made a rattling sound. When he looked to the side to see what I was doing, I slid the flashlight out of the pouch. He brought his right knee down and pinned my left arm. When he turned his head to look back at me, I swung the metal barrel across his grinning face. There was a soft crunch like a stepping on a snail. And the barrel broke off the flashlight.

"Wha!" He gasped and dropped the knife as his hands went to his face.

I twisted out from under him, scrabbled along the ground until I could get to my feet. I ran; ran like a deer veering one way then another. Slammed through branches, all the time hearing him behind; gaining on me. Heart pounding, mouth gone to cotton, side racked with a stitch—run! The woods began to thin; ahead a clearing, and then I tripped and fell hard.

I waited for him to land on top of me, but nothing happened. All I could hear was the racket of my breathing. Quiet. There was the road in front of me; the sliver of moon caught like a fallen kite in the tree tops as if nothing at all had happened.

Afraid of being seen, I moved along the line of trees parallel to the road; a sudden bend to the right and a big white cross loomed up out of the dark. There was a building. And another.

No light burned. All was dark. Too dark. I tried to remember where it was the girls were supposed to meet us. Turning back, at least immediately, was out of the question. That Covite would be looking for me and plenty pissed. Babu and Ween must have gotten away or I would have heard their screams.

Moving in the shadows, I eased closer to the main building—a dorm. The girls were going to get a surprise—only one guy. Then I found, wrapped around the building's doors, a padlocked chain.

Softly, I stepped across the pea gravel; the other building

was the same. Always seems to take me awhile to notice the obvious—no cars. The entire place was shut down. For some time, by the looks of things. Maybe it wasn't the school? Maybe this was some seminary for nuns—an old convent? I made my way back to the front where the cross stood. And there, on a large white stone stuck in the ground were letters that spelled out: **St. Mar s**. The Y wasn't the only thing missing.

Chapter 7

In a Dark Wood

F*UCKING WEEN!* IT ROILED INSIDE MY HEAD as I slogged back to the Academy; the gut churn and replay of anger—of betrayal. *Fucking liar!* I beetled over tree roots, kicked through kudzu, head full of snakes. How stupid I had been to believe him; so easily duped; so ready to be fooled!

And then, in this fractured state of mind, I found myself thinking back to Ron and Don's house: back when I was a nine-year old boy at play with my two little friends, two brothers, one fat and loud, the other skinny and mute. Somehow the term 'adopted' had come up and when I asked what it meant, Ron, the loud fat one, looked at me with stunned surprise and said, "You are adopted. Didn't you know?"

"No, I'm not," I countered with no clue of what it was exactly, but assumed by his tone that it was something I had no interest in being.

"Those aren't your real parents," the fat one explained. "You're adop-ted."

It's a cruel trick, was my first thought. After all, they were two brothers, and brothers working in collusion tended to be meaner than your average single child. Ron pressed the point, insisted on a history I knew nothing about; named his mother as a source, while the skinny brother nodded in mute confirmation.

How could someone know something about me that I didn't know?

I would have cursed them as liars right then and there, except—the air thickened, time slowed—the floor tilted as memories bobbed to the surface: the woman who came to visit, the walk to the park, the car ride with the 'nice people.' Up until that very moment, in my ninth year, I had thought they were just dreams I'd had, but for the fact that they all wound back to a distinct image of Her; always there at the hub where all memories circled back to the original memory—Mother.

It is early morning; she lies in bed. My older brother stands beside me at her bedroom doorway. Still in our pajamas, we watch her like prey, draped there in white sheets, perfect as statuary.

Unable to restrain ourselves another instant, we unleash cries and storm her bed. She's not really asleep. But we give her a start or at least she pretends we do—squeals at us, pulls the sheet over her head feigning terror.

We tug at her sheet, expose her head and keep tugging trying to pull it off, to reveal her—to see all of Mommy. But she laughs.

"No, no," she admonishes with a smile, "... leave Mommy's neenoos alone." She tugs the sheet up demurely. We give up the struggle and drop to nuzzle against the heat and smell of her.

After the memory washed over me, I walked out of Ron and Don's house without saying goodbye; drifted outside and squatted on the curb. Waited for my mother to come pick me up.

"Am I adopted?" I demanded with all the authority a nine year-old can muster. Stunned silence as she carefully pulled away from the curb.

She claimed she had been waiting until I was old enough.

Old enough?

To understand.

But they understood—Ron and Don understood it.

Who was the woman in the sheets?

The woman who took me to the park?

The boy that was my brother?

Are you my real mother?

She made careful answers.

"You were chosen," she said hands in firm possession of the steering wheel. "And those people you remember were a foster family. They were keeping you until you could be placed—they were not your mother and father."

Foster family, the temps of parenting. The one family deemed temporary from the outset and yet, was the cornerstone of my memory. My identity continued to shift, a kaleidoscope tumbling to new patterns with the same pieces.

Who is my real mother?

She lit a Salem, "You were born in Hawaii to an immature woman unable to provide adequate care."

Hawaii? Was my mother Hawaiian?

Mother nodded her head, exhaled a stream of smoky words, "Yes, the mother was Hawaiian. The father was not. You were tossed around a bit. That's all we know."

Well, you could have told me. So at least I would know what Ron and Don knew. I don't like being the last one on the block to find out!

And then I guilt-tripped her into springing for a model airplane with a .049 engine complete with ignition battery and can of fuel. I remember taking it home and, it being so cold outside, talked her into letting me start it up inside the bathroom where it made an incredibly loud high pitched whine: *WWW-WEEEEEEEEEEEENNNN!*

FUCKING WEEN! I shadowed the Sherwood Road; my head become a singular, unblinking eyeball bright with Benzedrine and rage. Finally, the woods thinned—there was Quintard Hall, dawn breaking across its face like a bad egg.

Foot sore and filthy with a swollen jaw where the Covite smacked me, I gimped up the back stairs, slipped into my room; kicked off the mud-covered boots, peeled the sweats from my shaking body just as the opening notes of "Fancy Pants" erupted from the PA—back in time for reveille.

Babu stood in ranks, his face a menu of abuses. A wan looking Drew limped across the quadrangle in leopard night shirt and slippers, dragging his bad ankle to the infirmary. He stopped and saluted us as we marched by, puffed his chest out and posed as if we were passing in review before him—Colonel Sicklist!

"Where is Ween?" I whispered to Babu over a platter of grease afloat with eggs fried hard as drain stoppers.

"I have not seen him. But I am exhausted I can tell you," Babu said with a touch on his swollen ear. "Those Covite bastards scared most of the shit out of me."

"I made it," I said under my breath, and then saw Nagle, presiding at the far end of the table, glance our way.

"Maybe Ween was not so lucky," Babu considered.

"No, Babu, what I mean is, I made it all the way to St. Mary's. I made it to the school."

"Shut the fuck up, Spic and pass the goddamn eggs before they ice over," snapped Nagle. "You and Babu can whisper sweet nothings back in your room while you cornhole each other."

"Sir, I have dietary restrictions regarding corn, sir."

"Shut the fuck-up, Babu, or you're gonna chug a ton of it come suppertime. How do you tell who the niggers are in Injuh, anyway?"

After breakfast, we found Drew moored in his bunk, the injured ankle wrapped and elevated. Babu and I slumped with fatigue against his desk.

"Well, amigos, my sojourns at the infirmary have come to an untimely end," he announced with a sigh. "Nurse Lyme has taken to counting the little red bottles and come up short. It seems I'm an outpatient now. Out in the cold anyway. Could use a swig of Ol' Redball about now."

"Spic made it to St. Mary's," said Babu.

"Shit me not, Spic?" Drew turned towards me.

At that moment, Ween or what was left of him—a bedraggled wraith, face laced with welts, eye sockets dark as a raccoon's—lurched through the door and collapsed wordless onto his bunk.

"Cadet Ween," piped Drew dryly, "You've missed reveille and breakfast. You, sir, will be marching PTs in hell—which is said to have a passing resemblance to this very place."

"Fucking Covites, chased me for hours—I couldn't lose 'em," Ween whimpered. "Got totally lost. Fucking hell, man."

"Hey, Ween, Spic made it to St. Mary's," Babu said.

"Great," Ween muttered without so much as a glance my way. I had wanted to see him squirm; see the guilt burn on his face. The last five hours of my life had been spent wanting to punish Ween for lying to me. To us. And here he was beaten, exhausted. Pitiful.

"The girls were great," I heard myself say. The room dropped into a well of silence.

"Get the fuck outta here," said Drew. "You saw the girls?"

I nodded my head to avoid having to say an outright 'yes'.

"You were hallucinating. The Benzedrine plays ocular tricks. I myself kept seeing a purple bat flapping before me through the woods," Drew fluttered one hand in the air and let it drop.

"They were waiting. Just like they said they'd be," I kept my eyes on the back of Ween's head. "Marla, Debra, Annie—all of them."

"Get the fuck out. You actually talked to them?" Drew sat up in his bunk and fired up a Camel.

"They were bummed you guys didn't make it."

"How did they look?" asked Babu.

"Annie wore this like—nightgown thingy, with a robe, but like you know—like visible stuff."

"What?" said Drew. "Ween, are you hearing this delusional chatter?"

"I was there. Hey, Ween, call her up. Ask her. Ask Marla. She'll tell you, we had a real good time."

Ween's face flushed red even through the grime and bruising.

"They had some beers stashed," I continued, warming to my story.

"May I inquire as to the brand?" asked Drew.

"Pabst Blue Ribbon—a sixer, tallboys. And a pint of Southern Comfort."

"Beeyootiful!" Drew swatted his leg, the one with the bandaged ankle and winced at the self-inflicted pain.

"How did Debra look?" asked Babu earnestly.

"Great hair. Long. And really excellent teeth."

"I knew she would be beautiful," Babu mused as he constructed a perfect Debra in his mind.

Maybe I should have felt bad lying to my friends. But it

didn't seem to have bothered Ween. There he lay, face to the wall, holding himself together like a torn package. He had played us. And what if I had told the truth? Revealed what I'd actually found? It would have destroyed the tribe. Though angry, I had a deeper need to keep the tribe intact. It was all I had in this place. And it was beyond me, at the time, to know it was a fool's game for things had already changed. Ween knew I knew and it would never be the same between us.

Winter made a reluctant surrender to spring. The smutty bergs of ice that hunkered in the shadows of buildings and under trees finally evaporated. All at once, the sun infused each bare twig and faded blade of grass with green. Even the ponderous face of Quintard Hall seemed lightened by blue sky and bird song.

Winter wool was put aside for lightweight summer trousers and starched white ducks was the uniform for Sunday's march to All Saints Chapel. There were moments in a day where I found myself seized, stopped in my tracks by a tree ruffling in the breeze or a waft of honeysuckle. The seasons had radically switched places, as if a massive carpet had been flipped to its true side and turned tatters to sudden glory. Hard to believe that these two seasons, so opposite, held joint sway and custody over the same ground.

Weather in the tribe was not so fair. Ween became adept at avoiding me. Drew and Babu saw this as resentment for my philandering with Ween's fictitious girlfriend. It was ridiculous. Pathetic.

And why hadn't I called the girls back?

And why wasn't I trying to set up another late night rendezvous with the nymphos of St. Mary's?

Somehow I was the one who had dropped the ball on everyone's orgy-in-the-woods-fantasy. The enthusiasm for a second expedition was quelled (with a hooded, but assuring nod from Ween) when I reminded them that the Covites would be on the lookout and if they ever got their hands on us, there would be deep hell to pay. I, in turn, resented them for not being able to see what a liar Ween was.

Drew got a restock on prescriptions. His moods changed with the color of the pills: hyper one day, silent and heavy-lidded the next. He'd dose himself into a coma then reverse and stay up on a twenty-four hour reading binge: all the plays of Tennessee Williams, the Beat poets. He would engage me in long rambling discussions; insist I listen to certain passages. Down the hall he would amble late at night puffing from a Camel, reciting sections of "Howl":

"I saw the best minds of my generation destroyed by madness, starving hysterical naked ..."

And then he would improvise:

" ... but then I took one look at Nagle and knew humanity was really fucked..."

Drew had broken rule #4: Never Say Anything Against the Senior Class. Retribution came late one night. Ween had been the witness:

"I woke up with a flashlight shining in my face. Thought it was one of you guys fucking with me. Then I see—must be six of them in the room. They throw a blanket over Drew and hold it down tight. They start whaling on him with socks—bars of soap knotted-up in the toe. They're swinging hard. Tell me to kiss my pillow or get the same. They're beating the shit out of him, man. Dust rising. Bunk's banging around, he's howling and shit. I mean what the fuck was I supposed to do, man? I couldn't do anything. Then it stops. And they're gone, but he's still howling. He kicks the blanket off and I snap on the lamp—he's a fucking mess, man. Whole body's shaking. Nose bloody. Crying. Can't see without his glasses. Then he gets up, walks over to the waste basket and pukes. Then turns to me and tells me not to say anything about what just happened. Not a fucking word he says. Nagle. Fucking bastards."

"Woke up in a shit storm without a hat," was how Drew described it lying in the infirmary. They seemed to have avoided his head, but his body was a quilt of bruises: greenish purple and black all over like a chameleon that couldn't decide its color.

"Hey, buddy, you got your ticket out of here," I told him with no little envy in my voice knowing the history of such hazing incidents usually resulted in the victim being secreted away to a faculty member's house until arrangements could be made for their return home, for their own safety and to avoid any fallout that might occur for the school.

"What? And leave you behind to have all the fun? Not on your life, Spic. I think I'll stick around. She's got the Redball stored up in the closet now, but I'll find the key. You know, I think Nurse Lyme has a thing for me. Really."

He told Nurse Lyme he fell down the stairs. I told him he was out of his mind. "Your parents can't fault you, the school can't fault you, so your record's clean—take it, go!"

"But what would Nagle do to occupy himself if I left? The goddamn place would fall apart. No, you got it wrong, Spic. We've got to keep up the good work—we're on a mission you and me. Besides, I've yet to pay my respect to the girls at St. Mary's," he said and winked at me, and then quoted Steinbeck with an idiot's drawl, "… tell me about the rabbits, George …"

Six weeks later Parent's Weekend was upon us. Ween's folks had driven up to the mountain from Mississippi. Took us all out to dinner at the Inn. It was out past All Saint's Chapel on the other side of the village. You could see the golf course from the dining room. Steaks. The smell of adults drinking cocktails, their confident blather; the tab picked up.

Later that night, I awoke to a flashlight shining in my face. "We gonna beat the shit outta you, boy."

I braced for an attack only to watch as the flashlight shone on a bottle of Southern Comfort dancing before me. Drew cackled.

"Wakey, wakey, the chariot awaits. Ween's got his daddy's car. We're driving to St. Mary's."

A warm night. All I had to do was crawl out of my bunk, slip into some sweats. The Tribe reunited for another adventure. Or had I longed for it so much that my mind had invented it in my sleep and this was actually a dream? It was too familiar though: the late night, the stolen car—the memory of that night back in Texas flashed in my skull: the cold metal slab in the Midland jail, the hopeless kid with the fuzzy teeth, the withering disappointment in my father's eyes; Mother's words.

And then I was shaking my head and saying to Drew, "No. No, I can't go. Don't feel well, not tonight. Sorry. I just can't …"

And Drew kept saying *come on get up* and *let's go! Tribal Council.* Then he pulled my blanket off and said, "Come on, get up, let's hustle, cadet."

"No," I said and stood up. I grabbed my blanket. "I'm not fucking going!" I said it too loud. Someone could have heard. Drew got it. He shrunk away from me, receded like a darker shadow out the door.

None of them made reveille. Probably exhausted, hungover and still in bed. I rolled out of formation and headed for Drew's room. His bed was unmade, as was Ween's. I checked the showers. The latrines. I went downstairs. Babu's room was the same. Breakfast formation and still a no-show. In the mess hall their chairs remained empty at the table. I wondered if they had run off without me, headed for San Francisco to find what was left of the summer of love. But Drew had said he was going to stay.

Then came the bad feeling: their three empty chairs seemed to elevate up, their legs lengthened stilt-like until they towered over us like props in a circus act waiting for the performers to come spinning back down out of the air and each land amazingly in his seat. But they didn't. Empty chairs in the din of forks and knives.

Chapter 8

All Saint's Chapel

DREW ISAACS' BODY WAS FOUND HALF-way out the back window of the car—folded once like an overcoat, back broken. They tried to sell a softer version, but with three hundred boys the ugly truth always finds a voice.

The car had been traveling at a high rate of speed when it swerved, struck the guardrail on the right side of the road and bounced off; it veered across the oncoming lanes and struck the guardrail on the opposite side of the highway.

Guardrails have seams where the sections of metal railing overlap in a manner designed so the edge of the seam faces away from oncoming traffic. This is to ensure any contact would just slide the vehicle along a smooth surface. But the car had crossed to the opposite side of the road and hit the rail going the wrong way. The impact breached the seam; the overlapping rail was peeled back and penetrated the car passing up through the driver's side door and out the back window impaling the vehicle and taking Drew along for the ride.

Robert Forrest (Ween) had been at the wheel when the guardrail smashed into his chest, flaying one pectoral muscle from the underlying bone. On the passenger side, Babu's left wrist was caught by the edge of the guardrail, his hand mashed to a paste along the length of the interior roof. The shredded white ligaments of his forearm were exposed and dangled like a ragged shirt sleeve when he was found standing by the hissing wreckage waving for help.

The drums beat a grim cadence for the march to All Saint's. The late morning heat had just begun to soak the inside of our wool blouses as we entered the narthex and felt the cooler air inside the great stone chapel. We gather, death, to acknowledge your most recent appearance. We stood and sat and kneeled in memory of Drew Isaacs.

The Headmaster of the school, the Rev. William P. Gunder, layered in cloth, gravely mounted the steps, took his position in the pulpit and looked out over us. He had a sense of occasion this red-haired comb-over rooster of a man; profoundly superior in demeanor, disposition and length of stride. Very little of his time was actually spent on the campus of the Academy. More often than not he was away on business: fundraising luncheons with well-heeled alumni, dining with chairs from the university or entertaining privately at his cozy cottage just in view of the academy where he lived by himself—opera and his enormous ego wafting from the windows thrown open on a Sunday afternoon. He wielded an intimidating intellectual power as palpable as the Commandant's physical one. And as for the priest's collar—it was difficult to imagine him tilting his chin low enough to pray.

"Cadet Robert Forrest will eventually recover from his injuries," the Headmaster said from the pulpit. Though he would never return to school.

"Babu Paksmideran," the Headmaster intoned, "Will recover from his injuries. But it is our great sadness that Drew Isaacs is no longer with us. He will, however, remain in our memories not only as a young man taken in the bloom of promise, but also as a warning to each and everyone of us—how quickly a precious life can be wasted in a moment of recklessness."

I reached for the hymnal not to join in the singing, but to read the sentiments scrawled there by a legion of cadets both present and gone on to other places—their thoughts left behind like scat to mark their time here. Maybe an entry by one of the tribe—a limerick, written by Babu's missing hand, conceived by Drew's dashed brains. I found:

If you are reading this then you are FUCKED.

I WANT TO COME BACK HERE AND BURN

THIS SHIT HOLE TO THE GROUND!

Why shoot yourself when you can Join the Army.

fucking hate fucking hate fucking hate fucking hate fucking

The entries went on and on, some written over others in what was a palimpsest of collective loathing. The Headmaster wrapped up the litany.

"O God, whose mercies cannot be numbered, accept our prayers on behalf of thy servant Drew Isaacs and grant him an entrance into the land of light and joy, in the fellowship of thy saints; through Jesus Christ thy Son our Lord, who liveth and reigneth with thee and the Holy Spirit, in God, now and for ever. Amen."

There was a lengthier entry in the back of a hymnal; the introductory episode of a serial tale, it traced the humble beginnings of a creature called "Cesspool Cid." Cid was spawned when "Miss Uterbuttons," a fictitious secretary at the Academy, disposed of her tampon in the same toilet that "Stinky" the Covite janitor had just jerked-off into and failed to flush his "spunk loogie."

The two co-mingled: the plump secretarial tampon and the janitorial ejaculation; they swirled in the "champagne pink waters" of the toilet bowl where a *spontaneous fertilization* occurred. The nascent little "happy sack of mucous" washed down the rusted pipes, all the way down to a "cesspool underneath Quintard Hall." There, Cid started to grow in earnest. "Begat with turds in his ears," Cid processed the filth around him, "through feathery neck gills he supped on shit and found it nutritive and familiar".

He was a furtive being, fearful of being seen; he knew they would make fun, torture him—they did it to themselves. His plan was to flood the Academy one night with sewage, plug all the drains and laugh as everyone drowned in a rising tide of their own excrement while he frolicked joyfully, the Prince of Crap.

Marked as *Episode I*, I was convinced this was a tale that could have only been conceived and composed by Drew Isaacs.

I rifled through the hymnals and prayer books on my row. And on the row behind me; went through others on my way out; would return to All Saints numerous times on town leave, slip into the chapel and systematically, from the front rows to the back, search through every hymnal and prayer book. And though I never found another episode of "Cesspool Cid", I did tear out the pages marked by the other cadets; pages of scrawls and crude drawings—the collective suffering of the hazed, the hopeless and oppressed of the Academy.

Back in my room, I would sift through these pages thinking that if so many had felt this way and if they were joined in one voice—in one unified howl—then the machine would have to listen. And if I couldn't find any more episodes of "Cesspool Cid," well, then I would make them up myself.

Chapter 9

Ramada Inn, Monteagle, Tennessee

LIKE AMIABLE STRANGERS, MOTHER AND I SAT poolside. Arlene anchored between her high ball and magazine while I gazed at detritus burping in the pool's leaf trap.

Earlier that day, commencement ceremonies at The Academy had come to a rousing climax when the final formation of the corps of cadets was given the last command, "Dis-missed!" And with a roar, 300 hundred white hats were hurled upwards and hung like a brief cloud in the June sky. It was over.

Afterwards, Mother and I in her station wagon, wound down the mountain to the Ramada Inn. Dad had gone on ahead to catch a plane, a full slate of prostates and kidney stones waiting back in Texas. She and I would spend the night before the long drive back to Odessa. "See the sights," I believe she said.

Though the commencement proceedings had provided the usual rituals of graduation and marked for me the fourth and final year of my internment at the Academy—all this had been overshadowed by the more significant event that had taken place several weeks earlier when the school had undergone its grueling annual General Inspection by Third Army. This inspection was the heartbeat of the Academy's junior R.O.T.C. program and the cadets had been harried as if preparing for a D-Day landing.

It had been a brilliant day for suffering: the sun blazed above a lush athletic field. Major Crane, the Commandant, watched from the reviewing stand, swagger stick in hand; his pair of hillbilly non-coms flanked him on either side.

The battalion of cadets: six platoons arrayed in precise rectangles before them, regular as bathroom tiles; ties snugged, brass buttons flashed in the glaring sun; all for the Third Army's Chicken Colonel who'd come to see if we were worthy of the R.O.T.C. program. The Chicken Colonel (that's a full colonel with an eagle insignia perched, wings straight as a razor, upon his cap and epaulets) was a slight fellow, short and fairly young—always a bad sign.

The Colonel seemed comfortable in light khakis, open collar and short sleeves. He prowled amongst us, eyes hidden behind a pair of Ray Ban aviators. A grin played around his mouth. Just out for a casual stroll it seemed when all of a sudden he'd halt, execute a sharp turn that brought him face to face with a boy. And that boy would, as if activated by a step-switch, pop to attention from his parade rest position, heft his rifle to port arms on a two-count, go on to inspection arms with a drop of his head down to open and check the chamber on the three count, and return his head to the upright position on the four. The Colonel would then proceed to generally fuck with him.

It was unacceptable to faint during the General Inspection. And I did feel some reluctance at being the first to hit the ground. Partly, I feared being the only one. Also, I wanted to see who might take the plunge first, either in protest or maybe just drop for real, overcome by the swelter as the sun hammered us. In addition to being an embarrassment for the entire corps at this crucial time of the year, fainting was also considered unmanly and was customarily rewarded with abuse for the remainder of one's days at the Academy—probably not many.

But it was a good day for fainting. The cicadas pulsed hypnotically, accompanied by an annoyance of bees buzzing your face. It crossed my mind to fake a bee sting, but that would be different from fainting and would require more acting, and they'd be likely to look for the stinger. Besides, it had to be the real deal for me—a voluntary act of civil disobedience, a strike against the system.

This was my fourth year at the Academy and during that time I had seen what the system could do. Saw what it had done to me or what I had done with it—on one night in particular. There was this new man named Cissey. That's right, cursed with a last name that you'd think at least one ancestor would have died to relieve his offspring of. And if that wasn't bad enough, he had been blessed with not only a prize-winning case of acne, but also a set of womanly hips way bigger than his shoulders. And to draw more attention to himself, he was always dicking around: out of his room after CQ (Call to Quarters) or going to the bathroom perhaps to pop zits or admire his large ass in the mirror. See, that's what I'm talking about: that was a mean thing to say about Cissey. He did not choose his ridiculous name or his big ass. Who does?

But he did choose to be a jerk—out of his room bumming smokes. And you have got to show some respect, even with me who could give two shits about the rules. But after a warning, I caught Cissey out of his room again. Pissed me off, being a goddamn senior and all, having suffered through four years of crap and I thought—this guy is just blowing me off.

"Hit the deck, Cissey and gimme twenty," I commanded. There was the back of his pimply neck as he did the push-ups. And I told him to do some more, and then told him he was still not done. But he said he couldn't do any more push-ups and got up before I said he could. Well, Fuck That! So I shoved him against the wall. And I shoved again, hard—a couple times against the wall. Then he tried to tear away from me, but I grabbed him by the front of his shirt, twisted it up hard in my fist and kept twisting until his collar was wound like a tourniquet around his zit-covered neck and his face was turning red.

Close-up his face was a cursed terrain—boils upon scars left by previous boils; blackheads burled like knotholes, festering clusters of whiteheads—his entire countenance a sort of seeping wound. Here was a boy already misshapen by life. You could tell he'd gotten a lot of shit. He always would. But something about him encouraged abuse—called out to others to come punish this thing they would never want to be. And it called out to me—the cigarette stink of his breath, the B.O. and fear. In my disgust, I twisted a little tighter and his face started to go blue; his eyes got a scared look and started to bulge like maybe his whole mess of a face would burst open.

And then it hit my nose—he'd shit himself. Tears trickled down his face, taking an indirect course around all the craters and whiteheads on the way to his chin. I released my grip and backed away. He eased down, shrinking into himself. Head down he turned away; slunk off wiping his nose as he shuffled back to his room, an oddly familiar figure of humiliation. And then I recognized who he was—*Me*—four years ago. He was me. I'd come full circle from tortured to torturer. Humiliated another human being as I had been humiliated. I had become the bully.

Too ashamed to tell anyone what happened, there was little sleep that night. *Me* who had defined himself as against the system. *Me* the anarchic voice of "Cesspool Cid," the underground newsletter I circulated—an obscene screed against the military system. And, yet, I was as much a part of the machine as any gung-ho saber swinging prick. Getting even for past crimes against your dignity is all it was, all it ever would be—a chain of suffering and grief passed down through the generations of cadets year after year; doing it because it had been done to you—since 1869. And what was the next step?

First, I went down to the bathroom where Cissey was quietly trying to clean up in a stall. I asked if he was all right. He didn't look at me, but nodded his head. "Go ahead and take a shower," I told him even though it was after lights-out. I wanted to do more; wanted to make it like it had never happened. Too late for that. But, the night before General Inspection, I slid one more issue of "Cesspool Cid" under the doors of Quintard Hall.

So there we were, on the parade ground, still as a set of toy soldiers. The Chicken Colonel turned up the rank in front of me, took a couple of steps, did halt/pivot and came face to face with Cissey. He was one squad in front of me, one man to the right. And Cissey (who had diligently maneuvered his weapon to port arms) must have thought he saw the Colonel's hand make a move towards his weapon (which you are supposed to release immediately, snapping your hands back to your sides as the Colonel deftly snatches the weapon out of your hands for inspection). But Cissey jumped the gun, so to speak: he dropped his rifle too soon and the Colonel missed the grab. Cissey's weapon fell to the ground, but not without first striking the Colonel on the instep with the metal butt-plate of the M1 .30 Garand—9.5lbs.

Every scared dick on the field knew what happened, even if it had happened behind you and you hadn't seen it; still you had heard the metallic rattle of a gun hitting the deck; you heard the Colonel say, *"Shit!"* surprised and annoyed at the same time. And you could almost hear Cissey getting ready to soil his shorts.

"Can you fight with that weapon, Cadet Cissey?" inquired the Colonel in a practiced 'I'm gonna fuck with you now' tone.

"Sir, No, sir!"

"Why not, Cissey?"

"Sir, the gun …"

"Gun? Did you say gun?"

"Weapon, sir."

"That weapon lying on the ground there, Cissey?"

"Sir, yes, sir!" Yipped Cissey at the Colonel, his voice going high as it cracked with fear.

"Okay, Cadet Cissey," the Colonel said, "here's what we're gonna do—I am the enemy, see, and I've got a knife right here in my hand, and I'm going to put this knife up under your rib cage and tickle your liver if you don't get to that gun before I get to you."

The Military likes to construct these kinds of situations to help obliterate any sense of reason you might have left. And I knew this was not going to go well for Cissey; I knew he was going to be marked and would be ruthlessly harassed and hazed from reveille to taps—woken up for a midnight reminder.

Do it now, I told myself. *Do it for Drew. Do it for Cissey, for that poor kid who hung himself out in the woods so many years ago. Do what you asked everyone else to do in the last issue of "Cesspool Cid."*

Out of the corner, I watched as the Colonel made his thumb into a pretend knife and held it out like he's getting ready to gig Cissey.

"You ready, Cissey?" said the Colonel.

"Sir, yes, sir!"

"Here it comes, Cissey, comin' atcha ..." taunted the Colonel.

I locked my knees and let myself go over, bent my knees at the last second to avoid landing smack on my face. The rifle I shunted aside so I wouldn't fall on it and knock out my teeth or accidentally whack Cissey in the back of the legs with it—hit the grass face-down just as the Colonel was ready to stab Cissey with his pretend knife.

There was this deep silence.

I lay there playing possum.

The Colonel looked over at me. The BC looked over at me and ordered my squad leader, "Sgt. Sashburn, see about your man!"

There was a pause, and then Sashburn fell over and hit the deck! Harder than me. Which was a surprise; I hadn't expected Sashburn to jump on board. He may, in fact, have actually fainted. The Colonel was still standing in front of Cissey when the BC called out to the platoon leader, "Lt. Ashcroft, see to your men."

Ashcroft double-timed it over to where I was lying, nudged me with his shoe, "Git the fuck up, Spic," he said under his breath.

That was when Massy and Jenkins in the first squad went down, followed by Menking and Callaway behind me.

The air took on a change out there on the field, got thicker, heavier. The grass where I lay was itching my face something terrible, but with my ear to the ground, I could hear them fall one after the other after the other—thumping the sod like dropped sand bags—hear the officers run around barking threats and orders, but there were simply too many of us. We'd had enough.

The Colonel looked out over the ones left standing, mostly officers and asslicks and Cissey who still stood there before him.

"Pick up that weapon, Cadet." The Colonel pivoted away. He had taken two steps when Cissey fell over and hit the ground. The Colonel kept marching; never looked back. Saluted the Battalion Commander and the BC, having worked up a pretty good sweat in the last forty seconds, returned the salute.

The Colonel pivoted again, marched towards the front of the battalion; as he passed the reviewing stand, he tossed a fuck-you salute to the Commandant whose face looked like it been doused with acid. Off the field the Chicken Colonel marched and up the hill to his olive drab sedan with Third Army stenciled on the side in yellow; his driver opened the door as the Chicken Colonel pulled off his cap, tossed it inside and followed it in like a dog fetching a ball. Away they drove.

"Have you thought about what you're going to do?" Mother asked as she sipped and flipped: highball and magazine. Cigarette. Highball. Magazine. The sun dropped below the motel's roof line. The pool area went cool in the shade.

"What's your plan?" Puff. Sip. Flip.

"My plan?"

"Maybe we should think about summer school. You need to get into a college and it may be your only route," she said not lifting her eyes from her magazine.

"I just got out of school."

"Did you want to go into the Army?" she said as if reading a story title from the magazine.

"The Army?" I repeated, she must have heard the disbelief in my voice.

"Best get some deciding done. You're out of the nest now. Always welcome to visit. But you've got to get on with your life—college, the Army, something."

An encroaching numbness, similar to the Novocain lip after the sting of the dentist's needle, as I watched Mother insert her long red nails to pinch a Salem from her pack—the burn scars from the accident visible on her hands. It had happened one summer afternoon: I had been playing on the floor in my room when I heard the boom of glass shattering. I turned around and looked up to find Mother standing in the doorway silently signaling to me with a pair of burning torches. Only after she turned and ran down the hall, after the scream broke the air, did I realize it was her hands she had been waving. Mother was on fire.

While filling the large silver cigarette lighter that sat on the coffee table in the living room, some of the lighter fluid had drained onto her hands. When she struck the flint to test it, her hands had burst into flames; she dropped the heavy lighter smashing the glass top of the coffee table. That's when she ran to my room. I arrived at the bathroom to find her on her knees, her hands in the toilet. "… My hands … my hands …" she whimpered as I stood there stuck in my ignorance of what to do—helpless to help her.

The Army? Four years at the Academy had seemed an eternity. Now, not only my time there, but the Academy itself was over. The Third Army had taken back its guns and manuals. Vietnam had left the country tired of war and war-like things. Our protest that day on the parade field had been the last straw. Next fall, instead of combat boots and sabers, it would be blazers and ties.

And though we had done in the military program, what surprised me most was to discover, out there by the pool at the Ramada Inn, that when you hate something for so long you really don't expect to miss it. And yet, it was the only thing I had known for four years—my bed, my board, my friends; both my enemy and my home. And I could never go back. As I looked over at the woman that was my mother with her bourbon and her questions, an ignorance came full upon me—I had no idea where home was.

Chapter 10

UT Austin

USHERED IN BY A HUMID SPRING, THE FEver of final exams was upon the student body. Meal attendance in the cafeteria had dwindled. The Coke machine was stripped bare; even the Mr. Pibb was gone. The amphetamines appeared everywhere all at once like wild flowers after rain: Dexi's green and yellow time-release pellets, the obsidian gleam of Black Beauties, the red/white of the two-toned Desoxyen tab; the white for speed and the red downer to smooth out the ride.

Science was with the students in our time of need. All was available without prescription and the drill was simple—pick your pill, rev your brain up and point it like a high-speed vacuum cleaner to suck-up a semester's worth of college reading material in a matter of days; suffer through the horrible crash with the aid of pot and Boone's Farm apple wine, and usually—hopefully, make the grade.

But things had unfolded differently this semester. I'd helped myself to the amphetamines all right, but the last reading I had accomplished was the letter from Selective Service. The seal on the letterhead said it all; the frowning eagle, arrows clutched in its talons. It was like a sinister gateway to a vortex—Vietnam howled on the other side. I had ten days.

Things had started to fall apart back in '69 when they held the draft lottery.

"Lucky number 7!" I barked with despair when they announced my number on TV. I had won a place at the top of the list for conscription. The only thing that stood between me and Vietnam was my student deferment: 2-S, college boy, 'Fortunate Son' as the song went. However, should I be so stupid as to allow my grade point average to drop below a 'C' for two consecutive semesters then I would be reclassified 1-A, promptly drafted, packaged in a uniform and shipped off to join the havoc.

And what had I done with this sword hanging over my head? Buckle down like anyone with good sense and make the grade? No, like some imp of the perverse, I began to fail. Not casually, but knowingly, with the grim helplessness of a legless man treading water. Course after course I failed. I begged for incompletes in the others—a desperate act of denial as I watched myself sink deeper, head ringing with doom.

The four years I had spent at the military academy left no illusions about the idiocy that I was in store for. The atrocities on the evening news. The callous disregard the military had for anyone's well being; rational behavior of the most basic kind like—*Don't Die!* And yet, I watched myself, mesmerized as if gazing upon a ghastly accident, I watched myself continue to fail.

Gone was my basic ability to read and comprehend a text book; pages would blur into an indecipherable smear that simply could not penetrate the noise of my own internal drama. My disease.

Only medical texts of a very specific nature could hold my attention. Studies on Huntington's Chorea, genetic research on neurological disorders, would grip me like a fast-paced thriller even though I had to read them with a medical dictionary at my side. I would meditate over a colored anatomical illustration of the brain, trace the ganglia, the cortex … *it attacks this area here which affects this here …*

I reread a monograph on Parkinson's, fascinated by anything that took its victims from the brain down. Any disease inherited was not just of interest to me, but a compulsion; that and the amazing ass that belonged to the girl in the white jeans.

She hung-out on the 7th floor of the dorm, the rec-room with the tangerine felted pool tables. Blonde stringy hair hung damp against her pink scalp as if she'd just stepped from the shower—all the time. Small-breasted, a tight cotton tank made the most of what was there. Not-so-great skin, her broad nose pushed-up at the end. She had the bloodshot eyes of someone who spends a lot time in the water—Gulf Coast surfer girl on an aquatic scholarship?

Without looking at me, she chalked her cue and asked if I would tighten the rack. She was showing off, but I didn't mind. Nice to get some clear direction in my life. Also, she had an excellent bridge with her index finger arched with a high elegance around the cue stick. She gave it a good crack on the break; a ball dropped. Then she critiqued her shape for the next shot. It wasn't like she was that good; to be so critical of her strategy. She wanted to be taken seriously, not just some chick fumbling around a pool table waiting for a guy to offer instruction.

As for my own shots, they dropped with uncanny regularity. The Black Beauty I had popped two hours previous focused what was left of my neurons. No need to stroke it hard, just a tap and they found the pocket. No hurry. Nothing else on my schedule, but count the days until I had to report for induction into hell. My universe had shrunk down to the balls on the tangerine table and the magnetic curve of her buttocks as she flexed around, arched her back, stood on tip-toe—a variety of poses that preceded each of her shots.

Admittedly, I was playing beyond my ability, channeling a game I'd never seen before. Somehow the compression of it all: the draft notice with its ticking clock, the hapless self-inflicted doom, the taut white jeans—it purged me of all but the moment. I merely lined up the cue and executed an ordained geometry.

Neither of us spoke. She was going to make all the mistakes by muscling it. Force. Disappointment. Self-anger. Renewed intensity, more forceful strokes and the ever fatal—going for the hi-risk shot. There was no ease in her game. All I had to do was let her lose. But then the thought streaked across my mind, *if she finally won would she quit?* What would I do with myself? Ten days left and I would be tagged and tossed like chum into the rice paddies of Vietnam.

All clarity evaporated. I scratched on the eight ball and lost the game. She checked the clock on the orange wall. UT Austin—everything was orange.

"I got 26 more cantos to read," she said. "Fucking Dante—trippy. I'm going to smoke a joint, if you wanna come up for a toke that's cool with me. My roomie's straight so we gotta be quiet."

Towed along by the low-slung roll of her hips, we arrived, shunted past the roommate bent at her desk and sat on the carpeted floor of the tiny hallway that provided access to the single bathroom shared with the adjacent room. She leaned against the wall, lit an expertly rolled joint and offered it. I was trying to find a way to take it without my hand trembling. She waited, her pink eyes upon me.

"Are you free," she asked exhaling a cloud of smoke. "Like really free?"

Was I *free*? It sounded like some kind of challenge, some how-hip-are-you test question and suddenly I didn't like her so much. It felt forced like her pool shots. Was I free? Stranded was a better word for it. I should be gathering wood, lighting a signal fire, desperately scanning the horizon for help instead of squatting in a bathroom puffing a joint and staring into her bloodshot eyes. But I didn't say that. I just nodded my head like—*sure isn't everybody 'free'?*

"That's why people turn to religion," she continued. "They're scared of real freedom. It means they have to think for themselves. We're all free, if you let yourself be."

"Uncle Sam seems to feel differently ..." I said and my voice trailed off as I thought about how soon I could get away from her and what else I could find to do at that hour, being extremely awake and all.

"The war is inside you," she countered. "Just surrender. Let go and you win. Give me your hand."

She seized my palm and focused her bloodshot eyes on it.

"... Strong life-line, but here, see this break? It means you have a big choice to make. But you have to make if from a sense of freedom, not fear. Fear's the way we die—like the song." Then, without a hint of talent, she sang a verse from the Youngbloods' song 'Get Together' while staring meaningfully into my eyes. I was so grateful when she stopped that it took a minute to realize that she had inserted my middle finger into her mouth and was sucking on it as she continued to stare into my eyes.

We got into this clinch; clothes were tugged aside, pushed down.

"Wait," she rolled to the side, reached between her legs and unplugged a carnelian-tipped tampon; with a sneakered toe, she kicked up the toilet seat, flung it in and tapped the handle. She rolled back onto her side and thrust her backside into my groin as the toilet finished flushing. Nothing sentimental about this girl; it was hushed, breathless sex bought with carpet burns, serenaded by a slow-filling toilet bowl.

Finished, she zipped the white jeans. "Recess is over," she said with a pat to her secured zipper. Disappointment must have flickered across my face for she stuck the rest of the joint into my shirt pocket and, like her zipper, gave me a pat. On my way out, I passed back through her room and glimpsed the roommate seated, purposefully bent over a book centered in the tight yellow pool of a Tensor lamp. How I envied her.

Down the hall I drifted, the roach smoldered with the draft summons still folded in my pocket. Should I flee to Canada? Could I ever return if I did? If I became a draft dodger, would my father ever speak to me again? He hardly spoke to me now. I knew him mostly by his doctor's scrawl on the bottom of the monthly check I received.

Back in my room, I leaned at the closet door and considered the dirty clothes that lay in drifts. And what would I take if I fled? Cold up in Canada. And what was their currency?

I checked the clock; it was after midnight. I now had nine days left. Hobbled with fear and indecision, I dropped into my bed. And as I lay there just attempting merely to breathe with slow even breaths, the phone went off like an alarm.

I dragged the receiver from its cradle—could it be the girl in the white jeans wanting to see how I was doing?

A girl's voice lilted on the other end, but it was not the girl in the white jeans. It was someone with a deep southern accent. At first, I thought she must have had the wrong number, but she mentioned my name. And then she told me who she was—Ween's wife.

I sat up in the bed, bolt upright as they say. *Ween was married?* And there were more surprises. For these I stood.

He was dying.

She didn't actually say that, but with a shaky gravity she announced in hushed tones, "He's not dewing real good and he just asked me to call yew ..."

Fucking Ween!

Chapter 11

The Delta

PANTHER BURN HAD BEEN IN WEEN'S FAMily for generations. All the old plantations had these names: Oak Alley, Swann's Point, Shadows on the Teche—most fairly obvious as to their origin. But Panther Burn had been named after a specific incident that occurred back when it was part of a massive Antebellum spread. There had been this panther, sometimes called a cougar or a puma, a breed of cat known to hunt alone, not in prides. And this one had proven to be cunning; not only adept at bringing down full grown deer, but with the pinch of civilization he had taken to looting the livestock around the plantation, carrying off children.

The Mississippi delta was all slow water and heavy air; Spanish moss draped the oaks. A hunting party was mustered; dogs were dropped. Near dusk, they ran the panther to ground in a cane break down by the river. Fires were set to converge and trap him against the water. Through the smoke and flames the beast could be seen as he turned from one ravening wall of fire only to be scorched and overtaken by another. His screams howled into the night. What else could he do as he burned alive, but scream and run in circles? Panther Burn.

"So good of yew to come!" Ween's wife looked all of seventeen, was grammatically challenged and visibly pregnant. His family lived in a red brick home, two stories with the quiet, understated confidence of an earlier time; a place where grown-ups lived. Inside, the rooms were warmly appointed with traditional furnishings and drapery. There was a library, a formal living room and a high-ceilinged hallway planked with dark wood that opened out into a comfortable family room. Generous windows, latticed with white sash bars, looked out at a backyard lush with trees. There was a modest guest house. Off the family room, a casual dining room adjoined the spacious kitchen where a massive black woman stood, perpetually bent over a counter, rolling out dough while having a discussion with herself.

"You stayin' for dinner?" she asked me with barely a shift in tone. "Nobody tells me nothin' but I's supposed to know everything."

"Yes, Lola. We gon need another place set," answered Ween's wife while Lola shook her head.

"Good thang I asked … uh hmm … good thang I bothered …"

Despite the natural light and warm domesticity, a somberness hung about the place. I was taken to an upstairs bedroom where Ween was tilted back in a massive Barcalounger. He was still in pajamas and robe at mid day flipping through channels with the remote as he cursed the TV. When he saw me at the door, he flopped around trying to escape the slippery leather of the recliner. Finally, he found the handle and catapulted himself upright.

"Spic!"

"Ween."

"Spic!"

"Ween."

He looked over at his young wife.

"Cloud, it's Bert," he said, "from the academy."

"Yeah, I know," Cloud answered tightly as she touched her swollen belly.

The light dampened in Ween's eyes when he saw his wife take in his sudden exuberance as he pumped my hand and patted my back. He checked his high spirits with an almost imperceptible slump to his shoulders as if just remembering he was not a well man. "Good to see you, man, really, great. Really. I'm glad you're here. Come on, I'll show you around."

"Don't tire yourself out, Bobby," Cloud warned both hands resting beneath the globe of her belly."

She called him Bobby reminding me that Ween's actual name was Robert Forrest and his family claimed ancestry with the confederate General Nathan Bedford Forrest reputed founder of the Ku Klux Klan.

"Oh, I'm feeling all right. Hell, Bert's come all this way, I gotta show him the place."

"No, celebratin' you two. He is not a well man," she warned me with a plaintive glance, eyes welling.

"Come on, honey, Spic—Bert is our guest so let us just take a little time ..."

"And be back for dinner. Even if you're not hungry. You got a big day tomorrow," she looked over at me, eyes hungry for sympathy.

"Startin' up his treatments tomorrow. All the way to Jackson. And then back," Cloud said as her voice cracked and she wiped at a tear.

Ween nodded his head in general agreement to all his wife was saying, would say or could say as he pulled on a pair of khakis and slipped the bony lengths of his bare feet into a pair of beat-up Weejuns.

"Yeah, yeah. Gonna be fine, honey. Don't you worry now, be jus fine."

"We gotta a baby comin'," Cloud sniffled at me as Ween quieted her with a reassuring, if abbreviated, hug.

"Gonna be fine. Gonna take some air, catch up a little with Bertie, men's talk, you know, baby."

Lola, her dark shape bent at the kitchen counter, nodded and shot us a look like we were heading out to knock over a liquor store and she knew which one.

"Dinner is hot at 6:30. Cold by seven ... Uh ... hmm ..."

A late model, lime-green Mustang with throaty pipes and wide tires—a fifteen-year old's wet dream stood in the driveway.

"Cloud's car," Ween said as he backed it out.

"You wife's name is Cloud? Is that like her Indian name?"

"Nickname. Claudia, I call her Cloud, as in a dark cloud hanging over my fuckin' head."

He brightened as the Mustang picked up speed and the house disappeared behind us. "Man, is it ever good to see you! Thanks for coming, bro. It's been awhile. How's college?

Couldn't hack it myself. Knew I'd end up workin' the farm anyways. The old man's liver blew up two years ago. Croaked. And Mom's been doing the back stroke across a scotch bottle while I run the whole fucking farm myself and cotton ain't what it used to be my friend. No, sir, the times they are a changin'."

Ween gave the nickel tour, related the legend of Panther Burn as we drove along a series of dry dirt roads that cut through the hopeful fields of young green cotton.

"Nothing much happening now," Ween said as I looked out the window. "Good time for you to come. Hell, anytime is a good time. I'm surprised you are here. Thank you, man ..."

A sob burped out of him unexpectedly, and then he teared-up so badly he had to pull the car over; he leaned his forehead against the wheel.

"Fuck! Fuck! Fuck!" He pounded the steering wheel, red face gone wet. "I'm so fucked, man!"

As bad as I felt for Ween, it was nice to hear somebody else say it out loud. Seven days before my date with the Selective Service and I wasn't exactly feeling blessed.

"How bad is it, Ween?"

"Fucked!"

"How fucked?"

"Very fucked!" he took a deep breath and exhaled the word, "Cancer."

"What?"

"Cancer," he repeated. "Fucking cancer, man!"

"You have cancer?"

He nodded his head 'Yes,' but then said, "No."

"Well, which is it?"

"That's what I told them," he moaned and punished the steering wheel again.

"You told your wife you have cancer?"

He nodded his head.

"But you don't have it?"

Nod and sob.

"So you lied?"

Sob.

"What the fuck is with you, Ween?" I released a hot bolt of

accusation. "Just like you lied about those girls that were supposed to be out at St. Mary's!"

It all rushed back: my anger at Ween, the death of Drew, my own ridiculously doomed situation. I needed to throw blame somewhere, somewhere outside myself. I needed to pass it on, gift someone else with the burden and here was a prime target, and deserving of all I could dump on him.

"... What was her fucking name?" I said coldly, "Your made-up girlfriend at St. Mary's—Marla? Amazing bullshit, Ween! What a world class liar you are. Like the Cassius Clay of lying. You have a gift, a calling—you should go into government. Jeezusfuckinchrist! And I don't know which was worse, your lying or our believing it!"

Big sob. Pause.

"But you never told on me, Bert," he choked out.

Big sigh as he snarfed mucous back into his lying nose.

"I didn't think we'd ever make it to that goddamn girls' school. "

"You could've gotten us killed! Those fucking Covites!"

"I thought it was just something fun to fantasize about. That's all—just a game."

"You did it to get attention. And here we are—years later, Drew's dead and you're still telling lies."

"It wasn't my fault! I swear to god, man. That night—something ran onto the road, an animal, fucking big, I swerved to miss it ... I swear ... it just appeared in the middle of the road ... it wasn't my fault! It just happened!"

Uncontrolled sobbing. It was cruel and unusual punishment to pin Drew's death on him. Even if it might be true, it was an unbearable truth.

"Okay. Okay. It's in the past. Gone. Over and done."

"That's right. I wanted you to know, man. I wanted you to hear it from me. And that's the truth. I swear!"

There was a pause. Ween's breathing returned to normal.

"Okay, okay. So your wife, Cloud, calls me and now here I am."

"Well, I had to tell her something, Bert. I was gone for three, four days at a time. Needed to get away. Do some thinking. "

"Cut the shit, Ween. "

"It was the fucking 'shrooms!"

"... 'shrooms?"

He popped the console and pulled out a plastic baggie and tossed it into my lap.

"Fucking mushrooms, man! Psilocybin. I was on a different plane—when I talked to people I was like really talking to them—in the moment, man. Listening to them. Figuring shit out. Understandin' stuff. Big stuff. You know what I'm sayin'? Passing a bottle of Dewar's around ... it was like ... deep, man. Cloud's not so great on deep shit. She is who the fuck she is, okay, she's Cloud, floating around. But sometimes I need to go off and talk about the Big Stuff. It was like when Jesus wandered out in the desert searching his soul. Only I was in New Orleans. It's all the same, that's the thing, it really is all the fucking same, man."

"So you ate these for three days?" I said examining the contents of the baggie.

Ween nodded his head.

"Scotch and mushrooms?"

"Fuck man, she would never understand! Try and tell her where I was at, what I was doing? All she sees is the drinking. It's all about the drinking, and that I'm not at home. And that I don't call. And she doesn't know where I am. Or who I'm with. Just thinks I'm just on another fucking binge after I promised her I'd go on the wagon. Fuck, I'm under a lot of pressure here, man. A baby on the way. Lotta fuckin' pressure."

"Yeah, but at least you're out of the draft. And you have a home—a job, this place."

"This? Panther Burn? I sold it, man."

"You sold the farm?"

"Had to. Needed the cash."

"You sold all the land?"

"My sister left her husband, moved back in. Cloud shops when she gets bored which is pretty goddamned often. Mom stays at the Four fuckin' Seasons in Savannah when she wants to change the scenery. Dude, do you have any idea how much a new tractor costs?"

"So you quit farming?"

"No, I rent the land from the guy I sold it to. But now I gotta make rent. Times have changed. Ain't the same as it was."

"So you decided it would be better to tell your wife, that you, her husband, have cancer rather than tell her you're going broke?"

"Seemed easier at the time. And I had a little side thing goin' on with this gal in the Quarter—nothing serious. You gotta help me here, Bert. I'm really fucked, man."

"Ween, as I see it, you got two choices: you either come clean or actually die."

"Yeah. Yeah. I know. Dying might be easier."

He reached into the bag of mushrooms, pulled one out, stuck it in his mouth and began to chew.

"... So, how you been?"

Chapter 12

Free Bird Home

IT WAS CUSTOMARY FOR PERDITA FORREST, Ween's mother, to install herself each afternoon in a white wicker chair that ruled the veranda. And though on this particular afternoon I was her only audience, silently hunched on a nearby ottoman, she seemed to be addressing a wider population somewhere just above and beyond my head.

"I have never worked a day in my life and neither will my daughter," she announced as if intoning the first line of a litany. In her hand was a silver julep cup, corseted with a gauze-like cozy to absorb condensation and insulate her fingers against the chill—meaning she never had to set it down.

At four in the afternoon the monogrammed cup appeared attached like a prosthetic at the end of Perdita's arm. It was kept filled with ice and scotch and would not be detached until just before bed time when the actual hand would be needed to steady her climb up the stairs.

Until that hour, she would wield the cup with the expressiveness of a conductor's baton: memories were evoked, current events parsed, politicians praised or dismissed; the boundaries of her domain were traced and defended by the graceful arcs and pointed jabs of the silver cup. And, of course, she used it to transport a steady stream of scotch down her gullet.

"My son is overwhelmed with medical problems," she lamented, "His wife is pregnant. Bless the girl, finally she's found something she can do," she finished with a slight roll of her eyes and generous swig from the cup.

Perdita possessed a fine head of gray hair: softly dappled, expensive looking like an exotic breed of horse—finicky and prone to injury.

"Somebody's got to run this place," the cup swung wide to indicate more than the expanse of land out there beyond my hunched form, beyond the screened-in porch, the white shutters, the immaculate lawn—beyond any actual physical acreage, to the mythic grandeur of a Panther Burn which was not so much out there as it was in her head.

Over the cup's rim, her eyes narrowed to assess how I was taking all this information. "You're a good listener, you know that? All the makings of a superb psychiatrist. Freshen your drink, dear?"

Earlier that morning I had driven her son to the first fictitious treatment for his fictitious cancer. Not wanting to subject his wife to its cruel rigors, "You're just gonna cry!" he had snapped at Cloud insisting that she remain at home to look after things which I took to mean the catalogues and magazines layered in drifts about the bedroom.

Ween's 'treatment' consisted of three hours frittered away in a crawdad joint two towns over. We drank beer, chewed Ween's magic mushrooms and threw horse shoes out back till I found myself bent over, staring at a horse shoe; marveling at its shape there in the dirt. Like the Omega, the last letter in the Greek alphabet, I thought profoundly to myself. There were seven days left before my body belonged to the Army. It was there at the bottom of every beer, waiting at the end of each song. It was like being on death row—all you could really do was count the days until the long walk. I stared down at the horse shoe and lost the ability to speak. Couldn't say anything as we drove back to the house.

By the time we arrived, Ween had acquired a glazed, limp look that passed for the after effects of some grueling medical procedure.

"I don't want to talk about it," he announced feebly amid Cloud's fussings. Then retreated upstairs leaving me to debrief Mama on the day's events: step into the circle of deception and implicate myself in the ruse. I had been called to help pull Ween out of this mess, when in fact, he was pulling me in.

Perdita resumed her appeal to those assembled somewhere over my head. "And my daughter, who married the town bully, seems surprised that he remains an insufferable asshole. I told her—people don't change, sugar, they only get 'more so'. A hobby is what she needs, outside interests. I myself am an avid gardener; tuberoses and Aggie's pants—that's what I call agapanthus. And let me tell you it's a chore. My back is killing me and not just the small of my back but the large—why the entire back of my body is often inflamed beyond description. But I never complain, not with my son fighting for his life."

Her eyes dropped down to consider the singular me, mute before her, "I think it helps, just your being here, Bert. He seems more hopeful."

I hadn't opened my mouth since we returned from the horse shoes for fear I'd never stop howling, or weeping, or both. The mushrooms combined with the crawdads and beer and now this additional layer of scotch—all landed on my senses to eerie effect: my body seemed to be shrinking inside my clothes and there was the overpowering smell of a cake baking somewhere; a delicious warm smelling cake.

"The cake smells wonderful," I heard myself mutter.

"What cake is that, dear?"

I had assumed Lola was busy in the kitchen baking. But just as Perdita informed me that it was Lola's day off, the screen door opened and Ween's sister, with immaculately manicured toes, stepped onto the veranda. If not the source of the warm cake smell, she certainly embodied its call to the senses.

"Hi, Mama."

"KayRae, this is Bert, Bobby's friend from school come to offer his support in our time of crisis."

"Hi," KayRae said sweetly, eyes gleamed with the momentary gratitude of a beauty queen. Then she turned back to her mother and dropped a tiny shopping bag onto an adjacent chair. Perdita acknowledged the bag with her cup.

"Well, it looks dangerously small whatever it is."

"That man is a pig," KayRae railed. "Fun is beyond his reach. Lacks the god-given gene to have a good time. And cannot abide any body around him having any. I got an assortment of perfumes to rid his stink."

Her face required my complete concentration to map the extent of her beauty, probe its edges, find the flaws. But I could find none; like an endless fall into a clear pool.

"Pardon my fury," she said with a pert nod in my direction. I realized I had been contemplating her like a religious painting and forced myself to look away, only to have my eyes spring back. Somewhere on a distant playground I heard the gleeful sound of children at recess while far overhead an airplane droned lazily—the entire world seemed to turn around the still point of KayRae's face.

When she smiled my first thought was would the Selective Service hunt me down with dogs—after my failure to show—would they run me to ground in a cane break on a cotton farm in Mississippi?

"I don't like lying to your mother," I said to Ween the next day on the way to his treatment. "And I don't like lying to your sister."

"No one's asking you to lie, I didn't say lie for me," he said changing channels on the car radio. "I'd never do that."

"You don't have to ask me," I persisted. "You put me in that position. They think I'm driving you to these fucking treatments. I nod my head at them and I'm lying."

Mostly, I was freaking out about the draft—six days left. My parents still thought I was in college back in Austin, but I was dead broke in Mississippi, hallucinating on mushrooms and scotch.

"I mean, Ween, I've got enough problems. I'm going to end up in Vietnam if I don't do something."

" 'Nam's a bummer," Ween said while chewing another mushroom.

"Thanks for cluing me in, Ween."

"Blow it off."

"Blow it off he says ..."

"You'll die over there. Stay here."

"Stay here? And wait for them to come get me? Is that what you're saying?"

"We'll hide you. Plenty of places."

"Hide me? I'm broke. I don't even have enough money to get to where I'm supposed to report even if I wanted to fucking report there."

"You can work at the shop."

"The shop?"

"The money from the mortgage—I got this partner, building contractor. Pre-fab homes, they go out in pieces stacked on a flatbed truck like a kit. Assembled on the lot."

He actually turned down the radio and shot me a meaningful look, "Once this thing breaks, we'll get orders for hundreds of 'em."

Ween peered into the question mark of my face, "I'm waiting on you to tell me it's a stupid idea like everyone else."

I opened my mouth to speak, but he held up his hand to stop me, "But don't because I can't handle any negativity right now," and turned the radio back up.

"Well, I know you're fragile what with fighting the cancer and all ..."

Ween, set his jaw and turned the radio off. He accelerated the Mustang into a turn.

"I believe in this thing, okay!" he shouted over the wind whipping in through the windows. "And it's my thing. Not my daddy's, not anyone else's. It's mine and it's gonna fuckin' work!"

"I can see it," he hollered and gestured wide with one hand like his mama with her silver cup. "I see them—hundreds of homes, people living in them, raising families ... and stuff like that."

Another turn and we pulled into the mud parking lot in front of an aluminum Quonset shed. There was a scattering of dust-caked trucks and cars. The whir and pop of power tools came from within.

"This is it," Ween said proudly. "Freebird Homes. As we like to say, 'A Freebird Home Flies to You'."

Ween stared at the metal shed with the misty glow of a true believer about to enter his church. "We'll pay you cash under the table, Bert, no problem. Know what I'm sayin', buddy."

"Okay," I said as I looked out over the dried Mississippi

mud surrounding the shed like a rutted race track. "And is there anything else I should know?"

Ween nodded his head slowly, "I think KayRae likes you."

KayRae drove her new blue MG convertible as if she were waving a banner of freedom in big, easy arcs back and forth across the dirt roads that wound through Panther Burn. Occasionally, she'd grind a gear when down-shifting, but KayRae didn't care. She was a woman growing stronger with every purchase, rising from the ashes of a dead marriage on the wings of her credit cards.

"Fuuun!" she squealed and cranked the radio to Neil Young's "Cinnamon Girl." Fun had little to do with how I'd spent the last five days sweating inside the big metal shed at Freebird Homes. I worked with a crew of two scrawny redneck boys who barely had a full set of teeth between them, and an older black man who wore a cap, bib-overalls and a long sleeve shirt every day in the swelter. By ten in the morning the shed was hot and by three in the afternoon it was like swimming around inside a damp furnace.

We built walls, all day long. Four walls laid out on horizontal jigs: one had a picture window with a front door, one had a bedroom window, one had a kitchen window and a back door and one had a hole for an air conditioner (not attached).

Each wall got stuffed with pink fiberglass insulation before it got one of three different styles of 'authentic' wood paneling stapled over with pneumatic guns. Electrical outlets, wall switches—the whole thing was wired and ready to be plugged in. The finished walls were then stacked onto a flatbed truck and rolled off to be glued together into a home and set on a show lot eked from drained swampland somewhere around Biloxi. A Freebird Home squatting more like a turtle in the mud.

I never saw one actually put together except for the picture in the brochure and that an artist's rendering of the home with imagined landscaping and an imagined car parked in the imagined driveway. Didn't look much like the stack of stapled walls we loaded on the flatbed which had more the look and feel of a really crappy mobile home; the kind you see on the news all blown apart by a tornado or a hurricane, or maybe just a drunken spouse on a rampage.

"Tornado fodder," I said to Ween when he would come to pick me up at the end of the day, "We're building tornado fodder."

"Man, I can feel it—this is gonna be big. Talk is the state might get involved, low income urban housing, animal shelters, lots of possibilities and we can deliver them anywhere 'cause, as you know …"

On cue I coughed out the motto, "A Freebird Home Flies to You." After all I was grateful he was trying to help me, even if he was besotted with his project. Each morning Ween would drop me off on the way to his 'treatments'. I'd work in the shed and he'd pick me up in the afternoon. We'd sit in his car, drink beer and eat mushrooms which only served to increase my anxiety.

"Starting to freak," I blurted out. "Supposed to report to the draft board day after tomorrow … freaking out now …"

"Ain't nobody knows where you're at. You get paid cash under the table. Just hang on now. The first Home Show is Saturday in Biloxi. And I'll make you a promise when this takes off, I'm gonna give you a Freebird Home. And a little piece of land to put it right here on Panther Burn—nice spot—trees, a little pond."

It didn't seem to matter to him that he had already sold the land. But I kept listening, wanting to hear something hopeful, reassuring.

"You can live there for as long as you want. It's yours. Hell you belong here, man. Fuck their war. You stay right here. Be a part of this family."

I swallowed his words like a hungry child. All my panic melted away and into my mushroom-addled brain there rose a vision of the future—like stumbling upon a secret map of your life: showing you not only where you've been, but where it is you are going. Like a cheat sheet from the fates themselves revealing the very reason why I had come to Panther Burn—it was my destiny to marry KayRae!

It was all so clear: fall in love, elope to Natchez or some other romantic gulf coast getaway (after her divorce was finalized). The vision was less specific after that; there was the Free Bird Home Ween promised me with adjacent pond, but it seemed certain that my membership in the family would be firmly established. That was all I needed.

I would encourage Ween to take the profits when Freebird Homes hit and buy back all the original land. I was meant to be here with these people. Together we would work to make Panther Burn a model of modern agriculture. Perhaps, even extending our crop rotation to include the very magic mushrooms that had fueled this vision. Why shouldn't Mississippi reap the benefits of this natural, spiritual tonic that allowed me to comprehend my place in all this? Forget the draft, fuck the war, it didn't matter. I was becoming someone else—a new and different person.

KayRae pulled off the dirt road; the car skidded to a stop that killed the engine and ignited her laughter. I toted a well-laden picnic basket while she unfurled a quilt for us to sit on. A fine bottle of Lancer's was uncorked. I marveled at my good fortune. Of course, I hadn't told her about Ween promising me the house or anything about my vision of the future. Just said I'd heard about the pond and wanted to see it. It was a picture of pastoral beauty, except for a few patches of pond scum and the occasional cloud of gnats. But mostly beautiful in the late afternoon as the sun bathed us in a soft glow.

Unfortunately, there had also been a certain glow in my pants. Actually, more of a burning sensation whenever I peed. The girl in the white pants. Back in Austin. Her love wasn't so 'free' after all. Sex with her had cost me a case of the clap. But I was not going to let it dampen my spirits or mar this special day. Necessary antibiotics would be procured and the problem solved. It would just take a little time during which I would, of course, abstain from any sexual temptations.

"To fuuun," KayRae said as she elevated her wine glass. We clanked. "And sweet freedom," she added with a dramatic sigh, plush throat thrust skyward. She drained her glass dry and lolled back onto the quilt to settle supine, arms spread, hair spilled around her head. On her lips a sinuous smile.

"*Tujours*," I thought I heard her say, meaning "always" and thought it very romantic.

"*Tujours*," I said back gazing down at her too pretty face in the too perfect light. When she turned the brilliance of her green eyes upon me, it became almost unbearable.

"Well, then?" she asked slyly. "What are you waiting for? Take me, I'm yours," she closed the green eyes as if sliding two jewels away in a drawer, and then lifted her chin offering her lips. 'I'm yours' she had said, not '*tujours*'. Perhaps a touch melodramatic, but she was lovely, who cared if it was a little corny.

"You look very beautiful," I said.

"Yes. And you want me don't you?"

"Yes. Yes, I do," I said a little too quickly. And I did want her. Wanted to freeze the moment and play it back again and again for years to come—this moment and the one before, and this one now ... but she was in more of a hurry.

"Well," she said with a lift of one eyebrow.

"Well …" I paused, casting about in the hollows of myself for a gambit.

"What's your problem?" she said going flat.

"I can't," I said, "Not right now … at this moment … here."

"What?"

"I am unable to do that which I very much want to do."

Up she sat like she'd been stung and now sought the perpetrator.

"You can't?" she looked at me through narrowed eyes, the green gone murky, "And why can't you?"

"Well, it would really be better if we waited, you know, for the timing to be just right … for us."

"The timing is just fine; nothing's wrong with the timing," she insisted.

"Well, it seems I have been visited with an unforeseen health issue."

"You're like sick or something?"

"A slight infection."

"An infection? What sort of infection?"

"Uh, well, it's of a personal nature."

"Is it? And where is this personal infection?"

"Down there?" I said with a dip of my head toward my nether parts. She considered my crotch for a moment as if it were a face that she couldn't recall the name of. Then her eyes flashed back up at me.

"Liar!" she snapped.

"No, no, I'm not lying," I insisted, but she began to gather her things.

"Oh, yes you are. And there's something wrong with you, all right."

"No, really, I just can't. I mean it would be wrong of me—"

"I've been going through this for three years with a fat, stupid bully of a husband—I don't need it from some boys' school fairy."

"I'm sorry?"

"Oh, come on. Gone all day with Robert? No girlfriend back in Texas? What was your major in college anyway—nursing?"

It was our first fight, but I had to trust in the vision and eventually everything would fall into place. KayRae, not having had the vision, was feeling rejected and understandably upset. Eventually, she would see she had me all wrong.

"That's just what I thought," she spat into my well of silence. Then she was up, a sparking flurry headed for the car. I followed dragging the quilt, a trail of deviled eggs leaking from the picnic basket.

"I just wanted to have some fun!" she bleated and slammed the car door.

Back at the house, we returned to find Perdita standing in the middle of the room, silver cup attached, shouting up the stairs to no one visible.

"Why would I get a call from a bank in Biloxi asking me questions about a mortgage against the property? What property is he referring to, son? Robert!"

"Musta been a wrong number," came the muffled reply

from upstairs. KayRae brushed past her mother and huffed up the stairs.

"He called this house," Perdita repeated. "He asked for you by name. I don't think it is a wrong number if they say your name. Tell him to come down here, KayRae. I want to speak with you, Mister!"

Ween appeared at the banister eyes hooded, donning his sick robe like a flak jacket, "I said I'd give him a call tomorrow and straighten things out. Don't worry about it."

"Don't worry? If you went and put a lien against this property I am most certainly worried, worried I will beat you senseless!"

"Hell, Mama—I could crap cherries on a china plate and you'd bitch about the pattern."

"I wish your father could hear such language, like a syphilitic field hand."

Cloud appeared beside him on the landing, "It's the treatments. I think they make him moody. And he's been drinking."

"What the hell are you talking about drinking, girl?"

"I can smell it."

"What is she saying, Robert?"

"It's the medication is all," Ween whined.

"Can't be good, the chemo and the liquor," Cloud accused.

"Well, I believe the girl is making some sense, Robert. Maybe you would like to give it a try?"

"EVERYONE JUST LEAVE ME THE FUCK ALONE!"

The room fell quiet. KayRae stepped out of her bedroom to see what was going on. Ween looked at me, his eyes pleading to be rescued.

The vision I'd had about Panther Burn: my belonging with this family, the Freebird Home by the scummy pond—KayRae; I could feel it all starting to evaporate. And as it evaporated something terrible was forming in its place.

"Tell them, Ween," I said.

"Yes. Tell us." Perdita said. Ween looked down then dropped his head. Perdita turned towards me.

"Okay, then you tell us."

"He doesn't have cancer," I may as well have fired a shotgun in the room for the ringing it left in our ears.

"What is he saying, Robert?" Perdita asked much too quietly.

"You don't have cancer?" Cloud mouthed in utter disbelief.

Ween had begun to shrink noticeably, retracting mollusk-like back into his robe.

"You told me you had cancer and I'm pregnant with the baby and all?" Cloud blurted and started to tear up. "What about the 'treatments'? Where were you all day?"

Perdita turned to me, "You were with him all day. You drove him to his treatments?"

"There were no treatments," I looked at Ween.

"You lied to us about taking him to his treatments," Perdita said her eyes still on me. "Why didn't you tell us?"

They were all looking at me.

"But I did just tell you."

"Well, you should have told us before now," Cloud whined angrily.

"Indeed you should have," Perdita concurred. "Our little talks out on the veranda—that was all lies?"

"It was not my intention to lie to you."

"Did you not sit there and let me believe you were escorting my son for cancer treatments? Shame on you! A guest here in my home; eating our food. And all the while lying to us. Is this the kind of friends you have, Robert?"

It was KayRae's glare that burned the worst, her unblinking eyes venting waves of hatred.

"He's a liar," she hissed. "A liar and a queer." With that she turned on her heel, strode back to her room and slammed the door.

It was well after dark when the pick-up truck dropped me off near the highway. He was a black man with gray salted through his beard. The news crackled on the old Ford's radio. And I literally could not believe what I heard. I asked the driver if he had just heard it too. And with a nod of his head he replied, "Yessir, the man said they done stopped drafting boys for Vietnam. Done called off the draft."

I had been due to report for induction the next day and they had just ended it. I asked the driver to tell me again. He chuckled and congratulated me. I was free. But when he dropped me near the interstate, and I watched as his truck lights disappeared down the side road, my elation at the news began to subside. It was that terrible thing I had sensed back at the house when the vision of Panther Burn and my place in it had crumbled: it was there on the empty highway that I stood on—extending off in either direction—disappearing into darkness. My foot began to twitch.

Chapter 13

The Strand

THE CHRISTIANS PICKED ME UP SOMEWHERE in the Louisiana countryside. Darkness had begun to fall and with it the fear of another night bivouacked in a field, shivering beneath my plastic poncho, waiting for something bad to happen: trampled by livestock, mauled by dogs, run-over by rednecks in a pick-up truck. A loop tape of imagined catastrophes whirred through my mind while fireflies lit themselves from within, heedless of my situation.

Hence, the bubble of gratitude that rose in my chest when I saw the approaching headlights slow, and then pull off onto the shoulder just past me.

Inside the late model sedan were two men, dressed in jackets and ties with the precisely placed hair of salesmen. Any momentary reassurance I got from their appearance gradually dissolved into paranoia as they questioned me. First, came the perfectly acceptable, "Where are you going?"

"Down the road," I answered with what I hoped was the weathered nonchalance of an old road dog.

The driver turned toward his companion and I caught the look that passed between them. I shrugged it off and while my ass was enjoying the ample upholstery of a full-sized, late model American car, my nose discovered that I had begun to smell.

"And what is your name?" asked the passenger in that round, over-modulated voice people use when addressing small children and domestic animals. I considered lying, but what did I care?

"Bert."

"And where is home, Bert?"

"Texas," I said sticking to the short answers, letting them

know I wasn't a big talker. Just a ride please. Nice ride too. Climate control. No snakes in here.

"And does your family know where you are, Bert?"

He was handling my name with overly familiar tones. Now I wished I had made one up. My hand found the door handle. I informed my ass we might be relocating soon.

And then, after a festering pause, "Where is it you're going again, Bert?"

A probing tone had now come into the driver's voice; he was no longer making polite conversation, but seeking hard information.

"Uh, just traveling right now."

"Bert, you sound like you don't really have a destination," said the passenger.

"Makes it easier to get there I reckon," I drawled trying to lighten things up. My effort was absorbed by another awkward silence. They had their own agenda. The driver gently cleared his throat.

"Not knowing where you're going makes it hard to know when you get there. Must get awfully lonely out there on a dark road."

"It does get quiet sometimes," I conceded scrunching closer to the door.

"And scared? Do you get a little scared out there? Fearful for yourself?"

I was getting a little scared right there inside the car; didn't like the drift of the conversation at all.

"How would you like to change your life, Bert?"

It was an enormous question that raised other enormous questions. I balked at the great pile of questions stacking in my head. My breathing stopped.

"Have you ever prayed to Our Lord Jesus Christ, Bert?"

Here we go.

"Yes, I have." I said with a firmness I hoped would allow us to leapfrog to another topic. And, in fact, I had prayed many times as a boy curled in my bed, prayed for all the selfish reasons a boy prays for: not to get caught for breaking, lying, stealing and cheating; for some coveted Christmas toy; prayed because you overheard your mother, tanked on bourbon, declare to your father that she's "done" with you; prayed that Kaydeen Bohner wouldn't get impregnated by your defective seed. I had prayed before, but privately, behind closed doors, like masturbation.

"Would you like to pray with us, Bert?"

The car was pulling off the highway. Freaking, I made an adrenalized review of all the personal information recently leaked to these two strangers:

That no one knew where I was.

That no one was expecting me.

Which implied:

1. I would not be missed for a long time, if ever.

2. I was an idiot.

Two polyester sex criminals, after some bogus Jesus-speak to calm their mark, were going to bind, torture and kill me in that precise way that only the neatly dressed psychos do. Then toss my 'difficult-to-identify,' semen-drenched remains into the kudzu for the ants to finish.

My hand tensed on the door handle ready to blow the hatch as the car slowed to a stop.

"Let's bow our heads now. Bert, would you repeat after me?" Silently, I complied, bowed my head in the backseat and waited for the blow to land: lead pipe, black jack, weighted Bible ...

"Dear Jesus Christ our Lord ..." intoned the driver, head bowed to the steering wheel. They were waiting for me to speak while my hand was ready to pull the latch, hurl myself into the dark. They'd never catch me, but it was warm in the car and so dark outside—mosquitoes, snakes, local law enforcement thugs.

"Dear Jesus," I repeated, my voice breaking, incredulous at my situation: praying in the back seat with two men who used hairspray. But I did. I asked Jesus to help me, to guide me and to, "... grant me forgiveness ..."

At first, I played along, faked it, but as I spoke the words, I heard the sound in my own voice—a quiver like maybe I really wanted to be helped, to be guided, to be forgiven. My face flushed hot with shame.

After a mutual "Amen," they must have heard my heart pounding for the driver turned his head back towards me, "Do you feel that tug in your heart, Bert?"

"Yes, sir, I do."

"That's Jesus letting you know he's listening. He hears you, Bert."

I didn't know if He had heard me, but I had heard me, heard the longing in my own mournful whine. And these two with their swoopy hair had heard me too. They pulled out their wallets, gathered and placed twenty-three dollars in my unwashed hand, money to be spent for a bus ticket home. Stunned, I mumbled thanks for the ride and for not killing me and for the money (even though they had made me pray to their God for it).

They dropped me near Galveston, a once grand city gone to seed with its fading Victorian mansions and moldy, sea-damp hotels. It was a dissolution that appealed to me and I decided to allocate a portion of my Christian funds towards a celebratory drink.

"Happy Hour Every Hour!" read the drooping purple banner outside a hole-in-the wall. As my eyes adjusted to the darkness inside, I began to see the patrons were all male.

"Salud," quipped the middle-aged gentleman on the barstool next to me, his yachting cap at a jaunty angle, pale watery eyes. He raised his glass towards me, then made a great show of speaking confidentially, "We're having a little barbecue later, just a few friends dropping by the house, you are more than welcome."

His younger, swan-necked companion in a blue-striped French sailor shirt, lazily bobbled his head in affirmation that indeed, this was all true. But as I searched for the right words to gracefully decline, the companion grew impatient and bobbled his head back to the skipper. "She's not talking," He announced haughtily.

She, meaning me. And I got the feeling that BBQ invite or no, I was crashing someone else's party. I tried to finish my beer without appearing to be in a rush while I couldn't help but notice the rising volume of the music as more male bodies crowded into the bar as if answering the call of the jukebox. My foot had begun to twitch uncontrollably.

With a polite nod to my disgruntled neighbors (they turned the other way), I hopped off my bar stool and began to work my way through a gauntlet of severely tanned men slippery and reeking of coconut oil. They pushed up against the bar three deep. Like thirsty waves, they rose and broke against the bar with an outreach of arms lilting over heads, and then receded back, cocktails in hand, bobbing to the thump of disco music now so loud it was felt as much as heard.

An emaciated young man ravaged by a diet of amphetamines, Bloody Marys and anonymous lavatory sex suddenly spun away from the bar in a momentary seizure of appreciation for the opening strains of "Rock Your Baby." He bumped into me and in reaction I whirled around to gain my balance. Thinking I was dancing, he shrieked encouragement.

"Go baby!" he yelped and clapped hands over the bleached hair lying thin on his sweaty head. I continued, sort of shuffling to the beat, to move past him on towards the door while "Rock Your Baby" soared in volume. George McCrae crooned his spell into the cigarette air; a beautiful falsetto voice calling out for love as I jigged my way through the oiled pectoral gauntlet, because if you weren't kind of bobbing and bumping along with the others you seemed judgmental, a grumpy straight guy. *'She's not talking'.*

So I tried to look like I was having lots of fun as I bobbed towards that painfully bright slit of sunlight that glared from the crack in the door jamb. And there, gleaming in that bright slit of light, was the very question the Christians had asked me in their car, "Where is it you're going, Bert?"

That pit inside my chest that had opened when I stood on the dark highway in Mississippi, and when mother had asked me what my plans were after the Academy—popped open again dark as an umbrella that filled my chest—where would I go after I passed through that door out into the blinding light? And at that moment the song soared.

... TAKE ME IN YOUR ARMS ROCK YOUR BABY ...

And his voice slipped into my body as a hand fills a glove

and spun me away from the door. If I had no place to go why not go into the song?

I became a puppet to the music like those inflated cloth figures seen in front of car dealerships: flapping scarecrows gesticulating wildly, movements dictated by the buffet of air runneling through them. Turn off the fan and they sink limp to the ground. But with the fan blowing they are robust, shivering effigies. And so was I flailing in the music's blast.

… *WOOOMAN TAKE ME IN YOUR ARMS ROCK ME BABY* …

A lavender-colored joint in a seedy beach town—sweet refuge poured from a juke box in a room filled with men. The song faded like love itself; the lights stopped moving. Rather it was I who stopped spinning. I grabbed the bar to steady myself. And there was Blas—posed, a stanchion of gravity at the center of the swirl.

"There are love dogs no one knows the names of," he said with a grave face. "Retsina?" The quote was from Rumi and the straw-colored wine he poured was Greek with a heady turpentine finish. I think he was waiting for me to make a face, but I downed it and pushed my glass forward. It was filled again.

He had an untrimmed furze of beard. Eyes deep set; dead serious and unblinking. A disc of yellowed bone hung from his neck on a leather thong. All of this set him apart from the other men in the bar like a pirate king among a group of nannies.

"So, you work here?" I asked.

"Work here?" He repeated, eyes brightening with the absurdity of my question. "You mean this moldy jewel box for old queens? No, my work is done elsewhere. I appear here and receive a stipend for my presence. And you? An avatar of Shiva come to remind us that we are both alive and dying?"

Something about my performance on the dance floor had impressed him. "Eros and rage fly off of you. You are like Artaud's actor signaling to us from the flames." Again my glass was filled. "With whom have you studied?"

With whom have I studied? I laughed out loud. He liked that too.

"Exactly," he barked. "Birds learn to fly by hurling themselves into the void."

"Yes," I said, "But do they get drunk first?"

Blas didn't laugh. He introduced himself with a pronounced Spanish accent when he said his name. He had a loft in the dangerous part of town. Two lofts, actually: the working loft and the living loft side by side on the top floor of an old building cavernous as a train station. It was on the bay side of the island, a wide old street called The Strand. There a scattering of dive bars and boarded-up buildings provided cheap loft space for those 'sooners' of urban renewal—artists and gays.

Blas thought he had glimpsed something of value in my gyrations on the dance floor. The surrender I had experienced hurling my body around the room said something to him; something he needed to remember in his work.

"A deliberate raid on the unconscious!" He assumed my movements to be a practiced art. Though eventually he assessed that I genuinely had no idea what it was I had done. Which only served to further enlarge his appreciation. So he found me worthy of mentoring.

"Movement is the origin of the theatre—the pure language of the body when loosed from the intellect."

I became his pet—the love dog no one knows the name of. A pallet was offered in a corner of the working loft, entered to from the living loft through a ragged hole banged in the plaster and lathe splintered like an artillery blast. There the piled confusion of paint cans, the gunked brushes—the art clutter—chaos but for the stacked canvases that leaned against the wall. One was a large figurative mural in the Mexican style: a church of crushed automobile bodies, angels flew on wings of bone. Other canvases were turned away. Blas tossed them about like so much discarded lumber to make some room for me in a corner of his life.

We ate like campesinos on bowls of beans brightened with cut limes and sweet onion; tortillas oily with lard, dense as leather bought for pennies out the back door of El Jardin a few blocks away. Yoghurt made by a hippie woman who mended his clothes as she grinned at me, dark-toothed and lewd.

Blas talked incessantly. I knew nothing; he knew everything. But he wanted to know what I thought about everything he knew, like he was trying understand himself better through me. He practiced a combination of praise and verbal scourging—both overblown, rhapsodic.

"YOU MUST DO SOMETHING! No, not perform in some trite show-goes-on-at-eight thing! Like a shaman you MUST APPEAR AND CHANNEL!"

"And don't use phrases like 'I don't know'," he would command, "It makes you sound ordinary. Read Rumi. Present an image. Don't explain it. Bewilder! People worship the mystery. Explanations are asked for, but never appreciated. No one wants to know you're confused. It's not interesting!"

He hated working in "that tired fag bar," but he also hated hustling patrons, sucking up to the reps and gallery owners in Houston. I watched him hurl a drink on one of his paintings when someone compared it to Frida Kahlo.

Thin skinned. Prickly. You could say nothing about his work. If you liked it, he would tell you what was wrong with it. If you were measured in your appreciation, he quietly launched a vicious attack on your character that began with your shoes and would terminate in an imagined bedroom with your disappointed mate staring forlornly at the ceiling. Didn't do much for sales.

The work, stacked about the loft with obvious disregard, was good, but he claimed he didn't 'do that' anymore. "If I'm going to repeat myself why not become one of those gutless, student-fucking academics?"

His current obsession was with three-dimensional works he constructed from desiccated animal bone and old quilts pierced by an array of 19th century surgeon's scalpels. Wounds.

"Carne!" he would shout out to the room—the overall effect of this work being a kind of primordial slaughter as found artifact—an excavation. Dramatic lighting would raise its morbidity to a quasi-religious level.

During the day cargo ships would glide soundlessly back and forth across the bay outside the floor to ceiling windows while I worked through my assigned reading list: Grotowsky,

Artaud, Rimbaud, Jodorowsky. Blas sat hunched in a battered canvas chair, glared at his 'wound' and shouted, "Carne!" Between tequila shots.

In the evenings, another vaporous bottle of Retsina would be uncorked; a box of Marlboro Reds unsealed and Blas would be off.

"Dance reciting the Tibetan Book of the Dead—tear rags from your body, screaming naked the chikhai bardo … we could rig something …"

Inflated art blather, but his words had an effect on me. Maybe I had something in me besides a self-destructing time bomb. Maybe the self-destructing time-bomb *was* the something in me, the thing that made me an interesting person. Or as Blas put it, "Not interesting! Chess is interesting. Be something they cannot look away from!"

While I was contemplating how I might appear and channel something they could not look away from, I needed a job. Blas introduced me to the other denizens of the enormous old building.

Reigning in the loft next door was Garren Waite. When I asked if Waite was a good artist, Blas responded tightly, "Do I think he's a good artist? It doesn't matter what I think. His shit sells."

Waite's success as a sculptor was evident from the interior of his loft: a white staircase curved up the exposed brick wall leading to two bedrooms with a full bath constructed over a raised and gleaming kitchen area. And as if torn from a Caravaggio painting, red velvet drapes spilled from the tops of three fourteen-foot windows onto the heavy planks of the floor. The view of the bay was the same view as Blas's, but central air filtered out the oily humidity; there was a lightness on the skin—it was easier to breathe.

Garren was older. He spoke with an elegantly crafted southern drawl which he unfurled by the yard, wrapped around those gathered in the room and gradually pulled it tighter until they revealed whatever it was he was probing for. Exposing people was his recreation.

"I have had thirty-three one man shows, produced lit-rahhly tons of art, whyyy the stuff I did on Mykonos alone—crating, shipping, it could have filled one of those tankers passing by. Thank god, it all sold. There was some breakage, always is, can't be avoided, the breakage, can it? And how are you fixed for space down the hall, Blas? You were wise to retain that second loft for storage."

Blas did a slow burn; waves of irritated heat rose from his head.

"You all have some of this grass," Garren said extending a joint. "It is very good, not too strong, but it's all I can do now that I've given up the drink."

Blas intercepted the joint and made his thrust with an aside to me, "Garren is forty now and needs to slow down."

"I am not forty!" Garren snapped back, the speed of his words outstripping the normally relaxed cadence of his accent. He shook himself like a wet bird and settled back into the sofa to launch his riposte. "Things seem quiet down the hall, Blas, should I send some people your way?"

Blas dropped the joint in a bronze deco ashtray, stood and performed a squeaky about-face on the tire soles of his huaraches.

"Coming?" He asked me without looking back.

"You all do drop by tomorrow. I'm having some folks out from the city," Garren called after us with triumphant cheer.

In silence, we marched down the main stairs to the street level and out into the appalling humidity of a Galveston summer. On the corner was Café des Artistes, a haphazard concern just coming together. There I was introduced to Janis, the dark-haired proprietress (the café was a venture funded by her family to keep her at home in Texas and out of Morocco). Janis moved with a slightly moist, easy-lay quality that suited her low-slung breasts and olive complexion. Blas told her I needed some work then stalked off down the street in search of something to bludgeon Garren Waite with, or so I imagined.

"Moody," Janis said regarding Blas. Then she handed me an apron, gave me a slow once-over with her stoned brown eyes, "... I usually fuck my waiters, but I'm seeing someone now."

I tried not to let my disappointment show at her change

in policy. There was a dismal scarcity of available females on the Strand. It had begun to feel like I was on an isolated outpost populated solely by men. Janis excused herself to sway upstairs and "see" the architect who was refinishing his loft above her café.

An hour later, the café ran out of glasses halfway through the lunch rush. We just waited until those people eating finished using their glasses so we could rinse, and redistribute among those waiting. I asked people if they cared to share a glass with their table-mate—romantic two straws? Few were amused.

Cafe des Artistes was granted a lot of latitude because it was new, boho funky and the first eatery to open on the block in forty years. But in the tropical humidity, with only the slow turning ceiling fans, there came a perceptible wilt among the clientele. They wanted a drink with their sandwich, and they wanted the sandwich they had ordered—the one from the menu; the menu Janis had concocted blasted on hash the night before and never looked at again.

I continued, optimistic as an aid worker, handing out the same ham and Swiss on rye. When the rye ran out, it was wheat. Eventually, Janis returned. She pushed the moist ringlets from her face, brushed at the sawdust ground into the back of her skirt, and asked what the problem was. I handed her my apron. I could accept being humiliated by my own incompetence but not hers; especially, while she was off fucking someone other than myself who not only needed fucking, but some decent tips for his efforts.

Garren Waite, who had come down and taken a table for lunch, grinned at me on my way out and flapped goodbye with half his sandwich. Job over.

But what was I going to do?

It had ceased to be a question and turned into a statement, a perpetual statement of a raging condition.

What was I going to do!

The angst, first directed at organizing my little corner of the working loft, moved on to Blas's stacks of paintings. I sorted through them, lined them up along the walls; paired certain ones, leaned them back-to-back against one another in a sort of an 'A' frame that ran along the center of the room. Then I changed them again: by contrast of theme, color, brightness; juxtaposing in a way that made the variety of the work stand out more. To my eye, it had an emotional movement, highs and lows—even humor.

When I was done, all the work was visible for anyone who cared to walk around the room. Blas looked at the arrangement and said nothing. He slouched in his battered chair, sipped tequila and stared at his wound.

I returned from my job-wandering late one afternoon; I didn't look for work so much as I wandered through areas of town hoping I'd stumble upon some kind of opportunity or maybe meet a girl and she would somehow save me. *Take Me in Your Arms Rock Your Baby ...*

But it was Garren Waite I found at his doorway, sending someone off as I came up the stairs. He turned the intelligent beam of his attention upon me; a small smile tugged at the corners of his mouth as if I brought to mind an amusing memory.

"Have you found other employment after that debacle at Janis' little lunch bucket?" He asked.

He needed some painting done in his loft, the entry room. "I am simply incapable of painting anything white," he said squinting up at this skylight. "Have you eaten?"

My body must have been noticeably thin, for Garren would set small plates of food down as I worked above on a twelve foot ladder. He would look up and say, "Oh, very nice."

"I messed-up there," I said pointing to a drip.

"Oh, no, I meant your legs."

As a man I had never been aware that I had legs other than for walking, running and standing purposes. And yet, as I studied a turned calf, it did not escape me how desperately susceptible I was to flattery of any kind. If someone had said, "My you chew your food very well." I would, no doubt, have been bolstered with a new found pride in that.

Garren's salon gathered in the late afternoon; the booze trolley was rolled out and people would start to drop by: wealthy Houston housewives stranded in the gulf between their husbands' golf and deer hunting and their own 'cultural' interests. They would show up in twos and threes crowding into the foyer, overriding the smell of my fresh paint with their perfume and Bain du Soliel; garbed in wrinkled linens, wrists and fingers weighted with gold.

They adored Garren Waite, his fey, but powerful hauteur, the quick wit and double-edged compliments.

Regarding a piece of his sculpture I overheard him say, "Whell, of course you love the piece, darlin', you are graced with an appreciation for wonderful things—take it home and see if he kicks a hole in it when the check clears."

Not all were dilettantes. Some carried a currency all their own; held positions in well-heeled Houston arts funding programs, influential with the vast pool of oil money, players in the underwriting of civic art works. Houston was a soulless, nouveau riche swamp exploding like a mushroom, social climbing for national recognition. It needed trophies to lend it substance and refinement. And Garren Waite had the good sense not to live there which made him even more irresistible to those that did.

After I had pushed paint around for a few hours in the foyer, Garren appeared and announced that it was time for me to refresh myself upstairs in his bathroom, then come down and join in. A clean white shirt was laid out and some draw string pants that were not quite pajamas.

After rinsing off, I came down to Garren heckling a wispy-bearded young man.

"Uh, now, let me see if I heard you correctly—you have dropped out of medical school and are now making jewelry. Both strike me as tediously practical occupations."

If the ex-med student was both chagrined and charmed, he was also a little shaken. I huddled on the edges of Garren's circle, avoiding the glare of his wit. He was not so much interested in exposing people's illusions, as he was in testing the mettle of one's grip on their illusions. He would poke and tease to see if it was just a mirage you were marching towards or something more substantial. His claim being that you had to play for keeps if you wanted others to share in your illusion. First, it was you who had to be thoroughly convinced of you.

"Well, did you bring any of this jewelry with you ... oh, I'm afraid you did ..."

And though Garren was certain of his own brilliance, there was, as the evening wore on and the women trundled back to Houston with a receipt for a piece of Garren Waite tucked in their designer beach bags, there occurred a perceptible slump to him; weariness with his own dazzle. The twinkle dimmed in his eye and something hung about him as fine and troubling as a strand of spider web—an inkling that it had all happened already and now he was on the other side of the Great Moment. He had made it. And there he was, after they closed their checkbooks, unstuck their adoring eyes and left. There he was climbing the stairs of his sumptuous loft alone—the artist.

"What a lovely evening it's been," he sighed. "Now I shall go upstairs and weep." On his way up, he paused, looked back and turned up the blue flame of his eyes for a moment as he focused on me, "You seem so dis-engaged, Bert. Is it ennui? Are you bored?"

I nodded my head as his words pointed to the amorphous feeling I had yet to name. Yes, I was bored, but it was a terrible boredom born of moving neither towards anything nor away from anything while at the same time being excruciatingly restless.

"Then I am very sorry for you," he said. "Very sorry, indeed. Uh, you may keep the clothes." He shuffled up the stairs to his bedroom and closed the door.

Blas was silently drinking when I returned. He stared out the window at the ships passing in the bay. A recording of Tibetan monks meditating was playing. It was a sound I could not imagine being further removed from meditation, like old armor being dragged across cobblestones and banged with sticks while crude horns blatted.

He didn't speak. Did not look my way. I went to lie on my pallet; sweat puddled in the hollow of my throat; the incredible stillness of the heat, my head buzzing *what will I do ... what will I do?* The record finished playing in the other room, I could hear Blas moving, a bottle shattered on the street below.

Garren, for whatever reason, actually began to send people wandering down to Blas's loft to have a look. These people considered his work through the filter of Garren's implicit approval and found themselves taken with the canvasses and their affordability.

But Blas chaffed under the tedious questions about his technique, his influences. He would just turn and walk away, leaving the prospect and me standing before the painting. In response to the ensuing pause, I opened my mouth and witnessed a stream of bullshit pour out about the difficult phase of work he was in or how 'this particular piece' had been an 'emotional Rubicon' for him. It was but a thin mimicking, a combination of both Blas and Garren's artspeak with some Jodorowsky tossed in. However, the paintings started to sell. Blas would return, see the check on the table and say nothing—just slump in his chair with the tequila, stare at his wound.

When a large canvas (depicting an anorexic Our Lady of Guadalupe, vagina stretched and bolted like a cathedral door, giving birth to an army of Conquistadores with fluttering gold leaf eyes) sold at a particularly good price, Blas excused himself from negotiations and returned later with a slab of hash wrapped in tin foil like a pound of chocolate. There were dates and more chilled bottles of Retsina. The hash was carved into pointy wedges and shoved inside the dates where the pits had been. We chewed them into a sticky mash and washed it down with the cold wine. Blas seemed in good spirits though in a measured way.

"So how's Garren?" he asked in a tone so neutral that it could be mistaken for nothing but disapproval. I told him my job painting his foyer was done. He nodded and pushed another hash-loaded date my way.

He unsheathed a record and placed it on the turntable. Egyptian music, the sinuous timbre plucked from an oud. With night came a distant wail of sirens. An orange color in the sky drew us to the windows. A wharf, stacked with bales of cotton was in flames. From a half-mile away, the heat was felt on our faces. The conflagration towered with the breezes; clots of burning cotton would loft up, carried by the heat into the surrounding night, then fall into the black waters of the bay. A fire boat shot arcing streams of water from its cannons.

Shunning the traditional sofas and chairs, Blas had strewn cushions and quilting like the floor of a Bedouin tent. We lounged against the big pillows, our glasses of Retsina on a low wooden table. The white walls of the loft wavered in the orange light reflected from the burning cotton, windows opened to the sultry, smoke-tinged air.

The hash dissolved through the cell walls of my digestive system. The edges of my body grew blurry, blending with the atmosphere. Whatever position I found myself in, I seemed as perfectly settled as a rock in a river bed. If I shifted, I would only find myself in another equally perfect position. Indeed, there was no reason to shift; the world seemed willing to cup me in the palm of its hand.

Thoughts of Janis materialized: after her return from fucking the architect upstairs—the after-sex smell of her, the sawdust on her back, the idea of her not even getting undressed, the panties stretched out of shape, if she'd worn any at all.

Had I quit the job too quickly? A falling-out with the architect would have likely led to a resumption of her old ways with the hired help. I would have been the next in line for her favors. Would being tossed the occasional fuck from Janis be worth suffering her incompetence as a restaurateur?

"My name is not Blas," came a bilious announcement from out of nowhere. "I'm not Spanish. I'm a Jewish boy from Houston."

I paused my porn film of Janis and shifted my head in Blas's direction to let him know I was listening.

"But no one wants to know who you really are," I said quoting his own words back to him.

"I want you to know. Actually, I'm only half Jewish," he said. "My father had some Spanish blood. But you see a queer, Mexican painter has a tortured authenticity. Whereas a queer Jewish painter from Houston without a New York gallery merely has a hobby. So ... I changed my name."

"Whoever you are, they like your work."

"Ha!" he snorted derisively and swigged deep from the bottle of Retsina. "Idiots."

A brown glass vial appeared in his hand, unlabeled. He twisted off the black cap, brought it to his nose and inhaled. Then reached it towards me.

"Sniff," he said and passed the open bottle under my nose. "Go on, sniff it." There was a vaporous dirty socks smell, and then, as I inhaled, my entire vascular system dilated all at once—a tsunami of blood rushed into my head. Amyl nitrate is not something you roll over your tongue while composing a suitable comment. Suddenly you're on the floor, the wind knocked out of you, crying uncle.

As the throbbing subsided, I was indeed on my back, arms outstretched like wings. My groin felt warm and heavy. I looked down to see Blas's hand, hairy and resting on my crotch. It was a good, masculine-looking hand appearing that much more out of place on my groinal area. Not that it felt unpleasant, but it was a man's hand, and years of training regarding this particular area: the appropriate display and touching of; cleaning and concealment of; its disturbingly independent nature i.e. visible and uncontrolled reactions to seeing parts of the female anatomy revealed or even the accessories that suggested those parts: the totemic power of the black lace brassiere, even alone and empty dangling from a shower rod—was it not the very emblem of wanton sex?

But this was a man's hand—a hairy man. But how exactly should I ask him to stop? And why should I ask him to stop if it felt good. And did it feel good? Whose rules was I living by anyway?

I examined while Blas undid my pants:

I had had 'feelings' for men that I admired. Charismatic men that seemed to know what they were about in life. Blessed with an ease and confidence that would bring them success, you could tell. Had they just been loved more? Adored from the day they were born? Is that what attracted me to them? The mantle of love; could I borrow it by proxy—tug a corner of their confidence to cover my insecurity?

If I watched them close enough, spent enough time with

them, could I crack the code of their mechanism? How they managed to be who they were. These attractions were intense. At times, I suspected they might be sexual and was confused, even ashamed of them. Maybe, I fell in love with them. But did I want to fuck them? Was that what I wanted all along?

And now that Blas was rolling my dick around in his mouth, an opportunity seemed squarely before me. Maybe there was a room somewhere inside of me, a secret door that I had been afraid to open. And what with the shortage of local females …

The Egyptian music, the double strings of the oud vibrated in an uncanny synchronicity with Blas's strokes. Yet, I was flagging. Too much in the head.

He paused his ministrations; the brown bottle was uncapped and passed under my nose. Again the locomotive of blood, wings beating in the heart; rising up towards the red throb of life itself.

Meanwhile, Blas made a series of maneuvers—his hips by my head, his head buried in my crotch like a feeding animal. His shorts unzipped, he was stroking himself, pressing towards me, inviting me to reciprocate.

Purple bloom of the head. Velvet scrotum. Who knew we men were so soft?

Moment of truth. Over the falls. Penis in the mouth. Sucking a cock...

Okay. Looking for the fun. Looking for that black brassiere feeling ...

Not getting it. I found no pleasure; merely, a foreign object—a guy's pecker in my mouth. I had one. Didn't need another. Mystery solved. Spit please.

Blas felt differently, he peered up from his ministrations, could he really be enjoying it that much? He was checking to see what had stalled down on my end. And I appreciated his efforts and all—felt complimented in an odd way. After all, he was paying attention to me. So I shut my eyes and there was Janis, her skirt tugged up, pubis thrust forward.

Did men think of women when they fucked each other in prison? Does someone have to put on the black brassiere, literally or psychologically?

Noting the obvious droop in my interest, Blas redoubled his efforts. And I turned up the heat on Janis: she rolled and pinched her dark nipples, coaxed dribbles of cream for me. Sent lewd signals with her mouth and tongue.

Blas had begun to stroke himself while with his other hand he reached again for the brown vial. He snorted, gurgled and groaned in what I took to be the throes of an epic climax. But fumes from the amyl flooded the room, suddenly stealing the air. I found myself upright watching Blas roll from side to side, hands clutched at his throat, face turning blue, mouth open in a silent gasp for air.

The brown vial, cap off, lay in a puddle, a wet stain darkened the front of his shirt, his face was wet. He had spilled the liquid down his nasal passages and couldn't breathe. The vapor was overpowering. I had to get to the window. I grabbed his legs, dragged him towards the windows as he gagged and retched.

"Breathe!" I yelled, tore off the amyl-soaked shirt, tossed it out the window. My own head boomed and swelled. I staggered over him.

"Breathe!" I shook him as hard as I could. He heaved himself up onto the window sill and drew a breath, retched, coughed, but again he gulped at the sweet air and washed his lungs.

In the distance, the flames from the burning wharf had been reduced to an orange smolder of timbers. Occasionally, one would give way and collapse with a hiss into the water below. I wiped the curtain of drool that hung from Blas's beard. We breathed.

Chapter 14

The Montrose

TWO BLACK GUYS, YOUNG AND LEAN AS GAzelles, sat in the front. In the back, I was nestled next to a doe-eyed male, the arm of his boyfriend draped gently over his finely-boned shoulders.

They had rolled out of Stewart Beach in a red '59 Impala convertible headed north towards Houston. The door opened with easy smiles as if they had been sent to pick me up. I climbed in. Not a word spoken. They just smiled. Relaxed as warm cats, their silence increased the simple shared pleasures of a gulf coast day: the salt-tinged buffet of wind under blue sky, the reflected glimmer of grassy marshes, the mulchy wet smell; the flocks of birds rose and fell in harmony with the exotic music coming from the car's radio tuned to a station that I have never heard before or since.

They dropped me off on Westheimer in the old Montrose section of Houston; left me with a supple quietness in my body, and though I had no idea what to do or where to go, for the moment it did not trouble me. It was a relief to be out of Galveston, gone from Blas's loft. He needed to glare at his wound in solitude.

The shops along the street were caught half-way in transition from post-hippie funk to yuppie-wine-bar. Mature trees lined the street of older homes. I happened upon a beleaguered little café with unmatched chairs and tables, tattered flyers stapled in layers on a well-chewed bulletin board. The place was making an effort: a quiche special was offered on the blackboard while patrons still clinging to their long hair sat on the porch, paused over journals as if trying to remember what it was they were writing about.

Next to the café, a larger building of rustic brick had a variety of males loitering around it. They read from pages clutched in their hands, mouthing the words and gesticulating like mental patients. A sign read Apex Theatre with an arrow that pointed down some stairs. I was passing when a young woman appeared at the top of the stairs wearing a vintage blue dress printed with white flowers.

"Did you get the sides?" she asked in a voice so clear and precise you might think she was British, but there was no accent. It was a voice cleansed of any regionalism. A trained voice.

She caught me mid-stare.

Between the fingers of one hand she held a Marlboro Light, in the other hand a clip board. Shod in a pair of leather combat boots like the ones I had worn at the Academy, except her boots had gone so long without polish as to have attained buckskin like knap.

I shook my head 'no' in answer to her question. I had no idea what sides were. I did, however, want her to continue speaking, preferably to me.

"Where are they?" I asked.

She shuffled through her clip board and pulled off several pages of text stapled together. "You will be reading for 'Curley'," she said, as she handed me the pages and asked my name.

"Uh … Bert."

"Are you sure?" her eyebrows arched in mock interrogation. I nodded as her smile spread wings and flapped into my chest. Brown irises flecked with a gold—a glimmer of sweetness, of goodwill.

She scribbled my name, dropped her cigarette, and gave it a precise turn with a boot. Then she reached down and picked up the butt. She held it like a dead insect and called out, "Randall" as if giving it a name.

One of the gesticulating males whipped around and eagerly fell in behind her as she retreated back down the stairs.

On the pages she had given me, 'Curley' was described as, "… a mean little guy who wore a leather glove filled with Vaseline to keep his hand soft for his wife ..."

Steinbeck's *Of Mice and Men*; the scene where Curley, the boss's son, enters snarling at people. He picks a fight with Lenny, the huge half-wit migrant worker. Curley forces a confrontation until Lenny, pushed to rage, grabs Curley's gloved hand and crushes it in his own as Curley screams in pain and drops to the floor. Abuse. Anger. Lashing out. I understood.

When it came my turn to follow her down the stairs, I noticed a slight limp—her right leg was not only shorter, but somewhat smaller than her left. Faintly withered, as if left over from an earlier, younger version of herself. But what was impressive was she had developed a method of landing and stepping smoothly off her right toe that almost completely masked the condition. This endeared her to me, not so much the leg as the endeavor to conceal its impediment upon her life.

The basement had a low ceiling, exposed pipes overhead and outdoor carpeting. Through a haze of cigarette smoke I could see a stage area had been painted on the floor. Sets of risers with folding chairs surrounded it on three sides. In the middle riser, towards the back, sprawled the director: one long blue-jeaned leg hung over a chair while he stubbed a smoke in a French Market coffee can.

"Okay, let's do it," he growled and lit another in what would be an endless chain of Pall Malls. Two actors, one big, the other smaller rose from chairs and shuffled quietly onto the 'stage'.

"Okay, Curley?" The smoking man looked at me with that awful kind of droopy-eyed self-confidence you see in some Texan males based on nothing more than bluster and a fancy pair of cowboy boots. Being tall and handsome had only contributed to his condition.

"Got any questions?" he drawled with a hint of challenge.

"Yeah, is there a restroom?" I asked.

"Show him, Paige," he said after an exasperated sigh that I enjoyed immensely. Again, I followed Paige, my eyes on her leg as she walked me through a disheveled dressing room with empty sockets around the mirrors. She gestured towards a yellow door as if I'd won a prize.

"Do your worst," she said with a half-smile and left me to wonder if she was referring to the sudden need to void my bowels or the impending audition. The toilet had seen some hard use as a receptacle for the cleaning of paint brushes. I emptied myself all at once and was concerned about the odor; the idea that Paige might catch a whiff horrified me. I unlatched a small window above the toilet and cracked it open.

Heads turned to greet my arrival from the bathroom. "An actor prepares," the director cracked. Mandatory chuckles and my foot started to twitch reminding me that I was doomed already so nothing really mattered anyway.

I joined the actors on stage, but in spite of my doomed perspective, as I lifted the script I noticed my hand shaking. When I looked up, both actors were gazing at me expectantly.

"Anytime, Curley," drawled the director.

I swallowed and read the first line aloud. Like an audible version of the unsteady hand, my voice quavered in the room. I stared at my next line, but before saying it, this time I turned to the actor playing Lenny and looked him in the eye.

When I spoke, it was to those eyes. My words slowed and my voice was weighted with an unexpected intensity. And though they were not my words, they were dipped in my anger. It didn't even seem to be words so much as a sound I was making, a sound from way down inside me that wanted to be heard and shoved aside all other considerations to do just that.

Then the other actor made a sound back at me and things got more charged and we got louder. It was like being in a dream, but knowing you are dreaming and allowing yourself to be led by the dream.

I seemed to forget, as did my body, who I had been before I'd stepped on that stage, before I had opened my mouth and the sound started to spill out larger than I had ever imagined myself being.

Afterwards, like waking, I got up from the floor where I had writhed and screamed in pain as the actor playing Lenny 'crushed' my hand. I felt oddly calm inside as if emerging from a warm bath. The basement was quiet.

The smoking director, Quinn, conferred in whispers with Paige who looked my way and nodded her head. I became nervous again, suddenly at a loss as to what to do with myself. Having no idea what the protocol was, I decided it best to wander off towards the door.

"Hang on," Quinn called out.

They talked a little more, and then Paige beckoned in her warm, clear voice. The role of Curley was offered. Rehearsals would begin the next day and I would be paid absolutely nothing.

"Welcome to 'underground' theater," said Quinn.

I had a part in a play. Now all I needed was a place to stay, a job and some food. The remainder of the afternoon I spent at the café next door nursing an endless cup of coffee, eyes trained on the comings and goings over at the Apex Theatre. At last, Paige and Quinn emerged at the top of the stairs. They waved goodbye to one another and went off their separate ways. At least they weren't a couple. After allowing enough time to be certain everyone had left the premises, I strolled over and made my way back down to the basement.

The front door of the theatre was locked, but an outside corridor ran around the back side where I came to the bathroom window I had opened earlier. The screen popped-out and, I glanced over my shoulder and crawled inside.

Inside the basement an EXIT lamp gave off a greenish glow. I located the light switch and found some old black felt material thrown over a sofa. Tired from my day, I lay down and wrapped myself in the musty cloth. Though guilty of breaking and entering, I thought it was fair compensation, at least temporarily, for my work as an actor. And eventually I would find a place. The rest of the night I spent thinking of my role: what Curley might wear, how he would stand and walk; debated whether or not to actually put Vaseline inside Curley's leather glove. It was a refreshing break from obsessing about my own past, present and future. After all, I was now, quite literally, in the theater.

I met Jimmie at the first rehearsal. A taut stretch of sinew and gray-eyed resentment. Pale-skinned with wispy locks, he had the automatic sarcasm that marks bright, smaller men who have identified their size as the source of all their misery. I was immediately drawn to his bitterness. Jimmie had the role of 'Candy,' the old guy who ran the bunkhouse.

Only a year or two older than me, we also had in common

our lack of acting experience. It was also Jimmie's good fortune to live with Paige, who was a force within the Apex theater hierarchy. Not only had Paige starred in several Apex productions, but she had actually studied acting in college prior to dropping out and opening an organic health food store with Jimmie. He had come into a modest inheritance, but organic health food had yet to find a profitable niche among Houston's blight of burger and fried chicken franchises. The health food store failed leaving Jimmie and Paige a lifetime supply of brown rice and miso paste. Paige's interest then shifted to the small theatre starting up in the neighborhood. Jimmie, who busied himself with odd carpentry jobs, grew resentful not only of her time spent away, but also the attention she received from the men around the theater.

Jimmie would attend her shows with a simmering hostility that boiled over one night after a performance. The cast had all gone out for drinks and Jimmie felt thoroughly out of it and wanted to leave. Paige, high on her performance and numerous glasses of the house Chablis, wanted the night to continue. Sullen, Jimmie drifted outside where he lurked around fitfully until he decided it was time for his own theatrical moment and put his fist through a window pane. Check please.

Not wanting to lose Paige, the Apex made a discreet decision to offer Jimmie a part in one of the upcoming productions. It was one of Quinn's boasts (the chain-smoking director and presiding egomaniac) that he could make anyone an actor, though he himself had a terrible time memorizing lines—too much pot or was it the speed? And so Jimmie accepted the role of 'Candy' with the proviso he would put his carpenter skills to use in building the sets.

Instead of wondering where Paige was at any given moment, Jimmie found himself focused on the intricacies of his character and the tack around the 'barn'. Being handy with tools, he used them on stage. And, of course, he had that complete deer-in-the-headlights stare when it came to opening night. It was a look I recognized in the dressing room mirror as I tugged the curlers from my hair ('Curley' after all, was my character's name).

Paige played Curley's wife with a sensual, forlorn quality that was less of the tramp described by the male characters and more of a lone woman caught in a man's world with no one to talk to. It was Paige who was first to suss out my nightly camping in the theatre. She must have spotted one of my little piles of discarded clothing. Lacking the facilities to do laundry, I simply bought clothes at the Salvation Army and tossed them when they ripened.

It was also Paige who got me a gig as a waiter at El Chico's, a restaurant ranked at the very top in sheer volume of bad Mexican food served daily. Paige proved to be as warm, soulful and decidedly braless as I suspected when we first met. She was a vegan who puffed Marlboro Lights through her brown rice fasts. A graceful hostess, I would watch her night after night as she crossed El Chico's huge dining room, menus in hand, with her special gait, the withered leg hidden under a mid-calf vintage black gabardine dress, beadwork sparkling across her chest.

One night, after the play had opened, I was invited for dinner. Paige had prepared the meal, remarkable for the total absence of meat or dairy. Even butter was eschewed by Jimmie who claimed it tainted his farts which he rigorously evaluated and commented on.

"Yep, that's butter all right."

Yet, the meal offered a beefy-tasting meatloafesque entrée complete with hearty gravy and vegan sides all surprisingly tasty and filling. And this was how they ate all the time. No dairy. No meat. No refined sugar. Though alcohol and Marlboro Lights had somehow managed to slip through the ropes.

We sipped scotch after dinner, engaged in lively discussions on acting and the theatre and who was fucking whom over at the Apex. The hour grew late and as I reluctantly prepared to make my exit Paige looked at me and said, "Going back to the theater?" Busted, I said nothing and could look neither of them in the eye.

"Why don't you stay in the extra bedroom tonight?" she said and rose to make the bed. I looked at Jimmie who smiled wryly, "The cat will munch your toes if they stick out of the blanket."

The following morning I awoke to the smell of French press coffee and fresh baked muffins, whole grain of course with clusters of blueberries oozing.

Together we crawled through different sections of the Sunday Chronicle: Jimmie deciphered the business trends with bitter amusement, Paige weighed-in on the shallowness of the latest movies and I tossed out mock quotes from the book reviews.

Afterwards, we saddled up our ten-speeds and were off for a bike ride. Actually, Jimmie and I had the ten speeds; Paige rode an old balloon tire vintage Huffy with a girl's dropped crossbar and a basket on the handle bars. Mine was some local chop shop special painted gray with no brand names visible (an affordable deal at sixty dollars) while Jimmie had a spidery new Raleigh with clamp-on air pump and water bottle. A Raleigh had good resale value Jimmie informed me.

Jimmie and I would sprint around chasing one another only to return panting on either side of Paige as she peddled serenely under the arboreal arches of the Montrose where we lived. Winded, we'd pull off along a section of Westheimer, enter one of the trendy shops, make fun of the disco garb on display; then mount up and peddle on to an herbal tea at the Hobbit Hole. All of life's hard questions, if unanswered, were at least masked for the moment by our being actors in a play.

As "Of Mice and Men" approached the end of its run, it was agreed that we needed to share another adventure. The Yucatan! Together we would explore the Toltec splendors of the Mayan ruins at Tulum, or Palenque with its huge ball court and the House of the Jaguar temple.

We would maintain the road less traveled, eat for pennies at local *mercados*; stay in small fishing villages. We would be travelers not tourists. I would scale the 91 steps of El Castillo at Chichen Itza. I would pray to Chac, the ancient rain god, to reconfigure the constellation of my genes, I would cut myself, splash fresh blood into a stone bowl of the reclining Chac Mool. I was full of shit; mostly I just wanted the three of us to be together.

In the weeks that followed, we read extensively, charted a

number of possible routes, plotted an itinerary. Restaurant tips were squirreled away. Jimmie and Paige had become my best friends. More like a best 'friend' for I saw them as a couple, adored them as a unit and was never so comfortable with either one separately as I was with them together. I, in turn, provided some refreshing stimulation to their relationship well into its sixth year and, as I gradually became aware, on approach for a reckoning.

"It's her mother," Jimmie confided one afternoon as the two of us worked on our bikes in the carport of their apartment.

"Paige's mother wants her to get married and can't relax until she's snagged a man like her sister up in Michigan. They've given up on me because I don't believe in marriage. It's bullshit. We've been together almost seven years. *Seven.* It's her mother-fucking mother fucking everything up."

Jimmie may have thought marriage an out-dated institution, but his living arrangement with Paige was traditional in its roles: Paige went to the market, kept the house tidy and cooked the vegan meals while Jimmie paid rent, maintained the car, killed bugs and hammered things. Viewing this arrangement, I was never quite sure why Jimmie was so dead set against marriage. Who wouldn't want this nutritious and harmonious relationship to continue? I certainly did.

It was decided we would fly to Merida, the colonial capital of the Yucatan. From there make our way by bus and hitching all around the ruins and back up to Texas. We'd travel light, one small pack, a pair of sturdy shoes. No cameras. We didn't need pictures, we lived in the moment! That was the snapshot—the memory of the moment. We priced quality back packs at an outfitters and put in orders for three in varied colors.

Meanwhile, my bargain bike had developed shifter troubles. As Jimmie helped me with repairs, he revealed an infidelity. I had met the couple, she a wild, cat-eyed redhead and he, a dull redneck with an inherited position in the family construction business that kept Dale in a late model truck and house payments and his wife Jeri in fresh shoes and dresses. Jeri made her physical attributes all too obvious, but also obvious was Paige's complete lack of interest in Jeri's husband, Dale.

I assumed Jimmie had been maneuvering towards a little 'swing' fling for them as a couple and it derailed into a side cheat for him and Jeri. It seemed a foolish risk—his relationship with Paige for a go at such a gold digger. There was no question in his mind that Paige was a worthy life partner whereas Jeri could never be more than a drunken tree fuck at the end of a summer party. But then I had never been with anyone past the time it took to have an orgasm, get dressed and flee, or, as sometimes was the case, be fled from. So I held my tongue and changed the subject, hoping it would go away and all would be happy once we arrived in the Yucatan.

The subject came up again at a happy hour I shared with Paige and Jeri. Jimmie had taken a roofing job contracted out by Jeri's husband and I guess he felt Jeri wouldn't wander off 'fucking-the-world' if she was with Paige. So there I sat sipping my third margarita grande listening to them chat, knowing Jeri had fucked Jimmie, knowing that Paige didn't know it and feeling the disappointment of knowing that people we think we are close to are often not what they seem; that lies are not so much told as beliefs are allowed to continue uncorrected and the road to hell made smooth until we are surprised to find that there is no more road.

I was in line for another shift in perspective when I heard myself blurt to Paige, "I'll always love you whether Jimmie marries you or not."

Paige said nothing, but Jeri responded while sucking her lime wedge, "Yeah, but can you provide for her?"

I turned to Paige fully expecting her to correct Jeri and inform her that she was referring to a lifestyle women had left behind in the 50's. But Paige quietly looked at me with those brown eyes flecked with gold.

"Are you saying that you require a man to support you?" I sputtered, incredulous. Both women nodded their heads in unison.

"... And marriage too," Jeri added slurping the last of her grande. Paige said nothing which was far more than I wanted to hear. This was Paige, an artistic woman with strong opinions about health, diet and the environment—she wore fucking combat boots!

The conversation congealed along with the nachos on the table. I made an effort to resurrect it with some small talk of where we might be staying in Merida, but this was upstaged by more prosaic concerns—ones that didn't involve me.

Paige and I pedaled our bicycles home on the down side of margarita euphoria. A shift had occurred; you could tell by the way we rode our bikes, further apart as I lagged behind like a pouting child.

Damn the knowledge! I cursed to myself as I pedaled. *Fuck all knowing!* Best to live in ignorance; like a cow, chewing and mooing until they blow a bolt through your brain. What was the effect of all this knowing, but a less blissful present? And what was there, but the present? What was awareness, but awareness of impending loss: sickness, death—betrayal!

A week later, the other shoe dropped; plans for our big trip postponed by a summons from Paige's sister in Michigan. Paige was to come up and help with the kids while her sister's husband was away on business. Paige said she would be gone for at least ten days, she wasn't sure. But she would be back, she assured me, and then we would take the trip.

"Could I take the rice pot?" She asked Jimmie pointing to one of the copper bottomed set of Revere wear that hung above the stove.

"Uh, I don't think so," he said without looking up from his newspaper. "I'm going to need that here while you're gone."

Paige left the next day, without the pot.

I never saw her again.

Her sister had hand-selected an eligible, marriage-minded, sufficiently moneyed man and apparently, the match took. Now it was Jimmie and I alone in the apartment. We ate out much of the time which made him even grumpier because of the strictness of his vegan diet.

"They cooked the carrots in butter—I smell it in my farts," he complained.

I tried once to make us a dinner. It was a poor effort I realized when Jimmie cackled at the grilled cheese sandwiches I set on the table.

We began to get on each other's nerves, argued about which

movie to see—I wanted the Bergman, he wanted the Eastwood. Paige would have gone for the Bergman.

Things finally came to a head one night as we sat in his truck trying to decide the least offensive place to eat. Concerning one option I remarked, "Yeah, it's not like Paige's cooking is it?"

Uncomfortable with admitting the loss, Jimmie snapped back, "That's why I didn't let her take that rice pot—I didn't want to break up that set."

"Break-up the set?!" I moaned. "Who gives a fuck about a goddamn pot! She's gone! Because you wouldn't fucking marry her. You were practically married already! What's a fucking ceremony, 'I do' and a ring? Where the fuck are you ever going to find someone, anyone to cook that obsessive fart-sniffing monk food? We were going to the Yucatan! I bought a fucking back pack! Was it her leg? Her withered leg? Was that it?"

And, as I had found myself writhing on the floor after my audition for Curley, I now found myself pounding the dash of Jimmie's truck wet with the sudden and embarrassing discharge of tears.

"You need to get your stuff," Jimmie said not with meanness, but matter-of-factly as if he'd come to the end of figuring a sum. It was over. Our little family had broken-up.

The ticket I bought the next day was not to the Yucatan, but to Los Angeles, a heartless place, I'd been warned; filled with shallow people, they all said. To which I smiled blankly and replied, "Good."

Chapter 15

Los Angeles

I AWOKE TO FIND MY THIRTIETH BIRTHDAY panting on my chest. An occasion significant beyond the sobering farewell to one's twenties being that I was supposed to be pretty much dead by now. That had been the extent of my life plan: dead by thirty or at least well on my way, a gibbering wreck or so I'd been told back in that message of doom delivered by Dad fifteen years ago—that dark banner I had marched under all the way to Los Angeles.

There were symptoms: unpredictable spastic twitch in the right foot had increased. Sometimes it would overtake the entire body with teeth-chattering shivers, especially on social occasions where I would have to duck outside and stand trembling in the shrubbery until it passed—people must have thought me very strange. And there was the deteriorating concentration, entire scenes missed in the movies I gazed at while a different movie played in my head—or was it just the senseless clatter of a mind gone off the tracks, careening towards oblivion?

The whipsaw of mood swings: sudden rages at inanimate objects, maudlin tears for a stray animal. All the signs for an early demise; but it was taking too long. Making plans is a human impulse natural as breathing—we shape an imagined future to walk into. So I found myself on my thirtieth birthday lit by a single desire: Do Not Be Alone. Then I called Callie. After all, it had been a year or had it been two since I'd last seen her? Just a friendly call. Checking in on an ex, nothing more, really.

Lies. All lies the brain tells the heart while the glands pace the sidelines just wanting to get in the game. And she actually sounded glad to hear from me. The fun we'd once had was there in her voice. It was all fine and great and you? Interested. Playful. After all, I had called her. And so I played my only card.

"It's my birthday ..."

She paused, letting me hang on the phone just long enough for hope to melt into shame at my desperation. *My birthday—how cheap—I never should have called.* My mouth was open in search of an apology when she chirped, "I've got a surprise for you."

I've never liked surprises, much less the anticipation of one. But if nothing else, it got my mind off the birthday and on to the rituals of grooming. Sex does that—for awhile.

I found myself back at the door of her historic Hollywood Gaylord apartment. After one knock, Callie flung the door wide, pulled me inside and greeted me with a lunging two-martini kiss; stabbed her tongue deep into my mouth and waggled it back and forth in a parody of passion. There was no mistaking—it was a big wet "fuck you".

After extracting her tongue, she shoved me a little too hard back against the door and pinned me there with a look, her eyes agleam with something hard, but more amused than hatred. Revenge came to mind.

And without breaking her gaze, Callie ran her hands up the length of her torso, opened her jacket and with a magician's flair, she flipped down the black cups of her bustier to reveal—the new breasts.

Tracing the curve under each aureole, a half-moon scar smiled up from where the incision had been made; markers of her once tiny breasts. Which I'd had no problem with, liked actually. They had seemed somehow innocent, vulnerable.

Callie was waiting for me to respond.

These new breasts were symmetrical, a matched set. But they seemed tight, like a too-small tee-shirt uncomfortably stretched—they were trying too hard.

"How do they feel?" was all I could muster, meaning how did they feel jutting out horizontally from what had previously been her nearly flat chest. Callie, however, took my question as a request to cop a feel.

"Oh, Bert wants to make some new birthday friends," she taunted with a practiced shimmy, then abruptly tucked them away like a shopkeeper with items you can't afford.

My heart plunged—she still cared enough to make me want her; brought me over to show me this new, surgically improved version of herself, to make me regret not being able to have all this. As if that had been the problem all along—that her tits weren't big enough.

She reached for a half-empty martini glass and my eyes squinted in anticipation of the sting of flung remains. The last time I had seen her she had screamed, as viciously as her Santa Barbara country club upbringing would allow, "You're a cardboard man! You'll be alone for the rest of your life!"

She had it dead right—cardboard: flimsy, corrugated pockets of narcissistic self-loathing sandwiched 'tween front and back. Cardboard Man slipping out the door of her Gaylord apartment, off into the neon haze of Koreatown, the dark hulk of the Ambassador Hotel shrouded in the death of Robert Kennedy. Young hope gunned down.

I should have told her the truth about me.

The remains of the martini downed, she grabbed her beaded clutch, turned to me and said, "There *is* a party somewhere, right?"

Strains of tropical lounge music floated over the ten-foot fence surrounding the Pacific Palisades compound. Having tempted me with her new improved self, Callie was ready to party. Valet parking. An attendant opened a side gate to a path illuminated with tiki torches. Callie extended a scented hand to steady herself. The smooth emolliated fingers, the Frenched nails she used to insert in my ass as if seeking the hidden me. The gate closed behind us with the metallic *zzzttt* of a pin tugged from a hand grenade.

Someone once said, "TV money is something you throw off the back of trains." That train had clearly passed through here: over-the-top retro 50's Trader Vic style luau, two professionally beaming long-haired girls wrapped in sarongs greeted us with fragrant leis, an outrigger canoe filled with iced beer was beached on sand piled near the pool where small islands of exotic flowers floated on various inflated pool toys. Groves of tiki torches flickered about the compound. Silly hats were issued to get the men in the spirit. A strategic scattering of thatched bar huts and a live band was set up on the tennis court with a dance floor.

"So that's him," Callie whispered making sure the new breasts made contact with my arm.

The host, a sitcom star who had recently made the leap to not-so-funny movies, was an enormous man, hair moist with sweat—he was the least comfortable person at the party; in constant retreat, ambling away from various groupings of guests who mirrored his slightest change in direction like synchronized schools of pilot fish shifting this way, and then that way with his every move.

From a Falstaffian sized tankard gripped in his mitt, "... a gift from Spielberg ..." he gulped beer with the urgency of a man unable to manufacture his own saliva.

If caught by an extended hand, he would pause momentarily; head cocked upward towards the heavens as though listening, then lurch off excusing himself as if suddenly recalling a duty or sighting a guest that required his attention. But he had no real destination, he was simply avoiding contact, wandering; a half-embarrassed expression as if, underneath it all, he suspected he didn't deserve all this and someone at the party might, at any moment, reveal him for what he was—a big fat drunk guy who got lucky. It is hard to be envied by others when living in your own skin is excruciating. You're a big success now, so what's the problem anyway? Ah, more beer.

Callie took no time in displaying her independence. After placing her order, she left me in the drink line and strode off into the crowd with all the assurance of a drum majorette.

She had spotted Blas, the painter I knew from Galveston—I guess I'll always think of him as the man whose dick I've had in my mouth. But he was my reason for being at the party. Earlier that week, I had hung his work in the entertainment room of the host's massive house; a two-story colonial that, despite its size, exuded the collapsible feel of a movie set, even to the fake ivy already sun-faded in the window boxes. Eventually, even the plastic wilts in Hollywood.

People had told me LA was a shallow place. That appealed

to me. I answered an ad for non-union actors that actually paid. The company specialized in the training of trial lawyers in mock courtroom situations. I read from some pages and they hired me to portray a variety of witnesses, defendants, plaintiffs, and prospective jurors. Not show business in the professional sense, but I didn't care. It took me out of myself, thrust me into an intense, if imagined, courtroom drama. And it paid the rent on my sparsely furnished studio apartment.

The company was impressed with my work. I seemed to excel at playing the 'hostile' witness. Called to the stand, the lawyers-in-training would ask me questions and at some point during the examination I would respond with a hostile remark. Like, *"… Because I felt like it."*

Or a snappy, *"I told you, I can't recall."*

Other times I would simply stare back at them and say nothing which had a generally unnerving effect on first timers. They didn't want a screamer who, in a real-life situation would simply be held in contempt or dragged off in cuffs by the bailiff. They wanted a quiet, measured hostility that forced the trainees to cope. I had the touch.

But after some months there emerged some inconvenient, what might be called empathetic feelings. I saw it more as impatience with certain lawyers-in-training—specifically, those with hopelessly gentle dispositions; the nice guys and girls doomed to get slammed in a real life courtroom. Victims, as I saw it. And I took it upon myself to bring this to their attention.

While on the witness stand I would suddenly blurt, *"You have no business in a courtroom! They'll eat you alive. You're a decent person, do probate for god's sake. Make out wills … something."*

My employers took exception with this vein of improvisation.

"Cut the shit or you're fired," was the way they put it. I replied they were misleading people with no concern for their obvious limitations, setting them up for failure, manufacturing delusion, running a victim factory. Case dismissed. Court adjourned. Job over.

Over the years, there had been the full complement of odd

jobs: catering, movie extra, house painter, cab driver. In many ways they were all the same job—diverting until I figured them out. Then they became dull and I would hate myself for doing them; for not having the guts just to be a wandering bindle stiff, a drifter. It's what I was inside, why not outside? I kept thinking I should leave Los Angeles, but I could never think of where to go or what I would do once I got there. So the days rolled on without much change from one to the next. Something LA's monotonous climate made very easy.

When Blas called, I realized more than five years had passed. I picked up the phone and his voice had the timbre of those compelled to ask something that agonizingly reveals they need your help. Finally, I thought, he's forgiven me for not being gay.

He was in LA, "Like a whore following the fleet," he crowed. "I have a publicist now. I detest myself. I should wear pumps and lipstick—suck cocks on Sunset Blvd. And how about you? Still pissing your life away? Never mind. Do you want to make some money?"

It seemed Blas was concerned about his own "hostility" problem.

"It's at a bank branch," he whined. "Those people. Fucking bean counters. Speaking of beans, I'm moving to Mexico. It's good for the image. You want the gig or no?"

Though not a major museum, it was a boon for an artist to be commissioned by a bank with multiple branches. But Blas found it just too bourgeois to be hung in a San Fernando Valley bank rather than some specially designed venue "... like Mark fucking Rothko!"

So his temper was already piqued, that and the fact that he'd taken the money. Overcome by self-disgust, he feared he would fly into a rage while discussing how to hang his work with a couple of branch managers in sensible shoes and name tags. Me? I needed some cash. So that's how I met Callie, the loan officer at the bank.

The hand-blown bottles at the luau's rum bar flickered in the torch light. It was a rum year. Scotch had been the year before with all that single-malt preciousness. I had chewed my way through an awful sangria period. And, of course, every year was a vodka year. But rum was coming out tonight and I felt an affinity, being island born myself, it was my theory at the time that rum did not so much make me drunk as it focused the mind; like a Buddhist meditation, helped settle one into the moment. And I sure could drink a lot of it.

A mojito was dispatched and I ordered another and watched Blas rankle at being introduced as "*our* artist" by the damp host.

"That's his stuff inside; go on take a look, hell I oughta get him to paint the tennis court … Blas maybe something wild on the tennis court?"

"How about BUDWEISER?" Came Blas's dead pan retort.

Chuckling under the tickle of this barb, the host directed the klieg light of his attention over at the band loitering in a cloud of contraband smoke as they puffed their way through a break.

"I can't hear you!" he shouted out.

"Waitin' for you!" the band leader yelled back and gestured toward the mike stand. The host grunted and waddled away; pilot fish shifted.

Blas turned to me and asked with a quiet disdain, "What's with you and the bank drone?"

She had come up to me that first day, Callie, the silk clad loan officer at the bank. Not very tall, thinish lips that seemed pursed against a social discomfort she was determined to overcome with aggressively good grooming and her excellent calves. When I arrived to hang Blas's work, Callie clicked over in her black pumps and, with an emotional sanction reserved for those worthy of a six figure loan approval, announced, "I love your work."

There was an invitation to dinner in the Diebenkorn blue of her eyes, at least to anyone hungry enough to see it. My first deception was to say nothing. Women will project a vast array of positive things upon you if you simply keep your trap shut. And fortunately for women, men are usually incapable of doing just that.

We all do it—view others in the light of our own morality, assuming everyone is just like us until the 'other family' materializes from out of nowhere, the mistress, the illegitimate kids. The Hawaiians greeted the missionaries with 'Aloha' and their half-naked bodies; in return the missionaries shamed them with religion and appropriated their land. *Oh, but we thought …*

Laughter burbled out on the tennis court. The host, fully awash in brew, grabbed the microphone and slurred some nonsense. Forced laughter burst forth from the invited like the laugh track on a failing sitcom. The band lurched into a song and the host belted out the opening verse of a sweaty blues number with a surprisingly decent saloon voice. He was actually talented. The masses gathered in.

I bit the end off one of the Montecristos from the bar. For all the hype about the Cuban cigar thing, it required constant re-lighting—more like tending a damp campfire than enjoying a luxurious smoke. Fashion cons us all. I stuck it in my mouth and watched Callie position herself toward the front of the band making subtle adjustments to her new cleavage like antennae being tweaked to receive clearer reception.

Of course, the real thing missing in Callie's life was not a C cup or even me—it was Callie. But doom attracts doom, the physics of enmeshment. After we met at the bank, I accepted her invitation and showed up at the HMS Bounty to meet her and her 'friends' for a drink. The Bounty is an old school red meat and martini joint on Wilshire; the entrance tricked-up to resemble the stern of the famed square rigger.

The Bounty was also conveniently adjacent to the Gaylord apartments. Callie had only to walk a few steps and she was home. Saved on DUIs. And the 'friends' she was to meet consisted of the bartender and some sagging regulars who had been seated at the bar since Jack Webb left his brass-tagged memorial chair.

We slid into a booth and a vodka negroni appeared before her. It was a vodka year for Callie. And the drinks continued to arrive with uncanny timing. The negroni gets its red color from the Campari. As she polished off one of the red drinks and then another, the color seemed to flow up into her cheeks and flush her face. The tight lips plumped and loosened. She informed me of her Santa Barbara up-bringing and her society page mom roaring around in "that embarrassing Rolls Royce."

With the third drink came her competitive younger sister on the east coast living out some horsy Ralph Lauren ad with a lanky fiancé. It was all grandma's real estate money. By drink four, the loan officer had shed her skin and before me was a playful flirt looking for some action outside the banking loop. If sloshed, she had also become pretty.

I myself had just begun to relax when the goddamn foot started up. Sometimes it would move up the leg, seize me with shivers the way a cold body would try to warm itself. It began like a cramp only it didn't curl in on itself, but insisted on outward expression—a vile and distracting movement. Like a fretful muscle anxious to be worked, you could stretch it any way you wanted, beat it with hammers, clamp a Denver boot on it—still the cells in the muscle fiber would twitch, the rogue gene in the DNA spinning destruction on chromosome four. Beyond my control. All I could do was hold on and try to mask it; walking deliberately as Paige with her withered leg had crossed that dining room floor back in Houston.

Callie, sensed a lapse in my attention, and asked what I thought of the art on the restaurant walls. I answered that it went with the menu. She giggled with amusement. Laughter is the first surrender. The sex probability meter ticked up.

And so did the twitch. But at that moment, what I thought I dearly wanted was to get laid and I knew that obvious bodily shaking wouldn't cut the mustard. So I braced my right foot against the bottom of the booth, used that leg to lift my ass just barely, but not so you would notice except for the fact that I was sitting up really straight, ass hovering just above the bench.

Callie interpreted this as a signal to get the check.

An awkward silence swooped down upon us. A blank space in the evening where I should have said something clever, made a cynical observation, asked if they dry docked the Bounty every few years to have the barnacles scraped from the barstools. However, I was entirely pre-occupied with the twitch so as to keep it from expanding into the shiver. And the awkward social moment had lurched beyond where I was supposed to say something clever into that even more uncomfortable place where anything one said would now appear so clumsily constructed as to reveal social discomfort—fear, flop-sweat, desperation. The wrong bait for sex.

But people assume, if you allow them. Callie gazed at me over her drink, caught up in her own movie. She set her glass down, leaned forward and looked me square in the eye.

"So I live next door," she blurted with a directness that transformed her as much as if she had suddenly yanked off a wig to reveal a naked scalp. There is a power to stating out loud what you want—it's the risk.

Bless her in that moment. Callie, lonesome as a prairie, dropped her mask, took a chance on me twitching in the booth across from her, or who she thought was me.

I held the door for her as we disembarked from the Bounty. She took a few steps toward her building before she looked back at me still clutching the handle of the heavy wooden door, the polished brass handle gripped in my fist to quell the shiver. She hadn't a clue about what she was dealing with and would not choose it if she knew, would not choose me.

From behind her down the street, a deep-throated howl erupted from a sports car. Headlight beams wiped across my eyes as it turned towards us and gathered speed. I let go of the brass door handle, released the twitching right foot and, without a thought, as if cued to perform a piece of perverse choreography embedded in the brain, I took one, two, three steps and was off the curb standing in the middle of the street directly in the path of a white oncoming RX-7.

The driver, still a half-block away, saw my body squared-off towards him and took it as a challenge, a game of chicken. He speed-shifted into third and accelerated maintaining his line, bearing down on me standing center lane, eyes staring back until at the last second, I pivoted, bull fighter style, around my planted left foot and the howling car brushed past at fifty plus.

The passenger in the RX-7, young dude, stuck his head out the window and whipped it around to look at me, incredulous at what he had just seen—that I was still standing. We all seemed surprised. Callie stood frozen, white-lipped under the lamplight as the howl receded down the street. The twitching had stopped.

"That car just passed through you," she murmured.

Should have known right there. She should have known after my mute lunge on the sofa, the awkward, but welcomed grope, the rushed aspect of it all, the unruly cushions, the final slide and settling on the carpet, clothes half-on, the nuisance of panty hose, the tangle of the tiny A cup bra. Chest like a boy's. Me half here—half down the street in front of the RX-7. Me in too much of hurry. Always the hurry. It's all being taken away. All disappearing. Hurry, before it goes. Before the shiver takes over the whole body. Before she changes her mind. Before the chance recedes, before she finds out who I am, before death. Hurry!

And what does Callie do, lying there beneath me? She opens her mouth, she speaks, "Slow down," she says not like a command, but like a benediction. Slow down.

And it all changed. Instead of moving at her, slamming into her with my blunt urgency, I began to move with her. This warm pocket, this lithe welcoming that rolled underneath me. Surged and subsided. A supple locking of soft gears in an exchange of tension and release, motion and stillness. Felt.

That's what she was doing—joining us together because it felt better. She made me inhabit my mistrusted body, settle into it, accept it in the moment and everything else disappeared. Sweet oblivion. And then that subsided and there we were, lying panting in a tangle of clothes, cross-hatched with shadows and I knew what I had to say.

"I am not Blas. I am not the artist," I reached for my pants.

"I didn't think so," She sighed. "Heard he was gay."

She should have known better, but it wasn't entirely her fault. When a woman starts to fall, for whatever reason: stepping in front of an oncoming car or slowing down when she asks—just continuing to show up makes you culpable. Upping the numbers over at the victim factory. That's what I had done.

And so the vodka nights rolled on, hanging like bats up in

the Gaylord, the coke dusted coffee table, the litter of nitrous cartridges strewn on the carpet—our chemical romance.

"Don't hit me in the face," she had blurted out one night deep into a session. Had she really thought I would strike her? Had she read that much rage in me? Or did she want me to hit her?

Doom attracts doom to create fresh disaster. We broke up a half-dozen times. We didn't get back together so much as we reconvened.

And why move forward when you can repeat the cycle? So there we were again after a year's respite. Or was it two? Because it's perfectly safe after a year or two—isn't it? We can just be friends—all lies, lies the crotch tells the brain, the brain babbles to the heart and the heart sags and murmurs, What the fuck, the worst has already happened—*I'm thirty and still alive.*

The Luau band was cranking out the old Martin Denny island exotica complete with background bird calls. The new improved Callie, well lubricated now, swayed out onto the dance floor, arms outstretched over her head; week-end warrior living large. Loan officer working a little too hard at having fun.

I never should have followed her home that Christmas, the backwards-facing train to Santa Barbara. The over-dieted mother in her cream-colored Rolls. The east coast sister fashionably outfitted to muck stalls.

That's where I strayed from policy. That's where I began to believe that, well maybe, since she was fucked-up and I was fucked-up, maybe we could go along just not giving a damn about anything—have a little fun on the short road to hell.

But, I had mis-read the map. Callie was interested in more than a quick trip to hell. Or at least she had a more conventional plan for it. It might all have been easier if Callie's mother hadn't dropped her on her face as an infant. Was it the gin and tonics or had she been reaching for the phone when she dropped the child? The face that couldn't be fixed until she was well in her teens.

At sixteen the face was corrected, the flattened nose set to standards. But the girl inside was not so easily mended. And there was the breast issue—in her teens and they still hadn't arrived. And mom was very busy. It was all right there in the society pages—the ball, the gala! And now, her younger sister doing swell in the East. Wedding ring. Belly swelling in the East.

So we had the talk, Callie and I; a champagne brunch, seaside hotel, breezy ambiance for what was really a bottom line business meeting. It was the loan officer seated across from me, checking the figures, assessing the risks. The prospectus read something like this:

Marriage

Children

Two children

Family

Timeline, goals, schedule—*you can shit on me if you want to …*

Pink dining room, pink table cloth, the blue Pacific swells outside the window, breaks upon the shore while a couple sits facing; the woman talks, stacking her words to build the outline of a vision, a future with the man seated across from her. A gull cries and the man lifts from his chair. The pink linen napkin flutters from his lap as he rises; Cardboard Man lifted by the thermal rising on the heat of Callie's words as she dreams, spins her plan. He rises, floats out through the open window, up high into the cool ocean air, foot twitching, teeth chattering, body quaking in a shiver.

Yes, my biggest cheat was silence. I never told her about the time bomb that ticked within. The Jack–In-the-Box gene I carried—disaster set to spring whenever. I didn't want to go there. Not that can of worms. Did not want to say, *I Can't Have Any Children because odds are they'll be born with a gene-gone-haywire-fuck-up- of- nature that destroys the very host that carries it along.*

Or, against all medical advice, let's say you decide to have a kid and the gene is passed on. Provided you live long enough yourself, you could well be in for the treat of watching your child, perhaps even as it is trying to grasp the wonders of the world, being disassembled neurologically—which is really the main switchboard if you want to start pulling plugs on everything from motor skills to mood swings.

And if you did have that child, you would watch it fiercely, your child and wonder, as I do my own inner workings, the endless checking and re-checking, seeking the symptoms, the ever-present doubt, the shadow of the curse. Yes? No? Yes?

No. Not another *me* walking around. Not that. That's why I nodded my head when the doctor pressed me a second time if I was 'sure' about proceeding with the vasectomy. I hadn't told her about that either.

Callie was on the dance floor doing The Bump with a round hairball of a man in a too-tight Aloha shirt; a journalist, police insider, nicotine gum-chewer, pink eczema raging on his ankle.

And then she slipped on that last martini. Embarrassed; waving help away, insisting she's fine thank you—she can be drunk and sloppy all on her own. She pointed accusingly—it was the dance floor's fault. A server was dispatched with a towel. She looked around. Was she looking for me?

The cruelest thing was to leave her guessing. Guessing as to why. Why not me? Leaving her mind to cast about for its own reasons, take inventory, glom onto and exaggerate her deficiencies, find the deal breaker. It must be the tits. That she could change.

But she did and yet, there she was embarrassing herself on the dance floor. I invited her out and she came. It's always the same. The disappointed girl reaches out for more and the Cardboard Man floats away, over and over and over again and they never know why?

Why not me? Why not love?

The compulsion. I'm a welcome mat on the porch of an empty house. The whole show, all of it, chronically botched and not even grandly—half failures, half loves. And so I decided, then and there, I would tell her. Say it out loud on the night of my thirtieth birthday—a birthday I was never supposed to reach.

With the help of some fine Jamaican rum I had come to clarity; it was time to let Callie know that it wasn't her fault. I was indeed the Cardboard Man! Incapable of loving not just her, but anyone.

So I reached for the nearest tiki torch and with a little back and forth, uprooted it. Stogie jutting from the mouth, I grabbed an enormous white towel from a chaise, wrapped it toga-style around my torso. An imperial declaration would be made. I would make a clean breast of it at last.

A picture of purposeful grace, I strode across the dance floor, passed the band leader, emphatically sawed my finger across my throat in the international symbol for stop whatever-the-fuck-you're-doing and pay attention.

They complied in a gradual dying wheeze of instruments.

I remember feeling good as I mounted the diving board, tiki torch brandished like a scepter. Felt better than I had in a long time. The moment really starting to gel, the silence deepened as I felt the gritty roughness of the diving board under my feet. Where were my shoes? Never mind that now. I banged the base of my torch on the board to claim the attention of any malingerers. One. Two. Three!

There was a slight problem with my tongue. Rum. But I was encouraged by the crowd's hush—the pilot fish shifted—all eyes upon me.

Callie and I locked eyes and I needed to take just a moment to organize my next sentence, pull the wool off my tongue. It was then I noticed the cigar had gone out and thought I'd buy a few seconds by re-lighting the stogie with the tiki torch, confidant in the knowledge that none of them had the slightest suspicion that this was not planned.

Blas smiled for the first time that evening as I tilted the flaming torch to the cigar. And then it happened—either I misjudged the distance or maybe it was the weight of the liquid fuel sloshing inside the canister as it leaned over and bumped against the end of the cigar. Anyway, the lid was dislodged—a thoroughly shoddy piece of workmanship that held the wick and capped the liquid fuel container—that part popped off …

It bounced off my chest, wick still burning. I lunged to

grab it, seared my fingers while fuel splashed from the canister, soaked my toga/towel and sluiced down onto my bare feet.

And here we were, back where I began all this; time slowed as I watched the lid with the burning wick land in the puddle of fuel sluicing around my feet, and then the *whoosh*, as the blue flame rose up to swallow me whole. The thin hiss of my beard burning. The foul smoke...

It was clear to everyone who watched that I was a man on fire. But being a Hollywood crowd, there was that jaded pause as they wondered—was I entertainment or a bad accident?

The towel, wrapped toga-style, was fully engulfed in flames and did not want to let me go; desperate tugs only served to snug it tighter. Useless flailing commenced with my hands and arms. People have an eye for genuine panic even in Hollywood.

A man was burning.

It was me.

My feet were on fire. Pain.

Someone screamed.

Was it me?

"Jump!" a voice called out. "Jump in the water!"

The water. Of course, right there, all the time—brought to mind the old joke about the man on fire who stands holding a bucket of water, screaming for somebody to help him. I stepped off the board.

Chapter 16
ER

THE HUMILIATION OF SELF-INFLICTED CAlamity. With an audience. Nearly equaled by the embarrassing need to explain everything in the middle of the crowded, baby-crying, gun-shot wounded, county ER. "… *hereditary neurological disease, progressive brain deterioration, bad gene, bad gene*!" Gushing like a broken sewer pipe while they snipped off what was left of my aloha shirt—eighty percent rayon, twenty percent cotton.

"Please, you must calm yourself," said Dr. Singh, resident shrink on-duty. "Now, tell me, Mr. Kelly, was this your first attempt at suicide?"

So surprised was I by his question that I momentarily forgot the pain. "It was an accident!" I sputtered to the young Sikh doctor. "… lousy tiki torches, a fuel spill, god knows what they were filled with: kerosene, white gas—probably made in China!"

I felt some ground had been gained with my statement when the pain made an astounding comeback.

"… Ah, you probably want something for the pain?" murmured Dr. Singh.

I nodded emphatically.

"I will give you something for the pain. But first, you must be completely honest with me, Mr. Kelly."

I had hoped the Huntington's story would buy some sympathy from the shrink; he would relent, hand out a scrip for Vicadin and head off to recruit some freshly stitched gangbanger for a def poetry workshop. But, Dr. Singh was not going that way.

"You say you did not consciously intend to cause yourself harm. You claim it was merely an accident. Perhaps, even negligence on the part of others. However, as I review your blood alcohol level I find it a wonder that you did not explode, Mr. Kelly. And was this irresponsible excess also an accident? Or perhaps the fault of some other person?"

"I'm just an asshole who accidentally set himself on fire."

"I think asshole is a good beginning." He dispensed a solitary pill and left me to consider my case. I would get the diligent man.

As the pain began to dim, I remembered Callie's face just before I became a human torch: her eyes wide, focused on me, her face lit from within as I was being lit from without. She seemed in that moment to be perfectly herself, not trying to be anyone else—not disappointed in not being anyone else. Maybe that is the most we can hope for. Then again, she was watching the asshole that broke her heart set himself on fire—who knows what she was thinking.

"So you think you have Huntington's disease?" Dr. Singh was back with fresh questions.

"I have symptoms," I answered slowly, more confident now there was a little distance between myself and the pain.

"Ah, you assume that you have symptoms, but as a professional I am not so certain. However, I want to inform you, Mr. Kelly, that a test for this disease is now available."

He referred to his metal clipboard. "A marker for the Huntington's gene has been located on chromosome four. This is a comparative blood test with a high degree of reliability."

"Comparative?"

"Samples are taken from all family members whether they suffer from the disease or not. These are then compared one to another."

"But I was adopted."

Dr. Singh took pause.

"I have no idea who my biological parents are or were."

Dr. Singh considered this information, and then spoke. "I think that can be remedied with the proper documentation. I will provide you with a 'medical need to know'. This will allow you legal access to any court documents regarding your adoption. The biological parents will be named as I believe would be any siblings, circumstances, etc."

It was my turn to be silent.

"You must find them, Mr. Kelly."

"My biological father is dead, Dr. Singh."

"Then you must find the survivors—your mother, any siblings. Their blood samples are necessary to the test."

"I told you, I have symptoms."

"You assume the spasm in your foot is a symptom of Huntington's disease. But it could be a symptom of something else."

I told him all I needed was a prescription and a taxi, but he wouldn't let it go.

"The County can continue to hold you for observation," he threatened with the complete confidence of those in power. "Self-immolation is not taken lightly by the county. You pose a danger not only to yourself, but to others as well."

"The County will designate me a fire hazard? I question the legality—"

"Oh, it is quite legal. You can agree to take this test and determine the presence or absence of this disease. Or you can continue to assume the very worst while you recuperate in the custody of this hospital. But speaking with absolute frankness, Mr. Kelly, I find this assumption on your part to be a defense. And this defense has become a part of your identity, part of this accident as you so call it. Have courage, Mr. Kelly. Go out and find them."

I nodded. And nodded again, agreed in full to whatever Dr. Singh, the keeper of the Vicadin, proposed.

The birthday card was still waiting for me when I returned from the hospital, unopened, casually tossed on the counter with the unpaid bills. But I knew exactly where it was; third envelope down, a peek of Mother's cheerful cursive was enough to trouble my stomach.

I read it on the plane after two vodka tonics:

"You're thirty now, teaching would have been a steady job."
Happy Birthday!

Chapter 17

The Big 'O'

I FIGURED HER FOR A LESBIAN WITH THE BOMBer jacket and jeans. Attractive in a masculine way with that chip-on-the-shoulder hunch. She punched the meter and pulled the taxi onto the interstate towards Odessa. Big hands for a woman.

Other than the new Midland International Airport, the most obvious change was the absence of soot that usually hung visible for miles over the landscape we were driving through—200,000 square miles of dun-colored veldt.

"What happened to the Carbon Black Plant?"

"Gone," the driver said. "EPA shut it down—unacceptable amounts of hydrogen sulfide—that 'rotten egg' smell?"

"I remember it well," I said as I gazed out over the site still marked with the heavy black soot. "... talk about your carbon foot print ..."

"Around one point eight million pounds of the stuff was the official estimate."

A Time magazine article had once ranked Odessa at the top of the nation's most polluted cities. The Carbon Black Plant had been the star player—they made black, the color. The cab driver was well informed, articulate for a cabbie.

"Yeah, but it was out in the absolute middle of nowhere," I countered. "So who really cared?"

"Not exactly," she said somewhat defensively.

"But you must admit there's an abundance of nowhere out here."

"People live here. That's the difference between nowhere and somewhere. People."

I had been corrected. Caught dissing the hometown.

“Class action suits, the health insurance companies got into it and that sealed the deal.”

She wasn’t from West Texas, didn’t have the twang. And the fact was, as a kid, the Carbon Black Plant had been a world class blight to behold. It was some miles outside of the city, a massive black cloud that loomed over the highway. At first, it was like following a large truck that was burning oil—a fleet of large trucks. It increased in density as we drove until it became dark as midnight at the blaze of noon.

Headlights had to be turned on miles before you actually passed the plant itself. The surrounding land caked in soot as if a huge fire had swept through the mesquite and left it charred, but standing and with blackened leaves. Then, off the highway you could just make out the windowless hulks of the buildings; the plant itself traced with catwalks strung with naked bulbs that twinkled like constellations in the black ether. At times you would even catch a glimpse of shadowy figures—men moving like beings in another world.

“So what’s there now?”

“Strip club,” the cab driver said flatly.

“Progress,” I quipped with some vague satisfaction.

“Different issues,” she said slotting it as a larger and more complicated discussion than she cared to get into.

We turned off the interstate and onto Quail Run, the street I had grown up on: a half dozen ranch styles—brick homes, mowed lawns, rose bushes. The same two empty lots were still vacant, overgrown with tumble weed and witch grass. And there was my house and even more suddenly there was Dad.

I was not prepared for it. The sequence was out of order. First, I wanted to see the house and think about that, and then, in my own good time, I would make my way to the door and when I was ready, and only then, would I step up and ring the bell.

But there he was, standing in the driveway beside a huge red and white SUV that was one flood lamp short of qualifying as an emergency vehicle. He stood arms akimbo, contemplating a pile of stuff with a steely concentration that could only mean that he was engaged in one of his most exacting rituals—The Packing of the Car.

It was like a puzzle whose intricacies I'd never grasped. I had always lacked the ability to read the hidden pattern, the placing of consumer goods and recreational gear one beside the other, ordered in a way based not just on shape and size, but on noise reduction and the priority of the object's scheduled need. "No, ice chest first, then the life preservers between the Hibachi ... no, you don't know what you're doing."

All this was vividly recalled in the back of the cab.

"Keep going! Don't stop! Keep going!" I barked at the driver as I dropped down to the floorboard, sank down low looking for a pocket of breathable air.

She pulled over after a block and stopped.

"Hello, back there?" She called out in a patronizing, speaking-to-a-child kind of way. "How we doing?"

"We are looking for my medication," I stalled.

"Can I help you?"

"No, thanks. Doing fine."

"Will you be getting out here then?"

She had put her finger on the question and I was not finding the answer there on the floor board.

"Sir? Can I help you find your medication?"

I tugged the pill bottle from my pocket and twisted the cap off. I put one in my mouth.

"Just some water, please."

She handed me a half filled water bottle.

"Thanks."

"So that's twenty-seven dollars. Keep the water."

I rose up and looked out the back window. Dad was gone. Had I actually seen him? Yes, all the stuff was there.

"Sir, I move from specific destination to specific destination. What ever this is you are doing let's get it done and settle up. Okay?"

The cold voice of reason. With her large, capable hands she no doubt steered many people to their specific destinations; they got out and did the things that needed doing.

I had things that needed doing. I coaxed myself into rising, pulled out my wallet and watched the situation make a grinding shift from questionable, to unfortunate.

“I’m sorry, did you say you don’t have the money?” she repeated like the punch line to a joke she hadn’t quite gotten.

“Yes. I’m afraid I’m a bit short.”

“How short would that be, sir?”

“Looks like, oh … twenty dollars.”

“So, let me understand this—you got into a cab with twenty dollars less than it was going to cost you?”

“I do have a credit card,” I chirped hopefully.

“Do you see a charge machine here?”

“Of course not. But …”

“Is this how you go through life?”

“Look there’s no need to get personal—“

“Yes, there is a need, Sir. You have breached an unspoken, but understood contract between a driver and a fare; I drive you where you want to go and you pay me what it costs. A simple concept your average normal citizen seems to get.”

“I understand your frustration—“

“Do you? Do you understand that because of your … irresponsibility, the flow of my day has been interrupted? Because now I have to deal with this … situation. I have to deal with You. I have to think, consider and react and a whole lot of other crap that I don’t want to do because I do not do this job to think. I do this job so I don’t have to think.”

By this time I had gotten out and stood by her window reciting in a variety of ways that I had every intention of paying her ASAP. I actually said that, “ASAP,” a kind of military thing I hate hearing or saying. I requested her card which was thrust in my general direction by one of her large hands.

I took the card in both hands and found myself bowing towards her in some Asian gesture of obeisance and then shuffled around to the trunk to retrieve my bag.

That’s when I heard the locks activate.

I tapped the rear of the car, called out if she might *pop the trunk*?

Up the windows went.

I shuffled back around to the driver’s side, tapped gently at her closed window. Down it glided four inches.

She'd be only too happy to deliver my bag to me as soon as she got the twenty-seven dollars I owed her.

A tight ribbon of panic unfurled in my stomach. The prickly singe on the tops of my feet called out—my reserve of pain killer was in that bag.

"Uh, I don't think it's legal to keep my luggage," I said drawing on my mock courtroom experience.

"Oh, really?" she said and drove off.

Dad eyed me with a familiar apprehension as I shuffled towards him, no luggage in hand, like I was simply taking a stroll and happened by after ten years (not good years judging from the shuffle, the bandages, the bent soul flickering in my eyes).

He was smaller than I remembered. Wispy strands of silver combed back over a tan scalp. Such a handsome man he'd been; blue-eyed with an aquiline nose and a masculine jaw line. Just no style in his manner; duty clumped upon him like the chronic dandruff that scaled in drifts above the ears, resistant to the variety of sulfurous shampoos that had fouled his walk-in shower over the years. And were those age spots that now mottled his surgeon's hands?

"Arlene!" He called out as he recognized me. Mouth slightly agape as he looked me up and down: the plastic shower sandals, gym socks pulled over bandaged feet, the gauze on my neck just under the chin.

"What the hell happened to you?"

His tone expressed the usual assumption of some misconduct on my part. And he was right, of course, eternally right—the Eagle Scout, the prominent urologist.

"Long story," I muttered as we fell into a clumsy, off-kilter hug that left us both looking towards the ground for something more to say.

"Why didn't you call?" The serrated timbre of Mother's voice sliced across the yard. It had never failed to release a spurt of adrenaline—that sound, the implicit accusation, the hurt, the fathoms of distress and disappointment, the need for love and the immediate suspicion at its offering.

Cradled in her arms, a foil-covered yellow casserole dish—

the moussaka. Thin she was, in the face and neck and below a little round tummy seemed to have absorbed what her buttocks had given up, a distended half-ball pressing against the front of her mauve velour sweat pants. The copper-colored hair gone to a base tint of blue-gray with pink highlights.

"I wanted to surprise you," I lied. It's simpler to lie. Since I can remember—simpler. Truth was, I could not bear to talk to her on the phone; the too-loud voice, that sound. Better to get it over with face to face. It required better manners. You couldn't assassinate and hang up. Had I called before I left LA, I would never have come.

The rest of her body was all hard edges and angles, like a starving bird. She never settled into my embrace. There was no stillness in her. Then, seized with a fit of coughing, she doubled-over in a phlegm-clearing wheeze—the nasty rattle of a thousand Salems.

"... Don't make me drop the moussaka!" she said regaining her breath, guarding the casserole from the dangerous onslaught of my affection.

"Say, take it easy," Dad warned her. Then he turned one of his rare, ironic smiles on me and said, "Well, you're just in time. We're going on vacation."

Chapter 18

Lajitas, Texas

MOM SANG IT OUT LIKE A MUSICAL phrase, *Lah-Hee-Tus.* A remote "getaway" down south just west of Presidio, the sun-baked border town seasonally referenced as the hottest spot in Texas.

The rustic resort sprang-up around an historic trading post nestled near a shallow crossing in the Rio Grande used by everyone from the Apaches and Pancho Villa to the back-and-forth activities of current day 'illegals' and drug dealers plying their trade. Lajitas, named after a towering mesa that looked out over the river and the austere expanse of Chihuahuan desert that spread out from it. The Badlands it was aptly named and it was just that—bad land. *Despoblado*, the Mexicans called it, the Uninhabited Place. Wander ill-prepared, too far from the river and you will die parched, scorpion-bit and buzzard-picked. My parents built a vacation home there. *Lah-Hee-Tus.*

Our trip there did not go smoothly. I climbed aboard Hillard's strategically packed Bronco and Arlene introduced me to Zeda, a lop-eared, drooling mutt the size of a buffalo-calf. The dog rode in the fur-matted portion of the cargo area, right behind my seat. A location that insured each bark would give me a moist earful. And he barked a lot, Zeda did; a bark born of ever-deepening pants that erupted into hard-edged bellows that blew foul breath and laced the back of my neck with saliva.

Baarrkkk!

When I complained, Dad's response was to reassure me that the animal had received a dose of Thorazine and would calm down as soon as we got on the road.

Baarrkkk!

"You injected the dog?" I asked.

"Oral. 50mg." He replied.

"And a Motrin for his hip," Mom added, ever the dutiful assistant.

Baarrkkk!

This Thorazine/Motrin cocktail did not stop the animal's barking so much as it slowed it down to a beleaguered and drawn out *YOWL ... YOWL....*

After twenty minutes of this, I began to wonder if my parents had gone deaf. What human ear could hear this plaintive cry and not respond in some manner: a meaty bone, a merciful gun shot? It was time to dispense with the honeymoon portion of our family reunion. I demanded Dad up the dosage on the dog.

"He's a big animal. You didn't give him enough. He needs more. Give the dog more drugs!"

YOWWWLLL! He filled my ear with a fresh load of warm saliva.

"If you calm down, *he* will calm down," Dad reasoned, barely audible over the discordant *YOWWLLL!*

"Oh, so it's *my* fault?" I barked back. "Well, it's not me. It's *him*! He's the one that needs to calm the fuck down!" And, as I pointed an accusing finger at the animal, he promptly clamped his jaws on my hand.

I retaliated with a hissing *FUUUCKKK!* And threw an elbow into his shoulder, pounded him on the head with my burned hand causing far more pain to myself than to his thick skull.

Dad, finally receptive to the melee taking place in the rear of the vehicle, breathed one of his resigned "Aww hell ..." sighs that translated as *Here We Go Again Coping with Your Endless Assholery.* Mom concurred with a bobble-headed nod.

The vehicle was pulled over. Dad swung down out of the driver's seat, threw open the rear gate—the dog and I were separated. My father, unswerving from his medical perspective, dosed both of us with Valium. In addition, I was given a Motrin for my hand now swelling with a tattoo of purple teeth marks.

Gradually, all was forgiven as a warm wave of well-being began to lap over me and the dog. Both of us, rendered motionless, stared out the window with a glazed serenity as the Badlands rolled by.

The roads became successively smaller and dustier—more turns and dips, the rocks thrown up by the tires bigger, impacting the undercarriage like hammer blows until finally, in a cloud of swirling dust, we arrived at what looked like the set of a cheesy western made for TV. *Lah-Hee-Tus.*

There was your plank boardwalk, your hitchin' posts, your "Badlands Hotel" with its false front, red brocade wall-papered faux brothel of a lobby. A Wild West Saloon, Sundries and Liquor, Livery Stables—Rent by the Hour or the Day, River Rafting! The folksy signs, done up like brands from a hot iron, framed with loopy twists of rope, as if to say this was a fun place with lots to do despite the sun-blasted desolation that stretched out far as the eye could see.

Across from the boardwalk stood a rickety, reeking livestock pen. Inside, a bloated Billy goat guzzled from a bottle of beer skillfully up-ended in his mouth to the amusement of a couple of paunchy white onlookers who looked to have up-ended more than a few bottles of their own. 'Clay Henry' read the sign on the pen, Mayor of Lajitas.

"Isn't this beautiful," Mom beamed.

I had hopes for the house when they told me it was a "natural" home built of adobe brick, but what I saw had been plastered and painted over in such a manner that it resembled a double-wide hauled in and dropped off a trailer truck. They had done everything they could to disguise anything 'natural' about it.

The house stood on a bulldozed bluff that overlooked a strip of a two-lane black top; across that was the river. Behind the house rose the crumbling grandeur of Lajitas Mesa, a towering brow of reddish rock skirted by a flinty talus that spilled down its sides. It did have a brutal majesty.

It was a dry heat, as they say, pushing the mercury up to 118 degrees at 1:00PM and I began to understand the beer swilling goat and how a muddy river might seem an inviting place to frolic. Inside, the air conditioner was roaring and I excused myself to wander off into a bedroom and slip into a dreamy Valium nap while being watched over by a painting of two Mexican children, their huge eyes dark and limpid as if to bait pederasts.

When I awoke, the heat had broken. Outside, Hillard and Arlene were two highballs into the cocktail hour. The ritual of bourbon, ice and water was in progress out on the flagstone porch overlooking the bend in the river; the *ahedo* land of Mexico folding away into the distant mountains.

"Makes you thirsty," Mom said, shaking the ice in her empty glass.

The dog, chained to a post, stopped chewing a rock and lifted one eyebrow in my direction.

"I laid out one of your father's shirts for you," she said cocking a critical eye at the one I had on, shredded from the dogfight.

"I know. Thanks. I tried it on—it's a little tight." My father nodded his head and pursed his lips at this information. I'm bigger than you now.

"Oh, well, there's a shop on the boardwalk, but it's closed up today. Chili cook-off in Terlingua. Everybody goes but us. Daddy doesn't go in for the chili thing, too spicy. Isn't that right?"

"Stinks up the house," Dad confirmed with a scrunch of his nose and polished off his highball.

"Say, you might be able to find something across the river there, the little village, Paso Lajitas. That's where your Mexicans live—we don't call them wetbacks because they take the boat. A little man rows them back and forth across the river. There's a restaurant over there, though you wouldn't catch me eatin' in it. And a store. Bet you could find a deal on a shirt over there." She rattled the ice in her glass again.

Dad checked his watch, "Say, when's dinner?"

"Whenever you want to fix it," she sassed back.

Dad tossed the ice from his drink out onto the pea-gravel that covered the front yard. He took her glass and started inside, "I'd like one too," I called after him remembering my Vicadin had driven away in the taxi.

"Those are the Chisos," she pointed to the range that rose up in the distance beyond the river. "The Ghost Mountains. The Apaches named them. Do you see any ghosts out there?"

"How are you, Mom?" I asked.

"Just fine. How are you?" She answered too quickly as if my question had thrown into question that she could be anything else.

"I'm fine," I said playing along.

"You look a little worse for the wear."

And then before I could answer, "Never mind. That's your business. If you want to tell me something that's fine. If not, well, that's fine too."

"Well, I would like to tell you some things."

"Really? Well, that's a surprise since I never hear from you. I figured you were fine and dandy, having a ball. Who knows? I don't. No one tells me anything."

I had forgotten how hard this was, the maneuvering, the blocking.

"Mother, do you know anything about the woman in Hawaii?"

"What woman would that be?"

"My birth mother. Do you know anything about her?"

"I know she wasn't much of a mother. A camp follower of some sort, who knows."

"Camp follower?"

"Followed the Air Force … Off We Go into the Wild Blue Yonder…"

Dad appeared at the screen door with the drinks.

"Well, I'm ready for dinner anytime you are," he said as she took the bourbon.

"How about you?" she asked dispensing a sudden jovial swat to my leg that seemed to officially terminate our discussion. "I bet you're ready for that moussaka."

"Always," I said wanting to please her.

She celebrated the compliment with a swig. Dad checked his watch, "Sun's setting tonight at 7:54. Orion should be visible."

"Okay, thank you," Mom said as she rose unsteadily to her

feet. "He knows it all: the time, the weather—when Orion farts. Just ask him." She took another swallow from her glass. "Guess I better get to work. No rest for the wicked."

"Okay, let's take it easy now," Dad cautioned as she wheezed off, grabbing at a chair for balance.

"Oh, you take it easy," she opened the screen door. "Is anybody going to feed my dog? Probably not." The dog raised his head as she tottered inside.

Dad and I stared out over rocky landscape in silence. It was a silence well known to me, a silence that could stretch on with no effort from my father to fill it, it was an impersonal silence. He was the same with everyone. I took some comfort in that knowledge, but it had been a hard lesson learned as a child sitting at the breakfast table every morning alone with him. Through the years it had become clear that you didn't really have a conversation with my father—you interviewed him. So I asked questions. The most inane.

"Are you going to work today?"

"Yes."

We would chew some more bran flakes until I came up with another question that he would apply one of the following answers:

Surgery.

Rounds.

Hospital.

Office.

Yes.

No.

Ask your mother.

Mother was no fount of answers either. Though one might be tempted to say my father's silence was the safest gambit with my mother: he could avoid the emotional trap doors one dropped through, the intricate games of blame, guilt and hurt feelings. And this may have even encouraged my father's silence, but I don't think it was the source. It was profound, this silence of my father, like a hi-tech foam bedding material: questions made a temporary impression, but then it quickly resumed its original shape; the silence sprang back, there was no change, no retention of the question's impact—it never reached a deeper surface if there was one. But this too seemed to be something that drove Mother to greater episodes of acting out.

However, this time and on this porch, I refused to do the conversational lifting. So we sat there trading in the same currency—Silence. We stared out over the greasewood and ocotillo, out towards the bend shining in the river. Silence. The pant of the dog. The rattle of ice against our glasses.

Finally, the dog couldn't take it anymore and whined.

"Oh, all right, I'll feed you." Dad, unable to pass up the escape of a simple task and, saved by duty, returned inside. The dog and I eyed one another like jealous siblings until he grew bored and dropped his head.

Every year was a bourbon year for my parents. Bought it by the case. Hillard and Arlene stored the Tom Moore in the garage along with the rusty golf clubs and insecticide.

From inside the 'natural' home there came rattlings. The stage was being set, props laid out for dinner and the floor show.

"Okay, I've put it all out so help yourself," she said with the upbeat resentment of an under-paid caterer. She sat down at the table, but didn't put any food on her plate except for a piece of garlic toast she pecked at.

"So how's retirement, Dad?" I asked finally surrendering to the interview format. "Do you miss your practice?"

"Well, I must say …" He began considering a complicated answer.

Mom darted into the gap to answer for him, "Oh, he loves it."

"Well, I do …"

"We're having a ball. Why you became a urologist I'll never know. All those prostates—yeck!"

Her teeth gnashed into the garlic toast, gave it a couple of good chews before reaching for her bourbon to wash it down. I sat thinking of 'all those prostates' of my father—a body of work out there walking around. Or not as the case may be.

Dad offered a measured defense of his career choice, "I had

actually considered radiology, however at the time there was an opening for an obstetrician and a urologist in Odessa. Would anyone care for some moussaka?" he asked while he traced a geometrically precise vertical rise and horizontal move of the yellow casserole dish towards me, where it remained stationary on that plane until my hands reached up and removed it. This accomplished, he initiated a careful dissection of the portion he had taken for himself.

"Obstetrics I found to be fairly passive. The baby just comes right out, as they have managed to for years, provided there are no complications. Not much to it really." He completed a deft exploratory incision into the moussaka with his knife and began to retract the opening with his fork.

"Okay," Mom announced to an imaginary audience, "He's going to talk about his medical career so let's all listen."

She turned towards him in a pose of mock fascination that made me want to throw my napkin at her; like the impulse to interview my father, it was a familiar feeling.

"Oh, never mind, I'm retired now," he said chastened.

"What would you like to talk about, Mom?" I asked in hopes that a redistribution of the attention might get things on a congenial track.

"Me?" She demurred. "I don't need to talk about anything. Your father's the one with the medical career. I just cook."

"... I don't think the moussaka is quite up to temperature in the center," came Dad's considered prognosis.

Mom, stood—her chair scraped loudly across the tile floor; she picked up the remainder of the casserole, lurched over to the trash, tromped on the foot peddle—the lid saluted her and she dropped it in.

"There dinner's done. Anyone interested in dessert?"

I may have traveled two hundred miles into the middle of nowhere, but there was no mistaking it—I was home.

"Come now, Arlene, you're getting too excited," Dad warned, but his eyes were on the recently fed trashcan.

"I am not the least bit excited. I am cleaning up—" She was cut short by a tearing cough, and then another as a progressive coughing fit shook her until she was half-bent over the kitchen sink. She retched and spat. Dad and I, moved by the dire sound, stood in unison and went to her.

"Where is your inhaler?" he prompted.

Mom gestured toward her purse on the sofa. Dad got it, put it to her mouth and squeezed. She wheezed in the medicine. Coughed and then inhaled some more. After several applications, the coughing began to dissipate, but her breathing was labored and asthmatic.

"I guess we better head back tomorrow," Dad pronounced as if sentencing a parole violator.

"... I ... I don't want to go back," she rasped.

"That's what you said last time and you ended up in the hospital."

She took another pull from the inhaler. As he guided her towards the bedroom, I asked Dad what I could do to help.

"See if you can salvage any of that moussaka."

Later, while Dad zapped the recovered moussaka to a suitable temperature, I stepped outside to watch the sun dissolve into a molten puddle on the ridge of the Chisos.

The path down to the two-lane black top was loose underfoot, shifted with the smooth rounded stones of a dry creek bed. I crossed the black top and found the stones refined into pebbles, and then even finer into soft powdery sand as I approached the line of salt cedars near the water. There the sand cloyed and darkened, humped itself up into deeply fissured mud, sticky as potter's clay and cracked from the beating sun, but then repaired itself and went smooth just as it dove into the brown river.

A glint through a cedar thicket—the metal of a row boat. A little brown man, wizened as a strip of jerky, turned his head in my direction. From under a stained straw brim his eyes found me—one milky and unseeing, the other bright and intent as a hawk's. He nodded silently for me to get in and shifted his body for work.

The boat was a floating Frankenstein stitched of metal parts. You could read the history from the welds that scarred the gunwales: it had been bent in half, backwards against its hull. Tremendous force. Snatched from its mooring by a flash-flood, bashed by rocks, tumbled and swamped. You could see it hung-up on a boulder where it filled with the on-rushing river, the groan of the metal as the pressure broke its back and the boat bent against itself around the rock.

The man must have found it when the flood waters receded, crushed like a tin can and tossed into a cedar thicket. But he saw something in the wreck. Or he needed to see something. Maybe it had been his boat before and he had to make it work again.

They must have yanked it straight between two pick-up trucks. Then with fire and hammers beat it back into the shape of a boat. The transom, ripped out by the river, had been replaced, the metal hack-sawed, then nailed to a doubled thickness of plywood; the seams staunched with roofing tar. Colorful patches cut from a variety of soda cans: Coke, Squirt, Mountain Dew, Orange Crush plastered like endorsements over the tears and rents in the metal skin. Oars fashioned from a sturdy length of dowel; U-bolts attached the crude plywood paddles, the laminated layers swollen with the river water spread apart like pages in a soggy book. Crude work, the boat seeped water from a dozen wounds, but it would get you to the other side.

It was the first beautiful man-made thing I had seen in this place. Was I merely romancing the makeshift efforts of a poor country? Was it just easier to love poor people? Was their suffering less complicated—more easily understood?

Mother's coughs echoed in my head. Even in this fragile state, she was still prickly and defensive. I found myself not wanting to return to the 'natural' house. Maybe Blas was right—Mexico was a good place to run to.

The boat's metal prow bit into the mud bank. Mexico. I reached in my pocket, but the boatman shook his head "no."

"*Regresse*," he said and made a circle with his hand. *When I come back.* He had more faith than I. Back across the river, on the Texas side, a purple haze veiled the broken face of Lajitas Mesa; from the saloon on the boardwalk out floated the garrulous sounds of drinking and laughter—traveled the distance with surprising clarity. It was quieter in Mexico. Poverty hit the sack early.

Tire ruts led from the muddy bank, through soft sand and on into the village. Evening wood smoke. There was an electric hum and pop as an array of florescent lights flickered on to illuminate a concrete basketball court incongruously dropped in the center of a ramshackle adobe village complete with goats and chickens.

It had the smell of gringo *mordida*—payoff from the Texas side. *Don't notice what comes across this river and we'll build you a basketball court.* All power wires webbed out from a single wooden pole that leaned from the tangled weight of jerry-rigged additions. Mexico.

In the little *tienda*, wardrobe options were limited to an already faded Power Rangers tee or a once-white cowboy shirt with red chili peppers embroidered over the breast pockets. I went for the cowboy shirt and a *La Milagrosa* votive that pictured the Miraculous Mother among the clouds, halo around her head, shafts of light shone from each of her hands; she had no feet, but was planted in a floating reef of roses.

Across from the *tienda,* a small *cemetario* had memorial offerings of sun-faded plastic flowers bunched among the graves; tiny *nichos* housed spent votives. Just past the cemetery stood an adobe *Iglesia* the size of a single-car garage, a crooked cross hung over the doorway.

Inside, four rough hewn benches faced a luridly suffering Christ. He had good cheekbones and an aquiline nose—a Caucasian *Cristo.* You'd think these people would at least have the self respect to give Jesus a tan, make their savior somewhat resemble themselves. Or must our saviors always look like something 'other' than ourselves because we just can't cut the mustard?

Dirt floor. Dim votives guttered on either side of a soot-smudged *nicho.* From the wall hung a jumble of crutches: wood, metal, plastic, homemade. Had their owners all walked away reconfigured by their belief in the healing power of this place? I had heard of psycho-genic death brought on by the power of the victim's own belief in a curse put upon him. Therefore, was it not possible to do the opposite—to heal through superstition? Or were the crutches merely standard set-dressing for any

Iglesia? Was I that cynical? Was I that gullible? Belief shaped by need. But what was the need? To be cured of the affliction.

I pulled a crutch down: the rubber under-arm cushion dried and cracked, a patina of use darkened the hand grip. Another was taken down. And another. Took them all down and rearranged them in a descending order of size, each slanted at a uniform diagonal towards the *Cristo* with the smaller crutches nearest the figure of suffering.

From the pocket of my wrecked shirt, I pulled the envelope given to me by Dr. Singh back in LA. Under his letterhead: "Medical Need to Know"; it was a legal key that would allow me access to sealed court documents: the circumstances of my adoption, the names of my birth parents—gateway to the past.

My ragged dog-fight-shirt was hung on the last nail at the end of the row of crutches. I put on my new shirt, tucked the letter into the pocket below the red chili pepper and snapped it; lit the Miraculous Mother votive and bowed my head to whatever power heals curses imagined or real.

Chapter 19

Odessa, Texas

"BUT THE CURE CAME AT AN UNFORE-seen cost," Mother's physician said quietly laying it out. Hardly older than me, he had a retiree's taste in footwear. Dad and I stood dutifully by her hospital bed, but he seemed to address himself mostly to me which suggested that both my parents had heard it all before. There always seems to be an "unforeseen cost."

"Because the axillary lymph nodes were involved …" he motioned with his hand to designate the armpit area beneath his white smock.

"… A real danger zone for the breast cancer spreading, so they hit her pretty hard with the radiation. And it worked, they did stop it. But her lungs were damaged by the intensity of the treatments, the right lung especially."

A respiratory specialist, he had the grace to avoid dispensing a sugar-coated version of her condition without being totally bleak, i.e. twenty years ago some over-zealous smocks had cranked the dials and fried Arlene's chest with radiation to obliterate the cancer. The result being she was still alive, but having a hard time drawing a satisfying breath.

"The oxygen helps her to breathe," the young specialist continued. "However, as we give her more, her lungs require more. Unfortunately, it is a cycle of diminishing returns. But she seems to be responding to the new medication. So we'll wait and see."

Ductal carcinoma. I learned the term at nine years old from my father when I asked why Mother was in the hospital. "Ductal carcinoma," he had replied. I was taken to the hospital to see her. She was groggy; her eyes, wet spots in the middle of dark circles. Barely able to talk, she asked for water. The plastic bedside pitcher shaky in my young hand, I poured her a cup. After several sips she rasped, "thank you" and let her head fall back on the pillow. I slipped out of the room and headed for the lab.

Being a doctor's son had endowed me with certain privileges at the hospital. The lab was on the first floor near the parking lot and having a ten year-old's fascination with laboratories I often hung around there, killing time while Dad made his rounds.

"Hello, Bertrand," Milly greeted me in her lab cap. "Come to visit your mom?"

I nodded and asked to see the ductal carcinoma. The other women in the room stopped what they were doing and looked at each other.

"I want to see what's hurting her."

Milly took in my request and moved crisply into action. She pulled a step-stool up to the binocular microscope I had amused myself with before; she opened a metal drawer filled with hundreds of glass slides that overlapped like scales on a large, rectangular fish; she selected a slide and clipped it in place on the microscope, torqued the focus knobs and turned to me, "Climb up and take a look."

Gray, irregularly shaped islands came into view clustered in a pale blue sea. They didn't look particularly deadly or even threatening, but you could tell there was something off about them: they had no common shape or size and were oddly clumped together without any natural symmetry; either bunched up too close to one another or too far away. There was no pattern which is what you almost always found when you looked into a microscope.

"That's right," Milly nodded. "There is no pattern. Cancer cells don't stick together like normal cells. They drift."

"Why?'

"They don't specialize, they never find a job. They stay immature and don't attach to their neighbors."

"Where do they come from?"

"Usually, billions of copies come from one cell that can't

stop reproducing itself. Like a bad weed in the garden, it'll take over if you don't pull it out."

The night she came home from her surgery, from the half-opened doorway I watched Mother change into her pajamas. She removed her bandage. My stomach clenched and I turned my head away. It looked like she had been hit with an axe. They had taken not only her breast, but had cut the muscle from her armpit, high-up into her shoulder; the skin burned red from the radiation.

Her moods were dark and often irritable. There was a ritual of bandaging, but she was cured, at least of the cancer. And now, twenty years later, this was the first I'd heard of the collateral damage done to her lungs.

"Wait and see," the young doctor repeated with a resigned sigh as if taking stock of his current proximity to god.

"She just needs some rest," Dad said vigilantly pulling the moment back from any drift towards poignancy. The doctor conceded with a respectful nod and roused himself to squeak out the door in his Velcro walkers.

My parents were joined in mutual denial about the seriousness of Arlene's condition. Denial had always been the current that ran beneath the surface of their everyday life. Don't mess with the surface routine and everything would be just fine: Dad's nap would be taken, dinners prepared and eaten; bedtime portions of thick brightly-colored novels read and coffee timer set to cue the beginning of tomorrow's cycle *doin' great.*

It had gone beyond functional optimism, morphed like a decrepit religion whose rites and rituals the followers have long forgotten the purpose of, yet the cycle continues. So, even though she'd been checked into the hospital again, her wrist banded like a caught bird, oxygen prongs blasting into her nostrils—Dad couldn't help himself, he checked his watch—the afternoon nap had been missed.

"You can go on home," he suggested. "I'll stay until she's had dinner." He spoke as if she were already in a coma, oblivious to our conversation; then he seemed surprised that I didn't have a car.

"Oh, that's right. Huh, you want to take the car and come back and get me later?"

"I'll just call a cab."

"Oh, that's an unnecessary expense."

I told him there was some business to attend to and leaned over the bed to say good-bye to Mom, gave her hand a squeeze, made an effort to infuse my gaze with care and concern, but she wasn't in the mood.

"I'm *fine,*" she cracked and shooed me away, her eyes on the wall in front of her.

Chapter 20

Odessa, Texas

THE YELLOW CAB PULLED IN. THE WINDOW glided down as I approached, revealing Margery Gardiner, her big hands at the wheel.

"My finances have been put in order," I said unexpectedly embarrassed as she weighed me in the balance of her eyes, and then, as if surprised by the appraisal, plucked the bills from my hand. "... I don't have your stuff with me. Back at headquarters for safe-keeping."

She stowed the cash and cheerfully offered to run me by her place in Goldsmith, one of the tiny satellite towns that surround Odessa like so many waning moons. But first she would have to pick her son up at school.

"Let's go," I said anxious to get the Vicadin.

Large hands set in motion, bossed the wheel into a U-turn, released it to slide through her spoon-shaped fingers on the rebound, squeezed it off at the right moment and accelerated. Big Hands in control.

That's what I needed. Big Hands to slap the world around a little, to get a grip on the steering wheel. My own hands, aside from burns and dog bite, were small and unimpressive, overly delicate for a man. I needed Big Hands and a plan. A plan to carry out my resolve. And there was Mother sick in the hospital. I needed big hands to lay on her thin, over-radiated body.

As if hearing my thoughts, Margery dropped her right hand out of sight.

"I hope it's not serious," she said out of nowhere and glanced back at me in the rearview mirror.

"What?"

"Your mother—I hope it's nothing serious."

Performing a quick review of the last few minutes, I could

not recall any mention of my mother's condition. Not out loud anyway. It was likely Margery had picked up scores of people at the Medical Center, no doubt heard stories. Had she developed an eye for the look people got when their mothers had run aground at the hospital?

"She's just in for some tests," And right there, I caught myself *denying*. I was as bad as they were—of course, I was their child; an imprint at the very least.

"Actually, she's having problems breathing," I corrected.

"I'm sorry," she said in a thoroughly sincere tone. Women are better at it than men—making that sincere tone. As a gender they are congenitally equipped for it along with lactating breasts; while men hazard through each day barely able to avoid a felony assault on another man.

"Thanks," I said sounding insincere even though I meant it.

"Of course," she said sounding sincere even if she didn't mean it.

Silence. Driving.

"Excuse me, Margery?"

"Yes?"

"When exactly did I mention that she was in the hospital?"

"What's that?"

"About my mother in the hospital—when did I mention that?"

"Uh, a few minutes ago."

"In the car?"

"Uh, yeah."

Pause.

"Did I say anything else?"

"Something about hands."

"Oh, yes, now I remember …" I flushed with shame.

"… I injured my hands recently," I offered as a camouflage. "… Cooking accident, dog bite thing—nothing serious. Sorry to bother you with it."

"Nothing to be sorry about," she said in a way that told me—*too much information.* Time to sit back and shut up.

It disturbed me, the idea that I had actually said out loud "big hands" to a woman who knows she has big hands—she's had them all her life, of course she knows. By thirty you know all your flaws or 'characteristics' might be the better term. However, an unconscious outburst is not a 'characteristic' that I had been previously aware of in myself; it could only be further evidence of neurological deterioration. So it was happening. How long before the occasional unconscious outburst worsened into an endless unedited spill of verbiage? A walking talking babbling stream-of-consciousness. And as anyone who has ever spent three minutes around someone who "thinks out loud" will tell you—they sound like complete idiots. But then, that is more or less what I was becoming and helpless to control it.

I clamped my hand over my mouth as the screech of self-doubt reverberated in my head on both the vertical and horizontal planes.

Vertical Plane = the big questions: meaning of life, states of being, considerations/estimations of neurological deterioration i.e., ability to control the physical person, level of sanity, hopelessness of the situation—the 'why go on' factor, suicide ideation, etc.

Engaging the Vertical Plane at this time was simply not advisable: Mom's in the hospital. Dad's in denial and I have no clean underwear.

Horizontal Plane = the tasks before you: en route to get your stuff, one singed foot in front of the other. Of course, vertical questions could insinuate themselves at any time like: Why was *stuff* so important anyway? Stuff is not inherently important. Ask anyone who has seen a plane crash or a ship sink with all that stuff—people's stuff—spread across a field or floating on the water. Remove the people and the stuff is meaningless detritus.

But, fact is, if you are alive, you need stuff. Plain and simple. Alive = Stuff. And though it seems obvious, it is sometimes necessary to get back to the obvious and examine whether it really is or is not obvious. One man's obvious is another man's head scratching. We all have blind spots. The key is to try to mark them before being blind-sided.

Therefore, (horizontal plane) I need to get my stuff because I am alive and I do not want to have to suffer again through the countless decisions of replacing said stuff: finding the right jeans—Loose Fit or Original? Socks of the proper thickness and poly/cotton blend; underwear with a comfortable waistband in colors/pattern not embarrassing to be discovered in should you get lucky or end up in an ER. And they all had to be washed at least three times before they felt like my clothes rather than the mass marketed commodities they are i.e., stuff.

Okay, fuck the stuff—there was Vicadin in that bag. Pharmaceutical relief, my name on the bottle, legally prescribed for my pain (with 1 refill). Yes, that lent this all a brighter purpose—pain relief. Horizontal plane. Move forward.

San Jacinto Elementary School. She turned into the parking lot of what was my pre-teen alma mater; pale brick flecked like Bit O' Honey candy. The grass was still dead. I had no memory of the grass ever not being dead.

First grade: napped a lot, it was an assignment and had to be taken seriously which made it difficult to do. Second grade: the kid who sat behind me threw up on me. Third grade: I threw up on the kid who sat in front of me. That got me to the fourth grade and Ms. Johnson, the first teacher, who for reasons my tiny mind could not fathom—did not like me. In fact, she disliked me.

Though a young woman at the time, Ms. Johnson had brittle orange hair, and a physical rigidity that belied her years. Her pale, near translucent skin ran to a blue green—the veins at her temples like a soft bruise.

Her formal disapproval of me was marked on my first report card: the letter 'C' in the 'conduct' box. It sprang off the page and caught like a fish hook in Dad's eye. He turned towards me, his eyes narrowed—he never contemplated me as clearly as he did when a punishment was being considered.

"Go to your room and take your pants down," he instructed grimly. Words that never failed to unleash pin pricks of perspiration.

His method never varied: pants puddled around my ankles, I would lean against the bed. He would apply the leather belt to the backs of my bare legs. At some point I had vowed to myself that I would not cry. My code of self-respect: I would not give him the satisfaction of hurting me. But all that began to falter on the third lash.

What you start to notice when someone whips you with a belt, repeatedly on a specific area, is that the pain compounds itself: the first lash has just begun to sting when the second lash falls accelerating the pain of the first. You think you can handle that when the third lash connects them all and before you know it, the fourth, like a bellows, blows on the hot coals of those that fell before. You try to hold onto yourself, but as the belt falls faster and faster, the coals burn hotter; the pain overtakes you, becomes bigger than your will, and then, try as you might, your body betrays you. You crumple. You curl-up within yourself and slide down onto the floor in a ball. You cry. Complete physical and emotional humiliation. Only then does it stop. Dad knew how to do it. Someone must have taught him. My rage was as immense as my sense of injustice. But I could only stand and glare at him wet-faced as he turned and said to me, "This hurts me as much as it hurts you."

But if that were true then how could he do it? How could he do it knowing how much it made me hate him?

The next semester another 'C' appeared. And again the belt was applied, the battle against the tears was lost, the glaring rage.

When I saw the third 'C' I put the card on the kitchen table and went to my room. Mother said nothing. I heard his car on the street outside as he pulled into the driveway. I knew I could not let it happen again, would not be humiliated. If he could hit, then so could I.

There was the rumble as the garage door opened and closed. I heard him greet Mother. Hushed voices. Then silence. His foot steps down the hall as he approached.

The door to my bedroom opened. The report card was in his hand. He looked at it, set the card on my desk and said, "This teacher just doesn't like you." And walked out. It was over.

One summer afternoon when school was out, I saw Ms.

Johnson shopping in Walgreen's, a headscarf on to protect her pale skin from the West Texas sun. Whereas, I just kept getting darker and darker as the summer wore on. She swept past me with her head up; in her wake the fusty, sweet smell of her perfume, like dirty dishwater that's stood too long. She tried to pretend not to see me, but I wouldn't allow her to ignore me.

"Hello, Ms. Johnson," I said prompting her to look my way and fake a sudden recognition.

"Oh, hello," she quavered. And with an awkward smile, snugged her scarf and moved on.

The first thing about Margery's kid was the hair. Like happening upon an orchid growing in the trunk of your car—you had to stop and marvel: a honey-colored, semi-afro floppy Tina Turner mane that bobbed and flexed as he made his sullen approach to the car. Not just unhappy, but a pissed-off, rock-kicker of a child—the begrudging air of one who has been defeated regularly and now suspects the game is rigged.

Andy got into the car, slammed the door. His feet were two complaints planted firmly against the dash board. He did not look at his mother who was intently reading the news in his every gesture.

"... And how was your day?" She asked. It was a real question, devoid of sarcasm. He stuck out his hand with a note attached, like so much dogshit, at the end of it.

She read it and said, "Okay, we will have to talk about this."

It did not have the sound of a threat, but of a desire for understanding. I liked Andy. Or the fact that he was pissed-off and miserable.

"I was just laughing," the boy huffed in defense of whatever charge had been leveled against him.

"Laughing?"

"She made a joke and I laughed."

"And that's all?"

"She thought I was laughing at her."

"Why would she think that?"

"Because no one laughs at her jokes and I was laughing too loud or something. I don't know. She hates me."

"No one hates you."

"She called me to the front of the class, told me to sit on a stool, face the class and laugh. By myself. No one else can laugh. Just me."

"Were you making fun of her?"

"No."

Margery set the car in motion. We were moving forward, but it was incidental to the exchange between mother and son.

"So why did you go to the principal's office?"

"Because I said no."

"No?"

"Said I wouldn't do it."

"Would not go to the principal's office?"

"Wouldn't sit on the stool in front of class and laugh."

"And so she sent you to the principal's office?"

"No, I dropped in on my own."

"What did I say about sarcasm?"

"Yes. She sent me."

"And what did the principal say?"

"Bad attitude."

"Bad attitude?"

"He said, 'A bad attitude undermines the entire class.'"

"What did you say?"

"Nothing. What's the point? He's on her side."

"So you went back to class?"

"No, I stayed and we tossed the Frisbee around." He slid a look over at his mother. "… Yes, I went back to class."

He nodded his head, hair flopping a motley fool's cap.

"But then she told me not to look at her that way."

"In what way?"

"I don't know. She just said 'stop looking at me like that.'"

"And what did you do?"

"Just looked down at my desk."

"What grade are you in?" I interrupted. The kid whipped his head around as if he just realized someone else was in the car.

"Who are you?" he asked.

"Just along for the ride, but I used to go to school at San Jacinto. What grade are you in?"

"Fourth."

"And who is your teacher?" I asked.

"Ms. Johnson," the boy said with a bitter edge.

She was still there, must have been in her sixties and still making some kid's life miserable.

"It's not about you," I said to Andy. "Not about anything you did anyway. And there is nothing you can do to fix it. Because, you're right—she just doesn't like you."

"Okay, wait a minute ..." Margery tried to stop me.

"Who knows why—your hair, your skin? She just doesn't like little brown people."

"Excuse me, but I don't think this is appropriate or helpful."

"Ms. Johnson. She didn't like me back in the day. I was there. And I could never figure out why. And it was the cause of no small amount of suffering on my part, welts on the legs, stuff you didn't want seen in the locker room. And I just couldn't figure out why? Until I saw our class picture and who was the darkest kid in the shot? You should see me in the summer—brown as a coffee bean, they used to say. 'And what nationality are you?' Christin Carlton always used to ask, and then never wait around for an answer. Ms. Johnson's pet of course—cute, blonde, vicious."

Margery had pulled the car over and stopped as I wrapped up my rant.

"Ms. Johnson, teacher, fourth grade. Perfume smelled like dirty dishwater."

"Totally," Andy said with a look back.

The three of us sat there in silence. Andy turned from me to his mom. She stared straight ahead, big hands on the steering wheel, still as a cat identifying a threat.

"... Told you," Andy said and flipped on the radio.

"Homework first, then TV," she recited the litany before the boy got through the door of their home.

"So who did you have in the third grade?" Andy asked me his new buddy, advocate and fellow sufferer.

"Never mind that now. Go. Homework. And you," she addressed me in the same tone as her son, then remembered I was an adult and adjusted it a half-click back from a command, "... follow me."

Generally, I bridled at anything that sounded like an order. But I found myself unexpectedly enjoying the certainty in her voice.

Outside, Margery opened the side door to a garage that stood separate from the house. She switched the light on to a shanty town of cardboard boxes.

"There," she said pointing to my bag.

"Sorry again for the trouble."

"No problem."

"If I could just take a minute, there's some medication in here …" I said working the zippers on the bag.

"… 'Cooking accident dog' …" she distractedly repeated the words I'd muttered earlier to cover for my blurt about her hands.

"That's right," I could tell she wanted me gone. Vicadin located, I fumbled as I twisted the top off, and then spilled the contents rattling down into a cardboard box crammed with papers.

"… Shit, sorry," I picked up the nearest pill and tossed it into my mouth.

"Are you in pain?"

"… Only when I'm awake," I answered as I dug around in the box for the rest of the pills. Files, papers, legal briefs. A box of business cards: Schnelling & Associates.

"You a lawyer?"

"Paralegal," she answered. "Listen, I'm sorry. I had no idea you had medication in that bag. You really should have said something."

There was a framed photo: Margery, Andy holding up a modest sized trout, and a handsome black man with his arms around them. Happy Family with Catch.

"I wish I had thought of it at the time …" I babbled to allow me a few seconds to study the photo. "… But, uh, that's the thing about pain—you forget it when it's gone and then all of a sudden …"

"It comes back."

I looked up to find the big hands covering her face.

"Hey, it's okay, my father's a physician," I consoled. "He helped me out. Of course, I was in line behind the dog ..."

There was a sharp intake of breath, a shoulder tremor—tears behind the big hands. I reached out, she pulled away.

"No. No, I'm fine …" she said with an effort to shake it off. "… it's just, the legal implications of depriving someone of their medication, I acted in anger, wasn't thinking … this is all so hard on him ...."

"The boy?"

She nodded her head, hands back over her face.

"That teacher is what I believe is commonly referred to in polite circles as a racist," I said.

"I have no proof of that. How do you prove that? A formal accusation would only serve to further alienate him."

"Meet with her. Ask some questions. Let her know you're paying attention."

"Of course I'm paying attention!" she snapped in a spray of mucous. "What do you think I'm doing? Driving a fucking cab so I have time."

I mumbled an apology, resisted the urge to put my arms around her.

"No, I'm sorry!" She countered. "Sorry. Sorry. Really, you just came to get your bag. And I don't know. Like this isn't hard enough. You know," she swept her big hands out to indicate the cardboard boxes, the records and mementos of another life.

I could see she was going Vertical as she surveyed all the stuff: the dusty golf clubs, the fishing poles and camping gear. Ex-husbands might leave a few albums behind, but not their golf clubs.

"When did you stop being a paralegal?" I asked softly.

"It's been two years," she exhaled like someone whose just remembered to breathe, and then it all washed across her face: the strain of single parenting while grieving the loss of a husband; a terrible grief that had become familiar. And there was something deeper under that—an almost sexual heat that seemed to emanate from her skin, but more mental in origin, and then I understood that it wasn't her skin, but her entire being that emanated a quiet suffering, devoted as praying wide awake at 3:00 AM.

I could see her lying there at night, hot sheets kicked aside, a life struggling to recompose itself from broken pieces, summoning a new vision for herself and the boy. How would they recover happiness? When? It was mesmerizing to see someone in the throes of something so completely and utterly private.

As if remembering where she was, she glanced down and found her hand at rest on a cardboard box. Lifting the lid, she reached in and pulled out a cellophane package.

"We have pajamas. Need any pajamas? Never been worn, still in the package, gathering dust. Take them. Make me feel better about withholding your meds."

She handed off them, moved to another box and opened it.

"Ties, ties, ties," she said lifting them up out of the box like a handful of dead snakes. "You don't seem like a tie guy," she dropped them limp back in the box.

"Thanks for the pajamas," I said and immediately regretted it because it sounded like I was in a hurry, ready to go and I wasn't. I wanted to stand there and watch her emanate.

She turned her head and looked at me; considered in full the man who stood before her: the bagged-out jeans, the no longer fresh chili pepper cowboy shirt, the scorched throat, teeth marks on one hand, Vicadin bottle gripped in the other. Finally, her eyes came back to mine.

"... What the fuck happened to you?"

Chapter 21

Medical Center

"WHERE'S MY LIPSTICK?" MOTHER rotated the turret gun of her head from the pillow and fired a glance at me. I sat next to her hospital bed, leafing through a rumpled three-month old issue of People magazine quietly loathing each celebrity profiled.

"My lipstick," she reiterated hoarsely. I tossed the magazine aside, wiped my hands and stood to pour her a cup of water, my go-to action when in doubt about her needs.

"When a woman wants her lipstick she must be feeling better," I sang out nestling the cup in her apathetic hands.

"What would you know?" she said, her spite had returned with her vanity.

She ate little, dozed often. When awake, she would slide smoothly back and forth between an astonishing clarity and an equally astonishing hallucination. Astonishing, not only because of their seamless proximity to one another, but because her tone of voice was the same for either one: for the imagined Girl in the Blue Dress or her very real lipstick in the shade of Evening Peach.

"This isn't it," she said with a frown at the cup I had just put in her hands.

"That is a cup of water."

"Where's my lipstick?"

"I have no idea. Let's look for it." I made dutiful sounds and motions rummaging through the nightstand.

"She moved it," she sighed with the resigned annoyance of one accustomed to suffering a repeated offense.

"Who moved it, Mother?"

"She hid it."

"The Girl in the Blue Dress?"

"She hides everything. And just smiles like it's nothing."

"You're confused," Dad piped-up like an Audio-Animatronic character that's been still for so long you're surprised by its sudden, nearly life-like movement.

He pivoted from his post at the window where he'd kept watch over the parking lot and the apparently captivating array of parked cars.

SHUT-THE-FUCK-UP! I screamed inside my skull, but locked my jaws around it, held it back like a fart in an elevator with ten floors left to go. Not here. Not now.

My temper had been primed by an event earlier that morning when, in response to something Mother had said, Dad had shaken his head and pronounced flatly, "You're not making any sense."

I watched this cold assessment land on her, saw her withdraw perceptibly beneath her skin, her spirit falling back—a retreating army giving up a little more territory. That's when I decided I would do just the opposite. I would board the train of her hallucinations ready to clatter along wherever it went. If she said there was a big fat hand giving her ass a squeeze under the bed sheet, then I collared the intruder and made a show of drop-kicking it out the door—*Bad Hand!*

If a Girl in a Blue Dress appeared in the corner, I offered her a beverage (which I was told she turned her nose up at). This immersion in Mother's hallucinations allowed the two of us to interact in a way that over-rode our layered history of disappointments and knee-jerk resentments; it kept us in a shared, if imagined, present. We were, in a way, playing together. And it annoyed the shit out of Dad.

"I'm fine here. Why don't you go on home, have lunch and a nap," I said to him in a tone so neutral, so nakedly filtered of ulterior motives, any rookie cop would have reached for his cuffs.

Dad checked in with his own personal God, a multi-function chronometer (tells time in 10 different countries, solar-powered, self-correcting.). He took a final assessing gander at Mother over his poised wrist as if the watch might divulge some new information about her if the appropriate function could be activated. She did not return his look.

"Okay, then," he surrendered to the powerful tug of the daily schedule, creaked out the door and down the hall considering a shorter route home that might, at that hour, recover a few minutes and set the afternoon back on course.

"Nothing ever gets to him," Mother sighed filling the room with a sachet of resignation. "It's all the same, that's whatcha get."

Then she pointed to the wall and said, "She's looking at you. Tell her to give back my lipstick."

"Okay. Where'd you hide it?" I demanded of the wall. "The lipstick! Come on, cough it up before things get ugly around here."

"She hid it."

"I know, I know, Mom, but why does the Girl in the Blue Dress keep hiding things?"

"Because she doesn't like me."

"I see. And why is that?" I asked rifling the drawers again, making a dutiful noise, joining her parade. Then I glimpsed the tube, a gleam of gold peeking from under the humiliating diapers. Evening Peach read the worn label on its base.

"Hey, I found it! She can't hide it from us." I put the tube into her hand. She stared at it quizzically.

"What's this for?"

"The lipstick. The missing lipstick?"

She looked up at me her eyes gone soft with a child-like bewilderment.

"Are you the mother?" she asked without irony. I nodded and took the lipstick from her hand.

"Yes, I am," I said and popped the top, rolled the frosty pink tip up out of its casing and into the light where it shone like a bullet: the shiny metal jacket, the ballistic taper of the tip—streamlined, efficient, ready to be loaded and fired—striking men unawares. I pressed the tip over her lower lip, but it was lax and rumpled like a bunched carpet under the pressure.

"Come on, firm it up, like this ..." I demonstrated: lips drawn taut in the customary manner, daubed a generous stroke of Evening Peach on my lower lip, a stroke on my upper; pressed the two together, smear and a pucker—time to blot.

This had all been learned as a small boy when I stood next to her vanity, observed her cosmetic rituals in the mirror. Blotting was my favorite part: she would pluck a sheet of Kleenex and press it between her freshly coated lips. The excess adhered to the tissue made a perfect imprint of her lips before being discarded into the waste basket.

These lip prints brought into high-relief the squiggled fissures that creased the surface of her lips, revealed their character in more detail than you would observe by merely looking at her. They seemed so personal—like finger prints—her unique mark, the residue left behind after she swept off to: Bridge Club, Shopping, Junior League, Altar Guild, Country Club ...

And after she left, I would return to her vanity, study her things—all meaningless and inert without her there to animate them, then I would bend to the waste basket and gather the tissues, take them back to my room where, in a sudden inspiration, I shoved all the clothes aside in my closet and Scotch taped the tissues to the back wall.

I harvested them daily like fruit fallen in the basket. I arranged them into an ever-expanding symmetrical pattern (unlike the wild irregularity of the cancer cells I had glimpsed under the microscope in the hospital lab). I made certain each imprint of Mother's lips was well-placed, equidistant from its neighbor. If I could not control what was happening inside her body, then at least here, in the back of my closet, with these markers she left behind, I could bring some order to bear.

It demanded tending like a fragile crop. There were constant adjustments: the shades of lipstick would change; the color of the tissues would change: usually pink, sometimes white, occasionally a pale blue (my least favorite). These colors had to be arranged in alternating sequences. Symmetry!

Some imprints were more faded, being the second or third blot in a series while others were deliciously coated with a rich impasto—all these needed to be placed with a balanced regularity within the circular configuration: the growing mandala of her lips on the back wall of my closet that ruffled lightly to greet me each time I pulled back the curtain of clothes.

Then, one night, she and Dad went out for an evening at The Golden Rooster (a place I had been repeatedly told, I, being a kid, was not allowed in). She was elegant, floating on a cloud of perfume, copper hair lacquered that afternoon by Kenneth, lipstick bullet and a fresh pack of Salems tucked in the clutch and the prosthetic breast tucked inside her black beaded gown—ah, the rustle and scent of glamour before I knew the word. They left me behind with a feeble babysitter who smelled faintly of moth balls and was snoring on the sofa by nine o'clock.

I went to my closet, shoved aside the curtain of clothes, tore all the lipstick tissues down, took them outside, piled them on the concrete patio and torched them. As they burned, pieces would lift, propelled upwards by the heat of their own disintegration up into the night sky until they flamed out and floated back as ash—she wasn't my real mother anyway.

A few days later, Dad discovered the burn mark from my sacrificial fire on the patio. I denied any knowledge of it and held up under the scrutiny of his stare.

"She doesn't like it," Mom said, done inspecting her lipstick application in the hand mirror I held before her.

"It looks fine. Who cares what the stupid Girl in the Blue Dress thinks anyway?" I said lowering the mirror.

"Everyone does," she said and wiped off the lipstick. "They all listen to her. It's like a spell, even the teacher."

"I think she might be jealous of you," I said and raised the mirror again. "Often comes down to something like that doesn't it? What was it about you?"

She gazed into the mirror. "I do have long hair. 'Rapunzel,' Daddy would say, 'let your hair down'. I wore it in braids to school."

"And her hair?"

"Thin. Blonde ringlets. And blue eyes. The way she'd look right through you."

"There it is, she wanted your long braids, tugging bait for boys."

"But she has the key. Look how the other girls circle round her," she noted as she stared at the wall.

"Yes, I see," I said peering at the wall with her, and as she spoke the girl came to life in front of me. I could see her, The Girl in the Blue Dress.

"Her father's wealthy—speaks without an accent. And her mother is so beyooteeful. Perfect house, like her blue dress. She hates me. Whispers when I walk by, says things to the others as I pass by. And then I hear it … 'Arlene." She calls out my name. She knows my name—it surprises me. I stop and turn. All the girls are looking. "It is Are-leen?" she asks with a smile. "Yes," I said, "It is."

"Then she looks me up and down, 'Well, Are-leen, it looks more like you Are-fat to me.' They're laughing. Laughing at me. Because I'm fat. Are-fat. That's what's wrong with me," Mother twisted in the bed and kicked her sheets.

"I can't breathe," she said.

I checked her oxygen. It was flowing.

"I'm fat and I CAN'T BREATHE!" She opened her mouth and tried to inhale more air in an almost cartoon-like manner, a caricature of someone gasping for air! At first, I thought she was just lost in remembered emotion, but there was real panic. She wailed and thrashed, tore at her covers.

"Wait a minute," I begged and pressed her back into her bed. "Just relax. I'll find the problem. I will fix it."

She settled for a moment as if remembering where she was. Then lying back, she looked up at the ceiling. The pajama top fallen open, her bony chest exposed, the rib cage where her breast had been—underneath the flutter of fear pulsing. She was frightened. It made me frightened. And that made me angry.

I milked the call button for the nurse. Sent a Morse code, a mongrel SOS flustering through the wire.

"It's all right. The nurse is coming," I assured her.

"The nurses are all fat! All they do is eat and eat. They don't understand. I can't breathe!"

"Okay. It's okay."

"I keep saying it and no one does anything!" she wailed.

I got up and started for the door, angry at something, at everything.

"I'll be right back."

"Where are you going?"

"To get the nurse."

"Don't leave me here!

"Mother, I'll be right back."

"You're leaving again?"

"Again? What do you mean?"

"You never liked me."

"I'm going to get the nurse. Stay in bed. I'll be right back."

"Go on. Leave again."

"Mother, I did not leave you! I was sent away remember?"

"That's watcha get," She rolled her eyes, mouth open to capture air.

"I did not want to go."

"You're with her aren't you? The two of you. Why are you doing this to me? Why?"

"I'm going to get help and I'm coming back."

"Wait ..."

"What?"

"I'm coming..." she said and started to get out of bed "Shoes? Where are my shoes ..." she was tangled in her oxygen hose.

"Stop," I said as the door swung out of my hands. The Filipino nurse entered the room.

"Okay, okay. The nurse is here and I'm not leaving." I turned to the nurse who was not fat. "She says she's hot and can't breathe."

"Meezes Kelly, you need to stay in the bed now, okay?" The nurse said as she eased a loaded syringe from her pocket, turned away, uncapped it, thumped it twice, dropped it to her side and approached the bed.

"I CAN'T BREATHE!"

"You're oxygen is flowing, but you joos have to calm down now."

"She's hot," I said my own face flushed with Mother's accusations, that I had abandoned her, that I was in league with her tormentor, the Girl in the Blue Dress—*is that what I had been?*

"We'll turn the temperature down in the room," said the nurse in her professional, but accented tone. What did I care about accents, she was Filipino—of course she had an accent. It was the Girl in the Blue Dress whose father spoke without an accent.

"I want to go home. I have things to do!" Mother sat up, swung her legs off the bed as if suddenly well-rested and ready to tackle the day. Clarity.

"You need to stay in bed now Meezes Kelly, okay."

"No, I'm going home now," she said quite matter-of-factly.

"Hold her," the nurse ordered. I pressed her back into the bed as the nurse deftly swabbed her arm and drove the needle home.

"I have increased your oxygen, just calm down and breathe slowly—"

"I WANT TO GO HOME!" She howled and then the slump, the last twist and a cry, "Leave me alone and let me die," she said and flopped back on the bed. "Just let me die …"

That unmistakable sound reverberating in the air—the ring of truth. All the oxygen in the world couldn't give her a satisfying breath. Gradually, she was suffocating: the weight of invisible rocks being piled upon her chest.

She tried to lift her head again, but was pulled down by the expanding Diazepam injection; lipstick case still cradled in her hand, the glaze of oblivion dropped over her eyes like a second set of lids. I walked out of her room in search of my own medication.

In an institution founded on the treatment of pain and suffering, where was the solace of an adult beverage? A comfortable chair, non-florescent lighting, ESPN flickering reassuringly in the corner at low volume? What's more reassuring than a ball game and a beer? Were they afraid they would never get the doctors out of there?

Glib—the slick side of fear.

It wasn't just that Mother had yanked away the blanket of denial—we've all seen the movies, we're supposed to cheer the dying on, reassure the horribly wounded soldier—"... *you're going to be fine ... just fine ...*"

But when they say it, when the soldier lets you know that he knows, well, it puts it all right square before us. *Let me die.*

It was a radical departure from the family script. But as I lurched outdoors into the blinding glare like a man hunched against a storm, there was something more deeply troubling in her words.

I found Mother's car and got in, ransacked the glove box and came up with an old pair of her sunglasses—primordial smudge on the prescription lenses formed a welcomed blur, an agreeable filter against a world too bright.

... Leave me alone and let me die ...

It was the *sound* of her outburst, the rattle of lonesomeness that erupted from her throat, caught in my ear.

... Leave me alone and let me die ...

The anguish of it. With the end of her life signaling, she reached out to what? To whom?

To nothing. To no one.

With a screech of tires out of the hospital parking lot, I braked and checked the rearview. There she was, in the back-seat—shocking as a corpse—the Girl in the Blue Dress.

Chapter 22

The Shadows

LIKE AN AFTERBURN ON AN OLD TV SET WHEN you shut it off, I figured the Girl in the Blue Dress would quickly fade. Everything's just fine. Out for a drive in Mother's car, out through the Westside of town, out past the frayed edges of Odessa. No hopeful Wal Marts or Home Depots, no gleaming temples to high school football here; this was the Awl Bidness side of town where the edge of the asphalt went scraggy, crumbled off and mixed with the white chalky powder of caleche rock.

Past the quonset huts, the metal sheds and rutty yards cluttered with equipment for getting at oil: winch trucks cables slack and frizzed, the mobile derricks folded-up like insect wings, the fingers of gate valves furcated upwards connected to nothing but blue sky; piles of saw-toothed drill bits stacked like weird fruit next to miles of sagging pipe. Underneath it all a crop of weeds sprouted while upon it the rust festered—the boom gone bust.

All windows down, the big Mercury accelerated out onto the Andrews Highway, a tar-weeping seam cut straight through the dun-colored hide of the oil fields. The buffet of warm wind tumbled the Girl in the Blue Dress out like a wad of Kleenex, blew her out the back window. "Don't Mess with Texas" read the litter barrels. Ha!

It is a vast, reiterated landscape: everything behind you looks just-like-everything-in-front of you. Driving becomes a moving meditation through emptiness.

I am going nowhere at a high rate of speed.

And then, just as you become accustomed to the monotony, a sign stands up on the horizon, seizes the eye.

"The Shadows"

A one-story cinder block cube, windowless as an armory. But with a swash of art on the exterior: two silhouettes painted in black—a man and a woman frozen in mid-dance, her skirt a twirl, his tie perpetually waving carefree amid swirls of lurid color—they were *swinging.*

I entered, sun-blind through the murk and bumped into a bar stool. Nothing darker than a bar in the daytime. Empty. Quiet as a padded cell.

The bartender turned with a vague annoyance; dull eyes slanted up from his paper, watch band half-buried in wrist meat. Not much of a talker. Perfect.

Bourbon Please. Mother's poison. As he rousted himself to fetch it, I realized I was not alone. On the stool next to me, up she hopped—the Girl in the Blue Dress. She focused the acetylene blue of her eyes upon me and farted in a high thin register.

Not wanting to appear shaken, in fact desiring to project a cavalier attitude, I called out to the barkeep, "… And a Rusty Nail, if you would, sir."

So what if she was a minor? No one except Mother and I could see her. I turned away, let my eyes adjust. Absorbed the décor done in the 'lounge' tradition: an upscale honky-tonk: liquor, beer, and all three colors of wine available for the ladies. A worn linoleum dance floor pooled out from the jukebox and a series of black booths receded back into—the shadows. Ideal for daytime cheaters or your pre-happy hour drifter doing his damnedest not to consider anything too close to the reality of his current circumstances, the questionable nature of past events or the slim options the future has to offer. I'll drink to that. Wordlessly, the bartender set both drinks before me, fingers thick as grilled hot links. A grunt and a suspicious side-slip of the eyes at the two incongruous drinks in front of the single patron. He crawled back into his paper.

I ignored the Girl in the Blue Dress.

Bourbon. Ah, that first sip—vanilla and fire. Gagged on it as a kid—that first stolen slug of Mom's highball. Gastric revolt. Doused one of Dad's camellias with my snarf before handing it off to Mother. "How can you swallow this?" I had dared her to explain.

"When you're older," had been her only response.

She was right. Years later, hunkered at The Shadows, what was once offending was now all sweetness and warm relief. A sunset in the tummy.

"Hit me again," I called out and wondered if age alters the child's taste buds or do we, by effort and application, "acquire" a taste for something once repugnant? A cultural rite of passage where repeated doses of the distasteful and offensive transmute it into something desired? Gag and suffer a few times then presto! A bad habit is born. *I'm all grown up now, Mom—I like bourbon and cigarettes! Or heroin. Or killing …*

"How about self-hatred?" the Girl in the Blue Dress chimed-in like a broken gong. The first I'd heard her speak and if you've spent five minutes on any playground you know the voice: Bored. Cold. Snotty. Anxious to punish you for her having to suffer the offense of your low-ranking presence.

"Self-hatred?" I mused, the hackles rising.

"An 'acquired taste' too?" she rattled on. "What I believe is now referred to as a 'lack of self-esteem'. Who knows, maybe it's genetic? Those pesky genes takin' the heat for nearly every little thang these days," she taunted with a Blanche Dubois wink and blew a burp of bubbles into the bottom of her drink.

"Uh, what's that got to do with my mother dying?" I spoke flatly, determined not to take any shit from a hallucination.

"Paleeze—it could take months if she has another recovery," she whined, straw between her fingers like a cigarette, she took a pretend drag and exhaled with an exaggerated hauteur that collapsed in a mock fit of coughing. A comment on Mother's long and intimate relationship with her Salems, purchased by the carton, coupons collected and redeemed—for what I can't remember. Ah, yes—cancer.

Hit me again, bartender.

"She knows what's happening to her," I said. "She knows it in her body."

"And so now you're wondering what happened to us?" the Girl whimpered.

"Pardon me, but what the fuck do you want?"

"What do I want?" she sneered breezing past my poker face. "Hey, pal, it was you brought me here—I'm stuck in your head like a fucking ice pick."

"But you are my mother's hallucination," I corrected while politely encouraging the barkeep to move it along with the refill. "You're from her life, Sweetheart—not mine."

"I'm all you got of your Mother!" She snapped like a steel trap. "Go ahead. Ring her up. See if you can reach her under ten tons of Valium. Have a chat, Sweetheart."

Slow Poke finally waddled over with my drink—next stop security guard at a manure factory. I focused on my drink, but she wouldn't let up.

"Hey, it's not like we're a couple of work buddies having a happy hour pop and shootin' the breeze here. You wanna know Where Did It All Go Wrong? And Did She Really Love Me? And Was It My Fault? Meaningful stuff. And you think I got some answers. Insights. So are we talking here? Or maybe you'd rather cut the chatter, get shit-faced and go hug the porcelain?"

Harsh words from a nine-year old in blue gingham and curls.

"Okay," I said softly. "So you tell me then, Where Did It All Go Wrong?"

"No, problem, pal. Right after you tell me WHEN DID IT EVER GO RIGHT?" she guffawed and smacked the bar.

Swallow deep the brown spirits, the acquired taste. Let it sluice through the brain, refine the rough ore of memory, pan the past for the glint of a golden time. Something shone, back there, in the rubble of my pre-teens. I heard my mother's voice:

"Would you rub my back, please?"

She had asked. Evenings after dinner. Sitting in front of the TV. Mother would turn, ask in her little voice, the voice she used when she wanted to be doted on, then settle herself on the carpet in front, me perched behind on the sofa mute as a loaf of bread, watching as she pulled up the back of her blouse, unhooked and loosened her bra so the straps wouldn't be in the way—soft lobe of her left breast in partial side view.

"Rub up here..."

She directed me to her neck and I touched the flesh at the base of her hairline—the sweet/sour smell of Salems and bourbon, of Mother. With my hands, fingers closed like a swimmer's, I stroked across her flesh, over the swells of her shoulders and down the warm spillway of her back.

"That's good ..." she purred.

And we went silent watching "Perry Mason" or "Wagon Train." The black and white dramas—good men, moral victories, lessons learned, catchy theme music.

"And where was Dad when this was going on?" The Girl in the Blue Dress interrupted.

Dad was around. This was not a secret thing between Mom and me. Sometimes he rubbed her back. Sometimes I did. What's the big deal?

"So what happened—Dad get tired of sharing? Maybe feeling a little crowded by this 'thing' between you and Mom?"

"Thing?"

"Come on, she had NO CHILDREN. We're talking the whole 50's "model" here—she had landed the doctor—that whole thing with the nickel?"

That's how they had met, Hillard and Arlene. The Nickel.

I got the two-martini version related by Arlene one evening in the Captain's Room at 'The Shrimp Boat' while Hillard sat silently studying the intricacies of the nautical knots displayed on the wall.

When she was single, Arlene had worked as a lab tech at a Houston hospital. One day, standing in the corridor just outside the lab, she found she was short a nickel for the pay phone. Uncanny timing: Hillard, an intern dutifully making his rounds, happened by.

Brazenly she asked this complete (if previously noticed) stranger, if she might possibly borrow a nickel to allow her to complete her very important call. Hillard, up for any clearly defined task, fished around in his pocket, sorted through Zippo, keys, nail clippers, nasal inhaler (self-mixed), penknife, money clip and came up with the requested nickel (he checked first to see if it was an Indian head before handing it over).

The next day, Arlene, with her long black hair loosely held back Liz Taylor style by a violet scarf, tracked him down at the cafeteria where he stood examining a piece of apple pie for freshness. She handed him back a nickel and offered to buy him an ice cream to go with the pie.

And it was at this point, in Arlene's recounting of the story, that she stopped and turned to her husband (engrossed in the sheepshank man o'war knot), raised her second martini and delivered the punch line, "And I bet you still have that nickel don'tcha?"

"Yes, she landed the Doctor," bleated the Girl in the Blue Dress impatiently. "But she needed a child to complete the picture: ranch style on the better side of town, station wagon. And nothing was happening in the child department. We're *not* getting pregnant. Sperm count wasn't on the table back then—it was all about the woman—feelings of inadequacy perhaps?"

"Hit me," I told the barkeep while she persisted.

"She needed The Kid. She needed *you* in order to feel good about herself. So she adopted you. And then you rubbed her back. You paid attention. She liked that. Cozy. So where did we veer from this well-manipulated arrangement? What jigsaw piece didn't fit in the puzzle?"

"She never told me I was adopted."

"Oops, maybe she forgot? So much on her mind: shopping, bridge club, altar guild, country club—another bourbon."

After being called 'spic' and 'nigger', after being asked, "What nationality are you?" at last I had a comeback. I was Hawaiian. And my resentment at her not telling me began to fade as an excitement about my new identity rose: Hawaii was more than a place—it was a way of being, a lifestyle with a cinematic history: "Blue Hawaii." Its assets were celebrated: balmy days, luau nights, girls in bikinis—a life lived in flip flops and jams. Hawaii was every school boy's autumn wish—"The Endless Summer."

"But Arlene had a different vision," quacked the Girl in the Blue Dress.

"I tell people you were born right here in Odessa—that's what

it says on your birth certificate. So why confuse people with the past." Arlene had said, seeking an accord with me for how to handle this new information.

"But you had no intention of confusing anyone," said the Girl in the Blue Dress. "You pranced about doing the hula, telling everybody how Hawaiian you were. How'd Arlene like that?"

Maybe I had left her behind there. Brushed Mother aside in my reach for the new me. Pushed her away. Made her feel less like my mother.

"So it's your fault she didn't love you?"

"Didn't love me? I didn't say that. I said I was difficult."

"You were an asshole, a bad kid."

"I had three mothers before I was two and a half years old!"

"It's a wonder you only had three."

"Fuck you."

"A bad kid! Ungrateful, rotten to your rotten core."

"What about the Armenian thing? Her Armenian father wouldn't allow the language spoken in his home. We were all supposed to be WASPs."

"Maybe she was just ashamed of you."

"Go fuck yourself."

"The ever present disappointment. The mistake of you! The constant reminder of her bad choice. Not only is the kid a hopeless ingrate, he's got some bad gene from that trash he's spawned from."

My foot started twitching.

"Face it, you're a fucking loser!"

"SHUT THE FUCK UP, BITCH!"

She threw her drink in my face. Alcohol stung my eyes. I grabbed the bony mean shank of her arm; she flogged me with her other. I fended, grappled—tried to protect myself from the onslaught. Okay, I grabbed her, I wanted to shut her up. I wanted to hurt her. I pinned her down, got in close to her face: she stank of bad grades and leather belts, of gun oil and regret—of a wasted life.

There was a felt blow, the soft internal crunch of cartilage;

an intricate web of pain dispersed throughout my face, frisson in the eye sockets.

A voice boomed, "Stop or I'll hit you again, buddy!"

Above a blur loomed, a face, a moving mouth. The Bartender. A pearl of spit on his lower lip.

"I told you to stop it! Now git up and git the hell gone crazy sum bitch."

Bent over me, the butt-end of a cut-down pool cue poised.

"… Did you hear me?"

The place was still empty. Sprawled in a puddle. No sign of the Girl in the Blue Dress. The patter of blood drops. My nose a bright bloom of pain.

"Hey!"

"Yes. Yes." I spat through the trickle, "I understand … I'm here alone."

Chapter 23
The Nativity

The Greatest Story Ever Told!
Come join us!
St. John's Episcopal Church Presents:
"The Nativity"
Food & beverages served afterwards in the Rectory

IT WAS THE INVITATION ANDY STUCK IN MY hand that night when I stepped out of Margery's garage stacked with all those boxes of memories. And since all information is filtered through my narcissistic fog before it actually reaches my brain, I had mistaken the nine-year old's invite as a wish to know me better—an invitation to friendship. Wrong. He was just hustling up an audience for his performance as Balthazar, who, if not the wisest of the three Wise Men, was certainly the one with the most lines.

"There will be a real live baby Jesus," Andy had said to erase any thoughts I might have of ditching the show.

As my feet sank into the blood red carpet in the narthex of St. John's Episcopal Church, I beheld the back of Margery's head, her hair secured with a heavy silver barrette. And, as if on cue, she turned and actually did a double take: first recognition immediately followed by a critical assessment—my bandaged nose (compliments of the bartender at The Shadows). A rash act on his part; could have been restored to my senses with a spritz from the soda gun. No need for that pool cue. Besides, it was Mother's hallucination that started the whole thing, but I didn't want to get into all that. Not here.

Margery trapped the disapproving expression on her face

behind a tight smile. In front of the altar, the stage area was set; straw-filled manger and several bales of hay strewn about as if some cattle might wander in. I settled into a pew two rows back and made a furtive check of my bandage to see if it had lost adhesion over the first traces of a flop-sweat triggered by Margery's disapproving look. What did I care what she thought anyway? I'd come to see Andy.

There was a good turn out and no wonder after the promise of a "real live baby Jesus". And after a meandering welcome by the florid Reverend Glass, the house lights were lowered and some sheep wandered in. Volvos in the parking lot had been stripped of their sheepskin seat covers so the kids playing the lambs had wooly coats. And there was the very real, if somewhat long in the tooth, Baby Jesus wriggling in the arms of the Virgin Mary, portrayed by a tall girl who seemed older than the other children and appeared to be drunk; slack-jawed, an odd tilt to her head. Must have been sampling the communion wine backstage. God knows I tippled a few with my fellow acolytes back in the day. Strong stuff, fortified. But you had to keep an eye out for Father Vander a short-tempered, chain-smoking priest rumored to have once strangled an altar boy.

Meanwhile, back in Bethlehem, Joseph and Mary were having some halting exchanges of dialogue and it became apparent that the Virgin Mary was not tanked. She was "special". Challenged. The poor girl had a disability and was trying her darnedest to get her lines spoken while maintaining a grasp on an infant tweaking on a sugar binge.

The actual mother was easily located: front row, leaning towards her child like a hungry leopard.

The Three Wise Men entered following the Star of Bethlehem, played by a large-beam flashlight operated by an angel dragging one wing. Andy was resplendent in a purple robe, previously a plastic shower curtain. Holding his gift for the Baby Jesus, a foil-wrapped cigar box. The other Wise Men were similarly wrapped in shower curtains of watermelon and avocado. And the Baby Jesus did not respond well to this color combination that was moving towards him.

"I offer this gift of frankincense to honor the blessed child,"

Andy said as he extended his gift. Then the Baby Jesus lost it. With one kick of his tiny legs, he broke free. We all watched the Baby Jesus execute a half-gainer, bounce with an audible burp on a padded step, roll over the wine-colored carpet and come to rest on his back, arms spread to the heavens.

A horrified gasp erupted from the congregation. No matter what you believe in, watching a baby free fall does something to you. Your arms extend, from hopeless distances—you reach out …

The infant's mother sprang forward. But Andy, being nearer, swooped down and casually retrieved the Baby Jesus like an errant basketball. We all waited for the tears, but instead, a big loopy grin spread across the infant's face.

However, the Virgin Mary was sinking into her own private hell: hands clasped over mouth, eyes brimming. And it was here that Andy did the most amazing thing: he walked over and handed the baby back. Back to the girl that just dropped it! It was like watching someone walk out of death row; tugged back from the brink of a crippling memory—marked as the girl who dropped the baby Jesus. Gratefully she took the child and delivered her final line.

"On this night we remember all children are blessed. And each is a gift … unto we."

The flashlight angel hit the switch and the star of Bethlehem became a black hole. The house lights came up to deafening applause. The mother regained custody of her beaming infant and the lambs began ripping off their seat covers.

I had that light-bodied feeling I get whenever I've forgotten about myself for over a minute. My eyes were still on Andy and I felt something like pride. I had just witnessed a child's spontaneous act of generosity. Rather than blame—he'd given the gift of a second chance.

The congregation babbled as they spilled down the aisles with all the excitement of a successful Broadway opening. The scent of candles wafted through the air mingled with the soapy smell of fresh snow graffiti sprayed from cans onto window corners.

St. John's had been the church of my childhood, of Sunday school sessions where we screened a roster of biblical short films. The most memorable episode being "The Stoning". Big stones, I remember thinking at the time—the size of grapefruits—viciously hurled by men and women alike.

It was a lead-in, of course, to the parable from John 8:7 where Jesus exhorts the gathered mob, stones at the ready to bash out the brains of an adulteress (I had always wanted to know the back story) *"… he that is without sin among you, let him cast the first stone …"* and shamed by his words spoken in a richly amplified voice, everyone kind of shuffled off, dumping their stones as they went. Then Jesus turned to the adulteress and said, *"… go thou and sin no more."* And you could tell, even with her face half-covered, she was kind of hot. It was the most requested film in our class.

St. John's had also been the site of my confirmation: my head had been firmly grasped in the aged Bishop's large hands that trembled with what I was not certain of—religious intensity or dotage or a hangover? Had it been a powerful moment or had I only imagined it to be so? Had I once actually believed? And then you find out that the whole baby Jesus thing, like Santa Claus, is a fairy tale told to children. My own childish belief had been shattered by a pair of cynical nine year olds. And years later, as a holiday hardened teen, I fired a question at Father Vander concerning all the frippery and seasonal dressings—"How would Jesus *feel* about all this stuff?"

I braced and waited for Father Vander to seize my throat, but he answered quietly, "The trappings of the church are merely reminders—an outward and visible sign of an inward and spiritual grace."

"Thank you for attending our Annual Dropping of the Baby Jesus," said Margery from somewhere behind me.

"Andy is a very wise man," I said. "You should be proud."

"Yeah, good luck getting that crown off his head any time soon."

I followed her eyes across the room to where Andy stood with the other wise men.

"How is your mother?" Margery asked.

"As well as can be expected," I said trying to catch my hand in mid-gesture before it reached my bandaged nose.

She gave the bandage a considered look.

"Ran into one of my mother's hallucinations," I answered suddenly finding the ceiling interesting out of a fear I might see the Girl in the Blue Dress across the room.

Margery nodded her head, "Yes, I can see where that might hurt."

"You don't want to know."

"No, I expect I don't."

"No, you don't."

For no particular reason, things got suddenly profound, the echo of our exchange bristled with all sorts of deeper meanings: *Why had I come here? What did I want? Why all the injuries?*

And then down dropped the big silence like a chain mail curtain surrounding us: we were two people confined in an odd solitude, connected by a weird energy yet facing away from each other in an outward and visible sign of an inward and spiritual discomfort.

Margery, a decidedly confident woman, was rendered uncomfortable by the memory of her exposed vulnerability that night when we stood together in her garage looking over the debris of her past, her tears. I felt uncomfortable for her discomfort and for my bandaged nose and suddenly, for just being there.

This state of suspension was gratefully interrupted by the approach of a fiercely smiling, energetic woman who landed next to us in a back-wash of floral perfume.

"Margereeee," she ironed her words out flat with a West Texas twang. "Now yew know 'bout the rummage sale, riiight? Next week end. Riiight here?"

Margery nodded into a slight pause that was somehow even more awkward than the one she and I had been trapped in prior to this woman's fragrant arrival. I could see the boxes in her garage being mentally sifted through.

"Okay, well jist checkin'. We need lots of stuff—any liddle thang—really," she said. Then promptly switched subjects,

"Wasn't it just great—the nahtivitee?" Her eyes ping-ponged between Margery and me.

"Wanda Bearings," extended a sinewy hand towards me and smiled with such an investigative intensity I thought her blue-tinted contacts might pop out and stick to my cheeks.

"Nice to meetchoo," she dropped my hand like a damp sponge. "See yawl on Saturday at the rummage sale—doncha forgit now."

Margery said nothing, but moved her head with just enough pitch and yaw to render it neither a yes nor a no.

"The Bible says they followed a star from the East," said the flashlight angel in deep discussion with Andy when I drifted up.

"I know what the Bible says," replied Andy. "And I'm telling you it wasn't a star. It was two planets."

"Bible says 'star'."

"Science says the conjunction of Jupiter and Saturn. The Wise Men were ancient astronomers."

"Where does it say the wise men were astronomers?"

"Not in the Bible."

"Exactly that's what I'm saying."

Margery stepped in. "Andy, are you ready?"

"Very."

When he turned and looked at me, I told him that was the best Nativity I'd ever seen.

"Thanks. But do you think the wise men were following a star?" he asked staring into my face with an earnestness you rarely see outside of children and salesmen.

I scratched the edges of my nose bandage and said, "Uh, I think the Wise Men were following something—seeing something they wanted to see or needed to see or maybe something that was ready to be seen. Who really knows? But you were a real Wise Man tonight—you handled that baby Jesus thing like a pro. I bet you did that without really thinking—right?"

Andy nodded his head. "Yeah, I guess so."

"I think that's kind of what the Wise Men did."

As Margery put her arm around her son's shoulders, I had

the distinct feeling I had drifted out into complicated conceptual waters—over worked my mouth and was now encroaching on their evening.

Outside, a vault of cloudless night rose above the church with such clarity the stars looked as if they were rushing toward you with the glittery promise of a white Christmas. From the parking lot came the tinkling voices of youngsters being loaded into cars, the deeper notes of parental urgings and explanations; complaints and promises as doors closed and engines started; cars set in motion towards homes where pillows wait for heads young and old to lie back feeling that all is right with the world at least on this night—an outward and visible sign of an inward and spiritual grace.

Chapter 24
Goldsmith, Texas

MARGERY'S BIG HANDS FUMBLED AT THE latch, gave away her discomfort at my appearance, unexpected, standing at her door, invading her day much like the brown plume of dust in the sky above.

Should have called first. But how could I begin to say what I had to say without standing before her, using the crucible of her eyes to refine the yammer in my skull. Don't explain. Appear.

"Yes?" She cracked the door, half invitation/half confrontation. Maternal suspicion pressed me back a step. A sudden gust barreled tumbleweeds along the street, mesquite pods clattered.

"I've come to ask you," I began, then choked—dust or hesitation gathered in my throat. I altered the approach, "May I have a glass of water?"

How could she deny a drink of water? After all, I had come to see her son's performance, my mother was in the hospital and there was a dust storm brewing. Even so, she took a moment to consider what exactly she might be welcoming in. But if she was nobody's fool, neither was she cold-hearted. And so, with a hint of reluctance, swung wide the door.

"Come in for a minute," she sighed, turned and padded barefoot towards the kitchen, heels raised, a slight twist to the balls of her feet as if summarily extinguishing a cigarette butt with each step.

Behind me, the door blew closed with a bang; the vagrant wind left behind to whine at the seams. The leather sofa in her living room seemed overly masculine and out of place—another reminder—there had once been a different life.

"Where's Andy?" I called out casually, hoping to dilute the tension.

"Play date," she said and re-entered with a glass of tap water, rigidly extended at the end of her arm. My request accomplished, egg timers began ticking in her eyes.

I thanked her, took an obligatory sip. West Texas tap water is unique in its awfulness, having not only an after-taste, but a smell that obliges you to go against the initial impulse to spit it out. Probably contributed to Mother's love of bourbon—made the water taste better.

Margery, arms folded across her chest, assumed an athletic stance, bare feet rooted to the floor, waiting for the pitch.

"I have a proposal for you," I said and set the glass on the coffee table "Work for hire. Cash up front."

It was a clumsy start at best, at worst it sounded like I was shopping for a hit man. And yet there was a self-important swell to my chest, like I had honest-to-god serious stuff going on. I reached for the glass and vamped with another sulfurous swig.

"I need a support person," I began again. Then uncomfortable with all the 'recovery' connotations of that gambit, I cut to the gist.

"I am required by the HD testing facility in San Antonio to bring a support person to the counseling sessions." There it was. Another sip of bad water and I found my eyes casting about for any place to look besides her unblinking eyes.

"I have absolutely no idea what you are talking about," she said and actually blinked to punctuate her lack of understanding.

"Of course you don't because I'm telling the whole thing backwards."

"Well, proceed to the beginning," she settled on a worn leather ottoman, back straight, level-eyed.

"Okay, in order to be tested for Huntington's disease—"

"Huntington's disease?" she eyed me as if considering an unfamiliar variety of fruit—exotic with a disagreeable exterior.

"... Neurological, degenerative, hereditary disorder. Woody Guthrie died from it."

"You are going to be tested for this disease?"

I nodded, "In order to be tested, it is required that I be accompanied by a 'support person'."

In hopes of injecting some legitimacy, I tugged out my scrawl of notes from the call I'd made that morning to the HD testing facility in San Antonio and read, *"... accompanied by a family member, spouse or companion to the initial counseling session and the five sessions that follow."*

"Huntington's disease. Hereditary." Margery mused. "This why your mother is in the hospital?"

"No. That's a whole other kettle of sick fish."

"But your father—the man packing the car, he looked reasonably healthy."

"He's not my biological father."

"Is she your biological mother?"

I shook my head.

"Oh. So you were adopted."

The intelligence in her eyes irised down to a sharper point, probed me with a gleam. And then, with a skeptical tilt of her head, a conflicted expression argued across her face as if hearing an off-color joke she found both amusing and inappropriate. Having reached a verdict, she laid a large hand over her mouth as if to hold back a sneeze.

But it was not a sneeze. It was a sort of burp. A burp that evolved into an elongated wheeze as she doubled over and whacked one denim-covered thigh with her big hand as her lungs emptied themselves of air.

Like an accordion being pulled open to fill itself, she arched back gasping for air only to double over again with a hearty guffaw. She was laughing. At me. Actual snorts as she tried to recover herself, but it was no good—she was overcome.

Usually, this would be considered a good thing—laughter being the first sign of a breach in the defenses, the beginning of someone liking you. But she was actually laughing *at* me and I was reminded how truly alone one feels when this happens; how it makes you want to disappear.

She grabbed my glass of water. Tried to put it to her lips, but cracked-up again and set it back down. She dabbed at cheek-tears, breathed in and out a couple of times, calmed herself and finally managed a swig from the glass. After clearing her throat, she waited a moment to see if there were any last spasms of glee before she spoke.

"You guys ..." she took one more sip of water and sat up straight for the delivery. "Never ceases to amaze me—you guys will say anything to get laid. And I admit I have never, ever heard that one before, but it's just so incredibly ... transparent. I mean did you read some article in a magazine—Huntington's disease? Unbelievable really ... and just so, very ..."

One more chuckle and the well of her amusement reached a dry, derisive bottom.

"... sad. It's very sad. "

She shook her head, again her eyes irised this time from amused disdain to something more damning—pity. And with that look, shame sluiced through my body, stung its way into the merest capillaries; my whole skin grew moist with a sheen of guilt. Was she right? Underneath it all—was I just hitting on her?

My foot spasmed.. It began to move up my leg. Had I reduced everything, cheapened my suffering, my mission, even leveraged my mother's illness into a pick-up line?

This woman had a child and a dead husband! It was socially retarded. Had my brain deteriorated that much? I smacked my head. Or was I just a fucking weasel?

When I looked up, her expression had made another shift: the last traces of a sardonic smirk melted from the corners of her mouth, her face slid into neutral. A long finger was raised towards me.

"Okay, wait, whoa ..." She stood up. Took another drink from my water glass, shoved her long fingers like combs into the tangled hair; massaged her scalp as if to organize the thoughts within.

"... You are actually serious?"

Was I? I didn't know anymore.

"But why come here? Involve me? This is what families are for, where you turn for something like this. And you—you lay this at the feet of a virtual stranger?"

She was getting her teeth into the subject; her paralegal training coming to the fore.

"But then again you—that day I picked you up at the airport, when you spotted your father, you had me drive past your stated destination: Quail Run. And you … hid yourself, dropped down in the back seat like you were afraid."

"I wasn't feeling well—"

She turned towards me. "You are afraid of your father."

"Not afraid exactly …"

"And your mother is in the hospital. You wouldn't want to burden her … and so you came here?"

"Completely inappropriate. Don't know what I was thinking."

"What were you thinking? Honestly?"

"I don't know."

"Come on that's a child's answer."

"I'm not sure I can trace my logic if there is any. You're a paralegal or were at one time. There are documents that need to get released from the court, there are these people I need to find, the test—lots of things really. And, I cannot ask my father to be my support person. Besides, someone needs to be here with Mother."

"Documents?"

"Adoption papers."

"Ah, court records. You need them to learn the names of your real parents."

I nodded my head, but I seemed to be leaving the scene; it had all become uncomfortably real. My impulse was to mumble an apology and slip away. Hit the road. Slide into a dark booth at The Shadows, hunker down to a bourbon rocks, a sad song—have the bartender work on me again.

"Wait a minute—so how did you find out about this disease if you never knew your real parents?"

With her big hands shoved in the back pockets of her jeans, she paced, her head down looking at her bare feet positioned side by side, lifting her heels, arching up on the balls. Stretching. She became taller.

"You're being for real right?" she asked momentarily backing up. "Yeah, you're too disorganized to be lying."

There she was expanding before my eyes while I felt like a child waiting for instructions. My once secret mission had become excruciatingly real. And with her keen intelligence, she would know if I faltered or wimped out. As she grabbed a pencil and looked about for something to write on, I quietly began to resent her.

Chapter 25

San Antonio, Texas

ALL ABOUT THE BLOOD. AT LEAST ACCORDing to Anna Soh, the professionally relaxed counselor at the San Antonio Genetic Testing Facility.

"The testing procedure is complicated and time-consuming," she said eyeing me through a pair of fashionable non-reflective lenses. She spoke in a thin, almost nasal voice that made me want to take a deep breath for her.

"There are many different forms of the marker," she said in a deliberate manner either to lend gravity to her words or perhaps she thought I was a bit slow mentally.

"To find out which marker runs in a given family, researchers need to analyze blood samples from all the family members who have Huntington's disease, and also what we term 'escapees,' that would be family members who are past the age of highest risk and who have shown none of the HD symptoms."

Margery jumped in, "Bert was adopted at two and a half. It was his father who was diagnosed with Huntington's and, considering the time that has passed since Bert was first notified of his biological father's condition, it is very likely that his father is deceased."

I had underestimated the degree of discomfort I would feel, having laid myself bare, asking Margery for help. To have another know the wretched you; it made me seem even more wretched to myself.

And then there was what she said before she signed on with my 'case' as she called it focusing her gray eyes on me, "This is not about sex. I need to make that clear up front, Bert. That doesn't interest me. It's your case that interests me."

Well, there it was—I had gotten what I came for.

"When was Bert first notified?" Anna Soh asked Margery.

"Fifteen years ago," answered Margery checking her pad. "And since the test for the marker did not exist at that time, it would be unlikely that the victim's blood was banked by the attending neurologist. So the question becomes, can the test be done without a sample of his father's blood?"

Margery was on her game, dressed in a dark blazer, crisp white shirt with jeans—boots on the bottom (water snake). During the three hours it took to drive to San Antonio, we had gone over the file of notes she'd gathered regarding both the disease and the test. She had prepped me as if I were going before a jury on a murder charge.

On the legal front, she had sent a formal letter to the Ector County Courthouse requesting all documents pertaining to my adoption. Included in the letter was a copy of the "Medical Need to Know" the same that had been stuck in my pocket by Dr. Singh back in Los Angeles before he released me.

For her help, I had offered Margery two hundred dollars plus travel expenses and dinner for herself and Andy at the Red Lobster on 'all you can eat' lobster night. Wednesdays I believe. At least Andy would be there to absorb some of her hyper-focused attention.

Ms. Soh continued in her oxygen-deprived drone. "Every effort should be made to confirm whether the biological father is alive and to find the physician who was treating him."

"The physician is no longer in practice and his records have been lost." Margery countered.

"Get samples from all the siblings. Have any been diagnosed with Huntington's?"

"Bert currently has no knowledge of the whereabouts of any members of his biological family."

It was no longer necessary for me to speak. I was preparing to excuse myself and go in search of a candy bar when Anna Soh shifted her attention back to me.

"That will make the process more complicated for you, Bert. Without blood samples, there can be no comparison."

"We are in the process of obtaining court documents regarding his adoption, names of biological parents and siblings," Margery assured her.

"This could require more effort on your part than you may have anticipated. Bert, before you move forward, I suggest you consider the emotional implications of this test."

"Emotional implications?"

"How you might be affected by a positive outcome for Huntington's disease and the impact this information could have on the rest of your life."

"Isn't it better to know?"

She finally took a deep breath. "For some people, yes. But others find it difficult to pick up and get on with their lives knowing that they will eventually contract the disease. There is sometimes the desire 'to get it over with.' "

"Oh, I know all about that," I said aware that my lifestyle up to that point was best described as alternately rushing towards, and then running away from death; either overwhelmed by a relentless consciousness of my mortality or a let's-go-to-hell surrender to oblivion. Fear and loathing followed by bouts of hedonism and regret.

"So," reiterated Anna Soh giving me the serious stare. "Should you make contact with family members and should you obtain blood samples, it is still very important for you to consider the effect of knowing that you have Huntington's disease."

As we walked down the corridor towards the exit, I recalled images from a film I had found in the archives back in Austin. Black and white documentary footage of Huntington's victims as they lurched down the street of a village in Venezuela's Lake Maricaibo region; their arms flailed wildly like drunks on a tirade about something that they would suddenly lose the thread of—forget whom or what it was they were cursing. And then a quiet, normal movement would settle in only to be interrupted again by a sudden jerk as if they had been stung or pinched by some invisible tormentor.

They were skinny; wasted from the physical effort of this constant involuntary movement. It was clearest when you looked at their eyes. You could see the soul trapped inside the renegade body; cognizant puppets betrayed by a deranged master—the defective gene.

Margery touched my back, a brushing that paused for a fraction of a second between my shoulder blades before dropping away. I couldn't look at her.

"We can find them, that is if you want to go forward with this," she said in a practical tone.

"Maybe they don't want to be found," I said.

"It doesn't matter what they want."

That night with Mom delirious in the hospital and Dad snoring at full roar in the master bedroom, I lay in a tangle on the twin bed of my childhood and dreamed I was standing over the toilet, waiting to pee, had just given it an encouraging shake when it detached in the most casual way—dropped like ripe fruit and splashed into the bowl. My dick.

No pain. No blood. I retrieved it, inanimate and cold as a frankfurter; shook it off and stuck it back onto the stump. It held. But I couldn't trust it anymore. I found myself seeking advice from my father.

"Pick it up and put it back on—get on with your business," was his response. I tried not to think about how securely it was re-attached or when it might drop off again. I knew masturbation was out and any sex would have to be approached with great care. Panic bubbled up in my chest. But I kept telling myself that occasionally a man's dick falls off. It happens.

Chapter 26
Memory Lane

MOTHER WAS MOORED IN THE HOSPITAL bed tethered by hoses; orange numbers blinked her vitals on the console overhead. Neither better nor worse, but disturbingly still for someone so compulsively active, she lay without magazine or open book; no playing cards being shuffled and turned, no paint-laden brush poised over a china plate. No cigarettes. No highball. The endless lists she shaped our days with. None of that. Just an upwards stare at the ceiling, her chest reaching for air.

The orange numbers flickered. Mother stirred, called out as if from a dream, "The moussaka ..." She brushed at her oxygen hose like a stray cobweb, kicked at the clinging sheet, but was stopped by the gauze restraints strung across the bed rails.

Arlene had marginalized her ethnicity to a casserole dish—the moussaka. Johns had been her maiden name, the Americanized version of Johanasian, the name her Armenian father left behind when he jumped ship at the port of New Orleans in 1914.

Johns, barely sixteen at the time, had been desperately launched like a human message in a bottle. His family had schemed and bribed to secure him a place as cabin boy on a ship bound for America. He would float away from Istanbul and into an uncertain future. But he would be out of the Turks' reach who were quietly marching Armenians out into the desert without the benefit of water.

With a war on, menial work was easily found by a youth of his size and intent. He felt best in the daylight with his body at labor. At night he often awakened in his cheap room. The walls, mere partitions that did not rise all the way to the ceiling encouraged the flow of air from cubby to cubby along with all adjacent noises: disgorging coughs, drunken caterwaul, peals of flatulence, the waft of odors among the half-strangled snores of restless men.

In his sleep, this human song wove itself through his dreams, twined itself round some nameless fear, then buoyed him up with a sudden urgency to burst the surface of consciousness—*had something shattered? Did someone scream?* Suddenly he would awake only to find himself alone in the summer swelter of New Orleans; heart drenched in panic as night sounds purled around him. Were they all right? The family back in Istanbul. Would they make it out alive? He must work harder—Get Them Here.

Johns stayed out of the bars. He arrived at work early, his imagination bent towards the day when the family could book passage—the day when they would be reunited in America. *Make the money. Send it home.*

If it was effort and savvy that improved his position, it was a discerning eye that continued to upgrade his appearance. Johns observed how a man in a pressed suit was deferred to, given a little more ear.

Opportunities were sought, openings gleaned—when to do something for free while others complained. A knack for languages, he would bend his accent to suit the listening ear—a little Yiddish when needed, or Greek, or Polish. Then he simply outworked everybody. And soon it was Johns who was negotiating with the farmers. It was Johns who was placing the orders. Johns who paid the vendors.

His English, however, could not be scrubbed free of an accent; something he saw as an impediment obvious as his size—over six feet now with thick black hair and a beard that required shaving twice a day if he went out in the evening.

When he did go out, Johns strolled along the river, stopped for an ice cream in the Quarter; so much creamier than the ices of Istanbul with their perfume of rosewater, ginger, and cardamom. It seemed America itself was cream, a thriving market, a salesman's dream; if you could work it, talk it—be American.

"I can sell salt on the shores of the Dead Sea," Johns told The Man.

"Just sell it in Iowa," replied The Man and shook his hand.

Johns wore the best suit he could afford that first summer in Decorah Iowa where he met Birchen in an ice cream parlor on the square. "Decorah," he would repeat the word to himself and shake his head. Birchen's mother spoke with an English accent, but Birchen was American born; her speech clean as corn silk. They strolled and lapped at their cones; sat before a whitewashed band stand and watched the gas lamps being lit as evening settled. He handed her a clean handkerchief to wipe her hands. He stared too long at her tiny feet in high-laced shoes and had to apologize.

By November 1920, they had been married a year and Birchen was pregnant. A telegram arrived from Johns' mother. Tirohi had booked passage on the Olympia, the sister ship of the Titanic. She was to travel to New York with his younger sister Arousiak. They would arrive in December. At last, his family would join him. After six long years they would be together again.

Arrangements were made for a train to New York. A new suit was purchased and Birchen, a milliner's daughter, brought stylish new hats for Johns' mother and sister. On the 22nd of December Johns and Birchen arrived in Manhattan. Two rooms had been booked at a modest midtown hotel and he would treat them all to a splendid holiday dinner—a feast to welcome them to their new country.

On the morning of his mother's arrival there was a knock at the door. It was a telegram from his sister Arousiak. During the processing, the doctor at Ellis Island had found a problem with his mother's eyes.

When Birchen returned to the hotel with their lunch, she found Johns sprawled in a chair, staring out the window, the telegram clutched in his hand. When he didn't respond to her questions, she took it from his hand and read.

Tirohi had been diagnosed with trachoma, an infectious disease that works gradually, the effect sometimes not evident until adulthood when the scarring caused by repeated infections deforms the eyelashes, forces them to turn inwards. In this perversion of design, the eyelids scratch painfully and relentlessly against the cornea. Slowly the eyesight is scraped away until the victim is rendered completely blind—one blink at a time.

His mother was denied entry. In addition, his sister Arousiak, out of concern for Tirohi's health, was compelled to return with her mother. The money for the extra room, the celebratory dinner—it would all go to pay for their return passage. The new hats brought by Birchen as gifts were left behind for the hotel maid.

Johns fell back to Decorah and took to bed. Only the birth of his son Russell would prove to resurrect him. Life trundled on. They flourished. Two daughters, Helen, and then Arlene the youngest—the woman who would one day adopt me.

Only English was spoken in the home. Johns, was decidedly American, his family would be American with designated American tastes; the only exception being the moussaka, a dish he would make himself: the eggplants and tomatoes fresh from his garden (leech out the bitterness of the eggplant with salt and the nutmeg always ground fresh, hand-stirred into the béchamel).

"It's not Greek!" He would declare like some TV commercial as he pulled it piping from the oven, the top perfectly golden. "It is Armenian—Mama's recipe."

And they would all gather round the table to behold the cutting and serving of the moussaka, the only thing in the house allowed to be Armenian.

As the children grew, so did Johns' tyrannical demands upon them: less than an A on a report card and you would cease to exist in the house. You were a forgotten person until a demonstrated excellence allowed your return to the world of the visible.

The boy, Russell, caught the worst of it; being a boy and carrying upon his face the burden of Johns' own profile; the high-bridged thrust of the nose itself providing reason enough for disdain. The boy was hard-pressed to perform any action to the complete satisfaction of his father. And at some point, he understood it was a game he could never win. He gave up and mutely endured his father's perpetual disappointment.

Helen, the oldest daughter was openly defiant, fought tooth and nail for her scrap of freedom—for her 'art' major in college. Meanwhile, the youngest, Arlene tried to pick up the pieces. Make Papa happy. Fix things—an exhausting task of many layers that often left her overwhelmed and resentful of them all: parents, siblings and finally, her own ineffectual self.

Johns cried at both his daughters' weddings, sponged his tears with a monogrammed linen handkerchief and used their choices in mates (both doctors: one medical, the other academic) to admonish his own son, who had only managed to earn a Masters.

"And who will marry you?"

Having had enough, Russell fled to the tropics. Found work in Panama teaching in the Canal Zone. But it didn't matter what he did, it didn't matter what any of the children did—they could never stop the ship that sailed from New York harbor in 1920, the ship that took Tirohi and Arousiak away.

"Go on live your life." the letters from his mother had told Johns. "Your happiness is our triumph." It was an awful burden.

Russell and I never met. Arlene said she would sometimes receive rambling, incoherent letters. He was alcoholic and died in Panama from multiple gunshot wounds, self-inflicted.

As a child, Papa Johns was the big man who came to visit me. He wore a silk robe, smelled of eau de cologne and ate three eggs in three bites. A melancholy man with a playful side, he engaged me in clever ways—made me laugh with a hide and seek involving the squeaking bladder taken from a toy. I searched his body for the source of the noise and eventually found it hidden in the fold of his knee. Having accomplished this, he looked me squarely in the eye, and asked, "Would you like to color?"

Yes, I nodded and ran off to fetch my crayons. When I returned Papa Johns was already at it. He was at work on his own coloring book with his own crayons—the 64 Crayolas box with the built in sharpener and those subtle colors from the far end of the spectrum: Burnt Sienna, Raw Umber, and Indian Red (discontinued).

My coloring style at the time was all about staying within the lines. I finished, first and presented my work.

"Finished?" he asked. "But where is the light?"

"The light?" I asked.

He picked up a dark green crayon and applied it thickly, then went a shade lighter over that, then took a yellow along the top and worked it in, the waxy smell of the crayons rising from the friction.

"See the light shines here. And the shadow is there. Without the shadow there is no light, no shape. You have just filled in space with your coloring."

The fun having gone out of things, I left him to his 'shaping' and 'shadows' and drifted into the kitchen to see what Mom was up to. Arlene was in front of her modern electric range, a furrow creased her brow, her hands in oven mitts were pressed prayerfully together. Then she lifted the oven door which swept smoothly upwards like the gull wing on a sports car. She raised a bright yellow casserole dish from the oven, tilted it to check to the doneness of the moussaka. She shook her head and admonished herself, "... it's not golden."

Chapter 27
Fort Worth, Texas

"YOU'RE THE MIDDLE BOY," MRS. HARrison said eyeballing me. "I asked you to take off your shirt so I could wash it. You snapped right back at me, Don't tell me what to do. Surprised me some, coming out of a little boy like that."

She had watched as my older brother, a five-year old at the time, dug through a garbage can while we (his two younger brothers) waited below. Mrs. Harrison recognized us from the house next door. At first, she thought we were just playing, making a mess like boys do. But then she noticed something.

"He was like a man at a job, the older boy was," she said. "I watched him pull an old bag of bread up out of that filthy can, tear it open and shove a piece into his mouth. Then he tossed it down for you other boys. Little Brion was crying. That's when I picked up the phone."

Our mother was nowhere to be found so Mrs. Harrison called Family Services. "Then I went and brung you boys in and made sandwiches."

The three of us were taken into the custody of Tarrant County, state of Texas. I was two and half when it happened and had no recall. But Mrs. Harrison recognized me when I introduced myself, my documents held out as proof of my identity. Margery's petition to the court had convinced the judge to release all information related to my adoption.

On the top of my formal adoption papers was a one page custody document issued by Family Services upon the removal of the three children from the premises. It officially declared us to be:

"*... neglected children dependant upon the public for support, are destitute, are homeless. And whose home by reason of neglect* *on the part of their parents, is an unfit place for such children."*

I kept reading the words over, weighing the implication of *neglect* and *destitute* and *unfit*, residing in the same sentence with other words like *parents* and *home.*

Destitute and homeless at two and half years old. I had gotten an early start. At least I couldn't remember any of it, but the older brother, the five-year old, how could he forget; the younger kids hungry, the crying, the confusion. *Where was Mother? When was she coming back home?*

Finally, Margery tugged the document from my hand and replaced it with the actual adoption papers. "This is the key," she had said pointing with her finger. "Here are all their names ..."

STATE OF TEXAS	CAUSE NO. 83
COUNTY OF ECTOR	IN RE: BERTRAND KELLY
	PETS: DR AND MRS. H. KELLY

IN THE DISTRICT OF ECTOR COUNTY, TEXAS
SEVENTIETH JUDICIAL DISTRICT
SITTING AS A JUVENILE COURT

Now comes S. J. Webb, Supervisor of the Ector County Child Welfare Unit who is the duly appointed investigator in the above matter, and presents the following report to the Court: CHILD: The said child for adoption, Bertrand Dewayne Browford, was born in Honolulu, Hawaii, October 26, 1950. He is of Oriental, Irish, Indian, and Spanish descent. His physical appearance indicates his mixture in nationalities in that his hair and eyes are dark and his complexion is bronze in coloring. Little is known of the actual birth, but based on his present physical and mental development, he is a normal, healthy child with a better than average mental level. The said child has a warm, outgoing personality that has assisted him in this adjustment to the petitioners. Since placement in the home of the petititioners, his development has continued to progress. Acceptance by the petitioners has been responsible for the rapid adjustment of the child to the petitioners and the community.

CIRCUMSTANCES OF PLACEMENT: Due to the inability of the parents to provide adequate care for the said child and his siblings, it became necessary for the 17th Judicial District Court to take custody of the children. Custody provided for placement of the said child in adoption. The said child was placed in the home of the petitioners February 15, 1954 by Family Service Association of Fort Worth, Texas.

NATURAL PARENTS:

MOTHER: Nunnie Browford, nee Kukona, was born in Maui, Hawaii, October 23, 1929. She is described as being five feet, two inches tall with black hair, black eyes and an olive complexion. She completed the eleventh grade in school and was of normal intelligence. Her insecurity and immaturity hindered her in the providing of adequate care for her family.

FATHER: Baine T. Browford was in the Air Force. Little is known of him, other than he is of native white parentage, is five feet, ten inches tall and of slender build. He has sandy hair, blue eyes, and is fair complexioned. Sgt. Browford completed high school and was considered of average intelligence. It is believed he was a year or two older than the mother. Sgt. Browford and Nunnie Kukona were married in Honolulu on July 8, 1950, and divorced on March 27, 1952 in Tarrant County, Texas.

The mother came to Worth, Texas, in February of 1952. In May of 1953, unable to provide adequate care for the children, the mother released them to the agency.

SIBLINGS: Jonathan Wayne, born 10-5-47, and Brion Dane, born 10-1-51. In all there were three children, the said child being the second child. All the children have been placed in adoption.

ADOPTIVE PARENTS:

FATHER: Dr. Hillard Kelly was born in Denison, Texas, February 29, 1912. Upon the completion of high school, he completed four years of college and entered a medical college where he specialized in urology. He is six feet, one inch tall with dark hair, hazel eyes and dark complexion. His acceptance of the said child indicates his understanding and warmth for children.

MOTHER: Mrs. Arlene Kelly, nee Johns, was born May 4, 1917

in Waterloo, Iowa. Upon the completion of college, she married and had divided her time between her family and assisting her husband with his practice. Mrs. Kelly is five feet, three inches tall with dark hair and eyes and brunette complexion. Her warm accepting personality has contributed to the adjustment of the said child as a member of the family.
HEALTH: Mrs. Kelly's inability to have children is not a condition due to bad health. She is in good health.
EVALUATION: Prior to placement of the said child, a thorough study was made to determine the suitability of the child for adoption. The petitioners likewise were studied in order to determine their suitability as parent persons. After placement, supervision for six months was maintained. During the six month period, the said child has adjusted exceptionally well in the home and the community. This adjustment has contributed to the love and care given the child by the petitioners. The said child has received stability and security from the petitioners and has in return fulfilled their quest for a son.

The petitioners request upon consummation of the adoption that the said child's name be changed to Bertrand Johns Kelly.

Respectfully, submitted,
ECTOR COUNTY CHILD
WELFARE UNIT
Signed: A.W. Grice

Brion, my younger brother, had been the first one Margery located through his adopted mother Mrs. Harrison. Margery had tracked her with an amended birth certificate. I drove to Ft. Worth for the meeting.

"Well, he has your complexion," Mrs. Harrison described my younger brother.

"But he's big. He likes to eat. That's okay, I'm big too," she said with a laugh that sent a jiggle through her corpulence.

Mrs. Harrison and her husband had gone on to adopt Brion. The oldest, Johnny, she thought had been sent back to Hawaii and me, the middle child, went to a foster family somewhere in Texas.

"Brion moves around a lot," she added sounding a more concerned note. "He's still figuring on what to do with hisself."

She gave me the number of a friend Brion stayed with. When I called, it was the friend that picked up. He confirmed Brion had been sleeping there and that he was going through a hard time. Depressed.

I left my number at the motel and said it was important Brion contact me; medical emergency, a long lost brother—need to talk. And then I went down to The Country Skillet for dinner.

The waitress gave me a sideways glance when I ordered three dinners complete with desserts—apple pie a'la mode. After two bites of steak, I pushed back and watched the ice cream melt on the pies while I considered: Where do you go when you leave three kids alone for days at a time? What activity do you indulge in that muffles your conscience, blocks out any intruding thoughts like: Have they eaten?

Aside from a mental disorder, binge drinking or heroin addiction, the only other thing I could come up with was that she just didn't care. Or possibly all of the above.

The check paid, the waitress brought the leftovers in three separate bags per my request and set them on the table. I thanked her, left a good tip and walked out with the bags. Outside, I walked around to the back of the restaurant, opened the trash bin and placed the three bags inside.

Brion returned my call the next morning—the soft voice on the other end of the line sent up hopeful flares that fell back to beleaguered ground. A career with the Army hadn't panned out.

"I really want to be a minister. Have my own church, preach the gospel and all."

But he needed to lose some weight: 5ft. 3inches, 285 lbs. Obese. Adrift on a friend's sofa.

When I told him about Huntington's disease, the father dying, the genetic risk, I tried to soften it; saying that we might not have the same father. But his nearly enthusiastic response was, "No, I probably have it." As if he found comfort including himself in a curse. When told about the blood test, that it would provide certainty, he agreed to meet later that afternoon. A clinic nearby could take the sample.

"And I want to meet you!" I said sending up my own hopeful flare. "We are brothers!"

Brion never showed. Messages were left. No response.

"Brion is not feeling good about himself right now; he'll come around," said Mrs. Harrison. "He's got a good heart, just got to let himself be."

When thanked for what she had done, for reaching out and giving one of us a home, she waved it off, "Oh, I just like having kids around," she chuckled. "They're fun."

"Apparently, others felt differently," I said. Mrs. Harrison shrugged and with a pat on my shoulder said, "Good luck finding the older one—Johnny."

Chapter 28

Oahu, Hawaii

AFTER YEARS OF BEING REFERRED TO AS that 'Mescan kid' back in Texas, glossed with 'Spic' up at the Academy, even called 'nigger' by a neighbor's relative visiting from Oklahoma, I had finally come to Oahu, the Pacific island of my birth, only to be greeted by Auntie Mary Jane with, "Oh … you're a *haole*."

Haole (how-lee): Hawaiian for a white person. This after logging some dedicated hours poolside basting myself in Hawaiian Tropic Dark Tanning Oil.

"I look like a *white* guy?" I asked holding up what I considered a bronze forearm.

"… Yes, a *haole* with a sunburn," she confirmed laying waste to an identity I had been constructing since the age of nine.

The only contact Margery had found in Hawaii, Auntie Mary Jane, though polite, was not an outpouring of the Aloha spirit. An undercurrent of suspicion laced her eyes, the whites of which had a custardy tint giving her that native look that would elude me no matter how many UV rays I absorbed. Not even a tan, but 'sunburn' she called it. White people got sunburns—*haoles.* Clearly not one to pussy-foot around, she corrected the lie of her spectacles as one might rack the focus knob on a microscope—the better to see you my dear—and made her report.

"A few years ago Nunnie, your mother, came back from the mainland for a visit. Things didn't go well. There was conflict in the family and she left on not such good terms."

The opposite of a balloon, Auntie Mary Jane seemed to expand and lift as she emptied herself of information.

"I have no idea where she is now. But you have a brother

living up in Moana. Many troubles. But I think you should go see him. Who knows."

As if offering some consolation, from her pocket she produced a snapshot. "My grandmother, your great grandmother, she was a beautiful lady. You may keep it."

Pictured was an elderly woman with gray, kinky hair and very dark skin, she could have been black—imagine that. How far from the tree I had fallen, from this great Hawaiian grandma smiling and spectacled standing before a modest house to this *haole* here reeking of coconut with a sunburn.

As per Auntie's instructions, I followed the road to the outskirts of Honolulu. There the asphalt went nubby, then dissolved into dirt and shrank to wind its way up a canyon. Houses seemed carelessly placed. Larger ones that sagged under the green mold and smaller plantation shacks gone wonky, their thin single walls chewed away near the ground. The ubiquitous blue plastic tarp appeared at various angles and covered a variety of objects throughout the area as if they'd been dropped from above by a relief organization. Small pick-up trucks were the mode. 'The other side of Hawaii' I thought to myself as the vegetation thickened and breathed cooler.

The dirt road became moist, then muddy, and then petered out in the tire-rutted yard of a two-story house in dire need of rehabilitation. All the windows were covered with foil on the inside. It looked as if some reconstruction was in progress on the driveway. However, a closer look revealed it was actually being torn apart by tree roots.

The tree itself, a huge primeval thing hung with veined purple leaves three feet long, smothered one entire side of the house. From its base came the gnarled stampede of muddy roots that shattered the driveway; that reached up under the skirt of lattice fronting the house and wracked the foundation. Once it had been a nice house. Still would be if they'd hacked that tree down.

An engine back-fired and rumbled to life. The effigy of a pick-up truck modeled in pink smears of Bondo choked and smoked from around the back of the house. A woman at the wheel, the heads of two children lurched like grocery bags as the truck swerved past. Her eyes, red-rimmed, landed like suction cups thrown glaring against the smudged window; her muffled shout through the glass, "He's out back—what's left of him!"

Across the rear window, splashed in wave-like letters the words, *Hawaiian Love*, in a hot pink decal caught the sun as the Bondo truck slithered onto the mud road and wriggled away in a cloud of blue exhaust.

Squatted low in a tangle of wire, sore-eyed and unblinking, he gave the appearance of a grizzled nesting bird that had outstayed the season. Around him the remains of all manner of household appliances: toaster ovens and disemboweled washing machines, motor coils and engine casings—kinetic debris—motion broken down to its dead parts and spread concentrically out; a junk yard blast site with him in a befuddled crouch at ground zero.

A low groan in his throat seemed to pull him upright—a man of my complexion—the next size up from me; slightly taller with broad shoulders, deep trunk set over well-boned legs. But moving closer, I could see his muscles were slack and wasted. Johnny Kukona or Johnny Kook, as he was known locally—my brother by certain documents, appeared old beyond the three-year difference in our age: his bald pate moist with a gritty sheen; what was left of his hair puffed out into sideburns that hedged along his jaw to twine themselves in a braid that dangled snidely from his chin. His greasy hands jerked to sudden action with body slaps as if attempting to kill a fast-moving bug.

"Gaawddamn it!" the low moan burst into full fury. "She took my last smoke." His eyes narrowed as he gazed towards the road, caught the pickup's blue vapor still haunting the air.

From his neck hung the barbed curl of a fish hook carved from bone, and from beneath a sweat-soaked tank top peeked the tattooed word SEMPER. The Marine motto's other word FI had been bitten off, along with one wing and half a globe by something large with many teeth.

"Mako, eight-footer. Bumped me off Maui. Didn't like the way I tasted." He said with an automatic tug of his shirt to reveal the finely etched oval of a jaw line wrapping front and back like a tester bite left in a sandwich; a brilliant scar—Christ, a shark bite! I wanted one. When he asked me for a smoke I noticed the gummy gap where his front teeth should have been.

"… It don't bodder me," he mumbled eyes still on the blue vapor over the road. "I got no love left in me. Two pair of panties all she had when we met. Bought her clothes. Bought dem kids clothes. Paid rent. I worked over time. And what she do? Off to da church. Not just Sunday. Naw, she got da Bible study. Picnics and meetin's. All da time makin' friends. Nice people. Nice. So I'm not good enough anymore. Not da kine she want now. The hell you think I work dem hours? And I never smoke it at home. Never front of dem kids. I carry twelve compressor casings at a time—work all night, double shift! So I need a little drink, take down da edge. She took my one weakness and used it against me and I DON'T FUCKIN' NEED YOU!"

Was it his agonized howl that seemed to stir the blue vapor or just my irises dilating with the fight or flight response?

"… Hell, I'm tired of it anyways," he sighed and let his eyes fall upon the dented biker boots. And then, as if just discovering himself astride a strange place, he wiped his gaze up the length of me and focused with a slight cock of his head, "… Who da fuck you?"

I initiated what I hoped was a casual introduction of myself—referencing our common auntie, Mary Jane, "… Whom I had seen just that morning, sends her best and encouraged me to drive over ..." But before I could get any further, Johnny's attention caught on the economy rental car at my disposal.

"Come on," he interrupted. "You needs meet a friend." He insinuated himself into the driver's seat and had the engine started before I got my door closed.

Give him plenty of room; ease gradually into the events of our mutual past was my plan. Monitor his resilience along the way. Not send him fleeing like Brion. I asked him about the Marines. He needed little prompting and launched into a story.

"They put me in lock down. Seventy-two hours in a totally dark cell. Can't see your fuckin' hand if you poke you finger in you eye. Fuckin' dark. Would have lost my mind hadn't been for dem buttons."

"Who put you in lock down?" I asked trying to look relaxed while fumbling to get my seat belt fastened before he hit a tree. Johnny heard the latch click, looked over at me and shook his head.

"What da fuck you worried 'bout. A hair dryer got more power than dis car." He wrenched the steering wheel, jammed it into reverse stripping a few years off the tranny. We went into a controlled skid for several miles down the muddy road. He told me how he'd been staying at a drug dealer's house when the police showed. The drug dealer was not at home, but Johnny was with enough cocaine to get him arrested and put in lock down.

"… Dats what dey do with any 'Nam vet dey take into custody—mandatory lock down. Cool you out in a dark cell for seventy-two hours before they even talk wid you. You wan know why? Because some crazy fucker almost cut a guard's head off using nothing but the zipper from his pants."

He yanked the car off the road, veered sharply down an embankment. I was bracing my body for impact when he slid the car sideways through a clearing and rolled up to an A-frame covered with mossy shingles.

"… Couldn't haul shit from a baby's bottom to da diaper," was Johnny's final assessment of the car's power train. He popped the trunk and exited, the door left open, the engine running. From the trunk he pulled a tire tool and headed off towards the house keeping up the chatter.

"… So I'm sittin' in dat dark cell and time's movin' awful slow if you know what I mean ..."

I caught up with him, fastened my eyes on the tire tool and told him that I too had been in jail, sharing these things we had in common: jail, Auntie Mary Jane. The tire tool really bothered me.

"… So I needs an activity," he said as we reached the back door of the A-frame. "… Sumptin I can do in dat dark cell so I don lose my fuckin' head … know what I mean?"

And while I nodded my head in that I'm-right-there-with-you-getting-it-all the way, Johnny took the wedge-end of the tire iron and with one deft stab, drove it into the door jamb and applied leverage. My skin jumped at the sound of wood cracking. My eyes flew to the car, estimated the distance and time it would take me to get there. Shouldn't have turned it off. Should have left it running.

"Maybe we could come back when your friend is actually at home," I said hoping to appeal to any remaining molecule of better judgment in Johnny's burnt-out brain pan.

"... Chill, brah. I don lost da keys is all. He don mind."

And with a final excruciating crack of wood, the door surrendered and against all instincts, legs jittering with bad feelings, I followed my brother into a felony: breaking and entering—apparently not his first.

"So," he continued glancing around the place, "I tear da buttons off my shirt—five buttons," he stopped in the middle of his 'friend's' mess of a kitchen to turn back to me and gesture with a spread of his fingers so I get the number clearly—*five.*

"I takes da buttons ..." he opened the refrigerator and with the tire iron, pried through the glacier of ice that was pushing its way out of the already deformed, never-ever-been-defrosted freezer compartment—were those pot stickers?

"... And I toss all five buttons against da wall at da same time. I'm sitting on the floor see, and when I toss da buttons I listens very careful to where dey fall. Cause it's dark, can't see ..."

Done with the fridge, he moved on—tugged a drawer open, shoved his grimy paw inside as if chasing a mouse, and then on to the next drawer, sweat started to sheen on his body.

He then turned all his mad attention on me, "... It's quiet in lock-down and it's night time, see. How I know it's nighttime? 'Cause I don here any sounds of traffic—off in the distance. No sounds 'cept the sound of the buttons when dey falls. And I can hear where dey each one fall. And I reach out and I pick it up ..."

Johnny wheeled and attacked the pantry—pulled out a box of Cocoa Puffs, gave them a rattle, dumped them on the counter, adding to the litter of empty SPAM containers and discarded cookie bags—Circus Animals. Chips Ahoy! Somebody had a sweet tooth but it wasn't Johnny; he hungered for a different treat.

"… So I changes da game. Now when I toss da buttons I has to reach out and touch each button with my finger—no running my hand along the floor, no feelin' around, no—I gots to reach out and put one finger on dat button where it fell EXACTLY!"

He illustrates this with his hands revealing a jagged pink shine of scar tissue on the inside of one wrist.

"… And I do it, brah, Ha!"

It wasn't when he took hold of the sofa and flipped it over; it was when he slashed the exposed bottom with a dirty steak knife that I announced. "… Time to go." And started to back towards the door. But he shushed me with a finger to his lips. As if he'd heard something outside. It stopped me cold. Voice quivering he asked, "How many buttons was dey?"

"Five."

"Right. But where was number five? You got to see it—in your mind—I locate each button by—"

"I know," I said. "You reach out, one finger … now really, Johnny …" But his face loomed up under mine, distorted with emotion as if seen through a rain-streaked window.

"… BUT I CAN'T FIND DA FIFTH BUTTON! And I'm feeling all around the floor of the cell, I mean every square inch … and den I start to think to my self—maybe dey was only four to begin with. Not five. Maybe I done lost it. Dinky dao! Gone *lolo.* Crazy man in a cage looking for a button was never there. But when dey come to lemme out, dey turn on da light. And I look around, and there, against da wall above is this trim, like a rubber bumper against da wall. And, peeking out I see da button. Ha! Caught in a crack from the wall. I was right, dey was five buttons! I'm not crazy I tells 'em. But dey don't unnerstan 'bout what I'm talking—da fifth button and what it means …."

His eyes emitted a cracked heat as he pointed a finger at his head. A chemical smell came off him like a burned shower curtain. And there was the knife in his hand.

"… What it means up here. Dey think I need a little more time. Ha ha! It don't matter, I done found da fifth button!"

I began to move myself, first, from within, as if I were packing a small personal suitcase: right foot goes there, left foot there, I would need a calm voice. Backwards slowly … and in a very calm voice, as I increased the distance between us, I placed his choices before him: either left behind to explain to his 'friend' the condition of his home or get into the car with me and leave. Now. It made sense, no? Slowly, I backed out the door. Johnny dropped the knife to throttle a plain-wrapped bottle of WHISKEY and followed.

"You my bruddah, huh?" he mused onto a new tack. I inserted myself into the driver seat and prayed we'd clear the area before someone showed.

"Yes. I believe we are brothers. At least we have the same mother, at least as far as I know. I know so very little really, but I do know that what you were doing back there—whatever it was—I'm not saying it's wrong, not knowing your friend and all, maybe it's customary to ransack one another's places—an island thing, but I do know it makes me very uncomfortable—" Then I remembered the tire iron.

"Where's the tire iron? Did you leave the tire iron back there?"

"What you trippin' on, brah?"

"I'm tripping on the fucking tire iron you took from this fucking rental car. It can be traced! Jail. I hate fucking jail!"

"Trace shit, brah. Go on, drive up da Pali," he croaked easing the whisky bottle up to his lips like an instrument he was fond of playing.

I wanted to turn back, wanted to get that tire iron—saw it lying back there on the floor with my name on it, circled in white chalk, flashing. But it meant going back to the house and I couldn't go back.

Between glugs of whisky Johnny guided me until I pulled off the muddy road on to a wide sweep of highway that curved up into the mist—the Pali. I felt reassured by the smooth pavement. Johnny had grown quiet. There were no police in the rear view mirror; cool air wafted through the window. I decided it was time to share more common history.

"We were taken into custody by the state of Texas when we were kids. You were five—the oldest. I was a few months past two with the youngest a year behind me. Do you remember anything? Anything that happened back then?"

Johnny answered quickly, "Nah. I don't remember nuthin' like dat."

"But you were five. You must have remembered something?'

"Don't remember nothing. I was raised in Waipahu by my Aunty—Hanai dey calls it. Sometimes kids goes to different folks in da family, you get raised by whoever can take you in. Dat's all I know, brah." Again he coaxed a gurgle from the whiskey bottle.

"Did anyone ever contact you about a hereditary disease? That your father had a brain disorder?"

Johnny looked at me. "I told you I don't remember nothing."

"There's a hereditary disease in our family. You and I, we could have it and not know it yet. But they have a test for it now, for the marker."

"Marker? Who da fuck send you?"

"Nobody sent me. I just came."

His whiskey lips curled up at the corners as if enjoying a shared secret—something sinister and unspoken. Then he drained off the bottle, set it carefully on the floor board as if it were still full and chuckled to himself. When we crested the ridge at the top of the Pali, Johnny wiped his hands on his shirt and croaked, "Pull in here."

A tour bus was parked, its occupants scattered about in wind blown clumps. Johnny opened his door, heaved himself from the car. It was a spectacular view: a ridge line of steep cliffs, furred in green, hung with mist, made a sheer drop to a valley below. The land flattened out as it swept to meet the gray line of the surrounding ocean. Further out, where the sky went cloudless, sun rays slanted down, stirred the ocean to a dark blue.

"You come like Cain come to see his bruddah?" Johnny rumbled.

"No, no," I reassured him. "But we each need to give some blood—"

"Blood you want?" He laughed in a high flutter, and jumped up onto the three-foot guard wall built of lava rock. A cold gust buffeted his kinky wisps, swayed his chin braid.

"For the test," I said. "They need a blood sample."

"For da test, huh. Everybody wants my blood for da test," he said facing me astride the low wall. "You tell dem, bruddah, tell dem they can have all dey want."

He looked up and closed his eyes, back tilted his head as if to take a momentary rest, but slowly he increased the angle of his lean away from me, and I began to lean forward with him to better fathom the degree of this backwards tilt when he dropped from sight.

I lurched for the wall, expecting to see Johnny on the other side, perched on a ledge a few feet below leering with a gap-toothed grin—a local joke played on *haoles*. What I found was a thousand foot drop to the gray rocks below and there, at the bottom—his tiny body—limbs splayed at cruel angles.

The tourists nearby were frozen in their colorful outfits—stunned like me, unsure of what they'd just seen. An older man in sparkling white sneakers, holiday windbreaker puffing in the gusts, shuffled to the wall, aimed his camera and snapped a picture.

Chapter 29

Aloha Funeral Home

ON THE LEEWARD OR SHITTY SIDE OF OAHU, the Aloha Funeral Home consisted of two beige double-wides (one for mourning, the other for eating) dropped on a freshly blacked parking lot.

Within five minutes of my arrival everyone at the service knew who I was which only served to amplify the high-weirdness of the situation. Though I knew in my heart I'd done nothing to help Johnny off that cliff, I could not shake the feeling that my presence had contributed, conjured buried memories—some post-traumatic-stress-disorder from Vietnam—that fifth button story? Or mentioning the blood test had triggered some paranoid delusion? Or was he just drunk and fell?

It was a dreadful, low in the gut sensation that resurrected a memory I thought I had successfully buried. It had all started when my father gifted me with a dissecting kit one Christmas, no doubt an encouragement to a young boy to follow in his father's footsteps—cut things open, poke around, see how they work. Encased in a neat wooden box secured with a metal latch were all the surgical tools required to dis-assemble a small specimen. And being that there was an abundance of horny toads in the area, the victim was determined.

A large one was soon caught, great thorny head like a massive sand burr with daubs of black on either side of his neck. A cotton ball soaked with denatured alcohol was applied to its snout—something I'd seen on TV? After a few minutes, the horny toad closed his eyes and ceased to move. I turned him over to expose the cream colored belly, and with the surgical scissors from my kit, I went to work snipping around the perimeter. With a final snip, I removed the entire flap of skin to expose the glistening innards. I turned to reach for the probe only to turn back and find he had flipped himself over onto his skinless belly and now sat blinking the black beads of his eyes at me, mouth slightly agape as if asking—*what have you done?*

There was no underside, nothing to hold his parts in place and he was still alive! With his little claws, he tried to pull himself forward, but the paper towel, my surgical sheet, was stuck to his underside. Dear god, he was dragging himself towards me—*what have you done?*

I scooped him up, forgive me, towel and all, to the bathroom, sorry, sorry, into the toilet and I flushed ... the agonizingly slow circular swirl of the body paraded ridiculously around the bowl, guts trailing, the beady eyes—oh, flush again. Unbearable ick factor. Washed my hands. Propelled from the bathroom, I strolled sweaty through the family room; they're watching TV, sipping martinis, as if nothing had happened, as if no murder had just been committed in the next room.

Back to the bathroom. Check and flush again. Woke in the middle of the night, those beady eyes—murderer! Into the dark bathroom. Flush again. He could have stuck, lodged in the pipes, worked his way back up again—found floating in the morning by the maid—I could hear her scream. Flush again. And then a blinding light! What? My father stood in the bathroom doorway in his pajamas blinking his own question.

"Are you sick?" he asked.

"... Yes ..."

"What's wrong?"

I should have told him, admitted it all. But it was such a botched job and how would he feel about horny toads in the plumbing, the useless death? The total absence of any medical aptitude? No knowledge gained. A wasted life flushed away. If only I could do that with this Johnny thing—flush it away, flush that feeling away.

There were not big numbers at the service. A scattering of soft brown eyes populated the pews, inward looking, mulling funerals past, bracing for those to come. They must have all known I was the last to see him alive. Were they suspicious of me or embarrassed for me? I couldn't tell. Didn't know myself.

The news reporter, an ambulance chaser who showed up at the scene of the incident had informed me, with a barely restrained enthusiasm that the Pali had been a favorite 'jumping off place' since Kamehameha had driven hundreds of Hawaiians off those cliffs in a battle to unite the islands under his rule. I wasn't sure what battle had driven Johnny over the cliffs, but I feared that I, too, would wake to its call late one night and have to answer.

"I didn't see you at the hospital," said Auntie Mary Jane installing herself into the pew behind me, ratcheting up my internal culpability. Yes, it was true, right after calling her, I had fled the hospital. Fled like a guilty child; the whole recovery procedure back at the Pali still playing in my head: the ropes, the orange restraint belts, the metal basket dragged bouncing and scraping up the cliff side—the gorgeous view, the giddy disbelief, the numbness of it all.

"I just met him ..." I told them at the hospital. "... He'd been drinking ... I believe he fell."

In explaining that he was my lost brother, it all got long and complicated during which I was reminded of why I had come to the islands in the first place—to get a sample of Johnny's blood. Of course, that seemed a tactless request that would require even more explaining, god knows what kind of red tape and what with the doctor already walking away, it just became more than I could sort. So after the call to Auntie Mary Jane, I stepped out into the most glorious sunset imaginable and began sampling the rum drinks of Hawaii.

Johnny Kukona lay in state, his pearly casket shone like a roadster, top down and draped in leis—ready for departure. A corpulent young man with a hairless globe of a face stood tented in an Aloha shirt strumming a ukulele and crooning a nearly recognizable Hawaiian styling of a hymnal standard. Crouched in an outside space in a pew near the front, I exchanged nods with the older, nut-brown man seated next to me. Both of us stared dutifully towards Johnny's gleaming white ride.

In a front pew I spotted the same woman who had driven past me that morning at Johnny's house and with her, two girls under ten. The younger girl had her glossy black hair held in place by a series of barrettes pronged with an array of little silver butterflies—each butterfly mounted on a short, flexible wire stem that allowed it to quiver and shake with the slightest movement of her head sending sparkles from the rhinestones mounted in their wings. Cute, I thought, until it became apparent from the shaking that the little girl was crying.

The haggard mom tried to console her, but the child fiercely shook her head causing the butterflies to shimmer and flash. She defiantly rose to her feet, took three quick steps toward the casket and froze for a moment before heaving a bright blue jet of vomit towards Johnny.

The ukulele guy froze in mid-strum. Everything went still in the room except for the sparkly butterflies quivering on the girl's head. She wheeled as if demanding an explanation from those gathered, her dark eyes blinking through a wrack of tears, reflecting our shame for all of us to see—a man had died too young.

Down the aisle she ran to the dry applause of her flip-flops, bursting through the metal door at the rear of the room. After a pause, it clanged shut behind her. The mother, hunched in bewilderment, followed her daughter's echo.

Gradually, people came to their senses. A low hubbub arose. An Asian-looking woman poked the uke guy. He unstuck his eyes from the blue puddle on the floor, tilted his face up towards the ceiling and resumed crooning. The nut-brown man next to me hissed, "Goddamn ice," and locked his fingers together as if keeping them from going off on their own to seek revenge. Me? No, it was 'ice' he cursed. Not haole relations.

A yellow plastic mop bucket was rolled out, the blue puddle absorbed. A cue was given and people stood-up one pew at a time to file past the open casket.

Johnny, styled into a "good" version of the man I had met, was nestled in a quilted puff of satin: hair trimmed and combed, chin braid snipped away, lips sealed over missing teeth, the impasto of make-up evened out his splotchy skin.

For the first time, I noticed his nose was like mine, and the strong brow hooded over the eyes—wasn't that mine also? How easily the face could have been transposed—me stretched out in the metal box; pick any one of a number of death-tempting moves on my part. Maybe Johnny had just gotten tired of holding back, tired of being slapped around by the hand of fate. Decided to 'get it over with'. And though Johnny had been freed from a tormented life, there was the collateral damage, the ones he left behind—the tribute of blue vomit.

The music stopped and left us stranded with only our human sounds, coughs and creakings, whispered words. There began a general movement towards the exit. Outside, people were clustering around the backs of various pick-up trucks. Coolers were dug into, plastic wrapped bins of food appeared, beers opened—a tailgate wake was in progress.

I approached Auntie Mary Jane and asked her if Nunnie, our mother, her sister, had possibly been heard from. She shook her head. "No one has heard from her, but come with me."

Swept along in Auntie's plumeria scented slipstream, I followed; the sunburned haole drawing nods and glances from the gathered as we approached a pomegranate red pick-up truck. Again the decal *Hawaiian Love* swirled wave-like across the rear window.

"Cookie Boy," she called out to a bear of a man foraging in an ice chest. "This is your cousin come from the mainland."

When Cookie Boy rose to his full height he looked to be about one Oreo shy of Sumo eligibility. Thick arms and neck—thick look in the eyes, eyes that did not totally focus on you, but read you more like a semaphore, an outline of you through drowsy Spam larded lids.

"Eh, cuz," he exhaled and absorbed my hand into his mitt. His beer looked like a miniature in his other hand. Hammy biceps wobbled as we shook hands drawing attention to the series of dots crudely tattooed on his deltoid and moving down his bicep—the eight Hawaii Islands, each island recognizable by its shape and position in the grouping.

"You da one wid Johnny when he went over?"

I nodded my head.

"Dat's cold, cuz."

"He was acting very erratic," I said seeking refuge in the facts.

"Yeah, dat Johnny Kook, he gone lolo. Him busup me place, tore it all up, brah." I nodded my head, not wanting to tell him I had been there.

"Did you happen to know if he was sick?"

Cookie Boy nodded and drained his beer can, wadded it like a gum wrapper and flicked it with a snap of his fingers into a corner of the truck bed. Two more were fished from the cooler.

"Up in him head fo' sure. Done lost him brakes," said Cookie. "Busup dat liddle one fo' real it did," He said and offered me a beer.

"Where you from?"

"Uh, Los Angeles mostly, by way of Texas, though I was born here, but mostly LA, I guess ..." I sputtered and ran out of gas just trying to explain the simplest of questions about a dubious self.

"LA? Why you come here?"

"Looking for answers. About our family. Thought Johnny could help me, but …" I motioned with my beer to indicate our surroundings and the larger psychic terrain of the unflushable incident.

"Johnny spend some time in da tubes, brah. Maybe somebody knows sumptin'."

He saw the question marks in my eyes and pointed his beer in the direction of the big island, Hawaii. It was a particularly clear day and off in the distance you could see white smoke from Kilauea slanting into the sky.

"… Lava tubes. Find most anything there, brah."

Chapter 30

The Big Island

COOKIE HAD A *CUZ* WITH AN OLD MARLIN boat, the fighting chair had a thousand notches and the gunwales chewed soft with use. I maxed-out the cash advance on my Visa and gave him fifty. That got us over to Kona on the big island where he planned to charter out to some haoles wanting a cheap boat with a genuine Hawaiian captain.

In Kona, we hitch-hiked to another cuz where Cookie managed to borrow a rolling wreck and five gallons of gas. Leaving a trail of oily smoke, we set out towards Kilauea's slanting tumble of white. I would have liked to have enjoyed the scenery, but mostly I was concerned about how the old pick-up sagged and swayed beneath Cookie's bulk like a hammock suspended between four tires. An hour later, it groaned and bottomed-out as he pulled off the road, seemed to give-up with a sputter and expired beneath a canopy of banyan trees. We got out, followed a foot-worn path that twined through ferns and ended at a dark hole in the ground. Cookie said it was a cave and actually wanted me to enter the hole.

"But I don't really like caves," I told Cookie. Cave as in cave-in. As in stuck inside a hole in the ground crushed to death by tons of earth. One seismic twitch and you're the meat in an earth sandwich. Or, in this case, lava rock because that's what was all around. We weren't that far from Kilauea, the volcano that produced all this lava and was still busy making more.

"What's da problem, brah?" Cookie Boy said. "Once you get inside, it open up, plenny big. No worries."

But there were worries. I had gotten stuck in a cave once, well, not me but the guy in front of me did. Ron the same fat kid that told me I was adopted. It was some stupid Boy Scout expedition for a spelunking merit badge. I won't go into it except to say, he got stuck and started freaking and that's not what you want when you are down there in this tiny space and some kid gets scared and you can't get him to move either way. And it's cold. And wet. And he shits himself. And I'm behind him. And we're in a cave—limited ventilation. Really ghastly. Finally, I guess relieving himself in his pants reduced his belly enough so he could shimmy through. So, gagging, we crawled out into the fresh air. Caves.

"Come on, brah, don be *haole* panty boy."

Haole was bad enough, but now panty boy? He'd thrown down the gauntlet. So Cookie led the way as we entered the hole, skidding down along a talus of loose lava rock until we reached the bottom.

Inside, the passage swelled into a cavern and, as my eyes adjusted, I could see the walls were soft-edged and sleek, a dark flowstone glazed with a metallic sheen. So this was a lava tube, part of an intricate array of tunnel-like caves that honeycombed beneath the surface of the big island; Hawaii had oozed out into being from such places. And I hoped there would be no more oozing from this particular one.

Overhead, a domed ceiling, punctured by a single skylight, filtered rays through feathery tendrils that hung down in a sort of reverse jungle made from the roots of trees on the surface above. It was getting warmer.

"Hey, Cookie, when was the last time lava flowed through here?"

"Chill, brah. No barbecue today."

"How far does it go?"

"Go to Pele's womb, brah."

Poetic for this great heap of a guy to whom I had yet to confess about my being with Johnny when his home got tossed. I wanted to make a clean breast of it, but didn't know how to begin. Maybe Cookie already knew and had merely lured me down into the lava tube to exact some kind of island revenge—steam me over a venting hole 'till I confessed. Trying to stop him would be like trying to stop a lava flow. Best to submit and surrender.

The third cavern was massive and occupied: candles flickered here and there in multi-leveled clusters, guttered and dripped from the lava runnels that ran along the walls. And up higher, a series of rust-red globular formations glistened like the wet heads of unborn children.

"Dis you muddah here," Cookie said reading my face. He waved his huge arm around. "See Pele's Tears," he pointed to droplets of lava that had cooled as they fell through the air, retaining their teardrop shapes as they hit the ground where they lay in piles.

"… Pele's Hair," he pointed to thin, brittle strands of volcanic glass strung from the ceiling. "Dis muddah of all Hawaii, what you stand on, what you see—everything Pele. Believe it, brah. She plenny live."

Plenny live was right; Kilauea being the most active volcano on the planet. And I had heard of 'benches,' crusts of hardened lava that seemed solid until some unsuspecting hiker stepped on them and found himself in a bath of molten lava flowing underneath. At least I would have a colorful obituary: *Haole* panty boy euthanized and cremated at the same time.

Voices echoed in the yellow glimmer. A half-naked woman rose and swayed towards us. Cookie Boy introduced Lani with her broad nose and coal black waves of hair; her breasts hung matter of fact, dark nippled and slack against her chest, a sarong knotted around generous hips. She smelled of flowers and dusky warmth.

"Dis Johnny's bruddah," Cookie said. "Wid Johnny wen maki."

"Johnny died?" she spoke in a voice surprisingly clean of the pidgin that Johnny and Cookie used.

Cookie Boy nodded, "Off da Pali. Maki die dead."

Lani shook her dark nimbus of hair with a sad, slow motion. Her eyes landed softly upon mine; their dark gleam prompted a statement.

"… Not sure what happened. He was drinking. Acting crazy."

"Bussup me place, brah," said Cookie with an edge. I waited to feel the smothering bulk of his arm close around my neck.

"I am so sorry," Lani said.

"We drove up the Pali, he climbed up on the wall ..." My words stopped. My arms gestured through a bewildered half-mime of the incident and floated uselessly back to my sides.

"Johnny was very good to me," Lani said softly.

"Was he sick?" I asked her.

Lani silently held my look for a moment, then turned and swayed away. I looked at Cookie; he nodded his head, "Bumbye, brah, bumbye."

When Lani returned she held a wooden box; carved on the lid was a fiercely grinning tiki, his teeth formed by inlaid bits of bone. We sat on woven mats. From out of the box came a pipe, bulbous like an apple blown from red glass and with it a small plastic bag filled with what looked like shards of broken glass or crystals. Lani shook a sliver into Cookie's hand and he held it up for me to look at.

"What is it?" I asked.

He dropped the sliver into the pipe.

Lani struck a lighter and circled the glass bulb with the flame. The sliver melted into a pool then vaporized; Cookie sucked in and held it. When he exhaled I caught the faint whiff of rotten roses as a smile bloomed across his face wide as the tiki's on the box.

"Ice," He said and passed the pipe. "Hawaiian Ice, brah."

Lani dropped in another sliver and made the lighter spark.

"Go on hit it, cuz."

When I exhaled the smoke, I felt refreshed as if I hadn't taken a really good, deep breath in a long time. Things around me zoomed into sharper focus: the air seemed tuned to higher pitch in my ears. I could hear the occasional distinct word that rose from the softly burbling clusters of people; there was the warm rhythm of flesh being massaged; a man polished a luminous curl of bone—his eyes flashed a dark beam at me, and then doused themselves back in his work.

"So Johnny used to hang out here?" My voice resonated in the cave with a bounce that surprised me, the full-throated herald of a newly arrived confidence. All of a sudden I was somebody. Whatever I had been before was something less than this.

Cookie Boy nodded his head at my question which I had already forgotten so taken was I with the tattooed pattern that decorated the length of Lani's arm. Intricate, as if the flesh itself had been woven through with strands of inky braid. She tipped the pipe to her lips, torched the bowl and sipped the vapor.

"Too much of this," Lani said tapping her head as she exhaled the bitter sweet whiff of rotten roses.

"But you do it," I said.

"Not like Johnny, brah," said Cookie. "Ice take you different places—like a riptide in da ocean grab holt you and take you wherever. Johnny tell me 'bout one time. Back in da 'Nam before dey wen battle, dey give dem soldiers drops from dis vial, clear liquid he say, da vial got German words on it."

"What was it?"

"Who knows, brah, was German words. But Johnny say make 'dem feel like dey bullet-proof, no thing can hurt dem. And dey throw away dey helmets. Crazy buggahs. And dat's where Johnny he need to be, back dat place where he bullet-proof, brah."

"Johnny is bullet-proof now. Nothing can hurt him anymore," Lani intoned.

My eyes moved over Lani's tattoo, tracing the dark pattern as it flowed around her elbow. She caught me staring.

"Maui is your island," she said and touched my shoulder muscle. "Here, it will make your arm strong to pull."

I looked at my right arm.

"Pull what?"

"What you need. Like Maui, I will give you a fish hook to pull up from the ocean the thing you need."

Johnny's death had scoured me of all desire to pull up any more stuff. No more damaged and broken people. I was like a blight visiting these people, making things worse in their already fragile lives. Johnny's body lying crumpled at the bottom of that cliff told me I had seen enough. I was done with the search. But I said nothing to Lani as she lightly traced, with one finger, a circular whorl over the skin of my shoulder and I began to see something.

"... Here," she said. "In the old way."

Moli, she called the implement: it was a huge tooth, a boar's tusk with a groove cut into it from the base to the needle-sharp point. And on the dull, upper end was an ink well attached to a wooden handle.

"Old way," she repeated. "Not so easy." And with that she set the point of the tusk against my skin and with a wooden wand, she tapped it sharply. Ah! Not so easy was right; the tusk pierced the flesh and drove pigment into the skin. Like getting bit by a single fang again and again. Each tap struck bright sparks in my brain. Tap. Tap. Cookie Boy passed me sips of *okolehao*, a sweet liquor made from the roots of the ti plant—Hawaiian moonshine.

"... You are *kama'aina*, Child of the Islands," Lani murmured to me in a low voice while she tapped. "Remember Maui."

"Maui the island?" I asked.

"Maui the god. Listen," Lani said. "Close your eyes, open your mind ..." With her hands she shaped a vortex of air over my head, like a hula benediction and gently closed my eyes.

"... See the *kai*, the great ocean. On the horizon see the tiny canoe. In the canoe is Maui, alone on the ocean. He is on a voyage to find the bones of his father. Maui had set out with his two brothers. But they feared a coming storm. The brothers were cowards, they deserted Maui. And now he is alone on the ocean with a black storm hard upon him. It beats at him and he is afraid, many doubts fill him. Huddled down in the bottom of his canoe, he is beaten by rain and waves. His canoe is so battered by the storm that it starts to break-up and Maui knows he must do something or die. *Maki.*"

Tap. Tap. Bites on my shoulder. Sparks in my brain. My body was filled with an energy, like a smoothly geared turbine suspended in the humming of its parts, it seemed to hover just above the cave floor. And as much as I wanted to listen to Lani's story my mind kept ratting off down a thousand different holes. I had questions—this Maui guy, how old was he? Did he share the same father with his brothers? And where was the mother? My mouth was drying up. Where was that bottle of *oke*? Cookie answered with another sip of the ti whiskey. Lani continued to tap and murmur.

"Maui had brought with him a rope braided from the intestines of his ancestors. And with this rope gripped in his teeth, he dove down into the ocean and wrapped the canoe with the rope, pulled it fast and made it strong again. But as he lifted himself back up into the canoe a big wave rose and struck him hard like a fist against the side of the canoe. His rib bone was broken and sticking from out from his skin ..."

Okay, I was on board. I loved the whole intestine rope thing. From the guts of his ancestors Maui finds the strength to keep himself afloat. And then the broken rib! Yes, hadn't I felt that when my father told me about the disease—something had snapped in me. A break. It was all so illuminating, vivid as the stain she was hammering into my skin with an animal's tooth.

"… And so Maui drifted for many days, lost; no land in sight. He grew weak with hunger. Soon, he knew he would be too weak to help himself. So from the broken bone of his rib he fashioned a fish hook. Maui tied the hook onto the rope braided from the intestines of his ancestors. He cast it out onto the water. The hook caught on something and Maui began to pull. With all the strength he had left he tugged hand over hand until up from the water, up from underneath him, up came an island …"

"Yes!" I sang out as I sat up. "That's it! The rope of my ancestors—it's the double helix of DNA, it twines around itself all our genes strung together—stretching back forever. The DNA is Maui's rope!"

Lani and Cookie Boy were staring at me with their mouths open. I glanced at my shoulder and there was the moli stuck, hanging from my skin.

"Sorry," I said and waited while Lani detached the boar's tooth from my flesh. Sips of *okolehao*. And again Lani closed my eyes with one hand while she placed the other on my pounding chest. A warmth flowed out from her hand and calmed my heart.

Tap. Tap. Tap. Bright sparks in the brain. The murmur of the story. Finally, Maui stood on his island. Dragged his canoe onto the land he had pulled from the sea with the rope of his ancestors and the rib bone hook from his own body. He looked around him and knew that he had found his home.

Brilliant! I got it. The rib bone—that broken part of yourself that protrudes from your very skin. The horrible injury that you survive and from it you make a fish hook; a tool for getting what you need. Lemonade from lemons; plain as day. Boy, was my brain working in some kind of high over-drive. That ice stuff was amazing. Could be addictive. Very. One more and that was it for me.

Lani stopped punching black holes in my skin and surveyed her work.

"*Makau*," she said and wiped it clean with the ti whiskey. "This is *Makau*—your fish hook. It will always be with you."

As the sting subsided, I almost missed the pain, the tap and bite of the tusk, the slow rhythm of her words.

"Catch the thing you need," she murmured as she loaded the pipe, applied the torch—I could hear the conversion of the ice into a liquid, the hiss as it vaporized ...

Chapter 31

Tweaking

THIS MUCH WAS CLEAR, THE PAY PHONE IN the KFC parking lot was a health risk. It was also the only functioning pay phone for miles and we needed it to call everyone and anyone who had known Johnny. That's what the 'ice' I had smoked was saying to me, *call everyone Johnny knew.* But it was also saying, with equal intensity, that the pay phone was absolutely fetid: the mouthpiece layered with the human accretion of all those desperate calls: the drunken tirades, the spit, the tears, the sniveling for drugs or cash—the pleas for forgiveness. Once I watched a homeless man in San Francisco stick a phone down his pants and rub it furiously up and down as he howled with pleasure.

And there I was, an open wound seeping on my shoulder—the tattoo—my fish hook. But Lani's tortured myth had reached beneath my skin; tapped into some reserve unknown to me. And with a boost from the ice, no doubt, I had emerged from the lava tube ablaze with the knowledge that I had to *do something* for Johnny, in honor of his wreck of a life. *Our* wreck of a life. For who knew better than I how easily it could become a wreck; needing no other reason than he was born my brother and at one time had dug through a garbage can to feed me. Johnny was one of the strands of that ancestral rope that held me together, that pulled me forward. I would find our birth mother—even though, at that very moment, my obsession, as I stood in the KFC parking lot, was the condition of the pay phone.

"Not in my ear!" I proclaimed to Cookie pointing at the jam crusted on the receiver.

"You so tweaking now, brah."

"It's crawling with bacteria: Staph, Ebola, that flesh-eating thing—have you seen the photos?"

Cookie Boy shook his head, amused by my fit of OCD. But I stood my ground and refused to use the phone without a thorough disinfecting—neutralized with Lysol or Clorox. I marched with high purpose towards the KFC.

Inside, I was disappointed by the response from the droopy-eyed kid working the counter. "Wet-Naps? That's all you have? No Pine-Sol? What do you clean the bathroom with? You *do* clean it don't you?" The kid shrugged his shoulders.

"*Dood*, I just work the counter," he whined and pointed at the colorful display above his head; it featured a variety of deep-fried items in different shapes and combinations. *'Make it Hawaiian!'* exclaimed one picture of a poultry bit drenched in pink syrup and what looked like tiny chunks of pineapple.

I didn't want to get started with him on the menu, its lack of nutritional fare not to mention the travesty of reducing a proud, indigenous people's cuisine down to pink corn syrup and faux pineapple chunks. After that last puff on the pipe, it didn't seem I would ever need food again.

I turned to the kid, "And have you seen the condition of that phone book out there?"

"Uh, no, sir, I haven't really ..."

"Well, it looks like someone may have used it to start a fire."

He squinted his eyes and looked up as if trying to recall a recent fire.

"... And that phone ..." I said as I grabbed double-fistfuls of the Wet-Naps and headed for the door. "Have it cleaned. Steam cleaned. Monthly. Hire a service. Take some responsibility." Nothing like being high to promote the liberal dispensing of free advice.

The kid nodded blankly as I backed-out the door, probably relieved that he hadn't suffered any worse from the bug-eyed maniac dribbling a trail of Wet-Naps and still babbling as I crossed the parking lot.

Back at the phone, Cookie Boy had forged ahead. Ignoring the level of toxicity, he'd dialed a cousin on Maui who knew another auntie of Johnny's, one that had not shown up at the funeral.

"Step away from that phone," I ordered. "Here, take these Wet-naps. Clean your hands, your ears. Any part of your face that touched it—do it now while there's still time."

He took the Wet-naps and complied with my directive while filling me in on the call.

"Dat *cuz* I talk wid gonna make some calls den call us back here, brah."

"How long do you think?"

"Bumbye, don go lolo. Buggah on it, brah."

"What was that gibberish you just spoke?"

"Be chillin', brah ..."

While Cookie held the hook down to keep the phone ready to receive the call, I attacked the receiver with a wad of wet naps. They seemed to have been sized to clean one finger at a time and I had just finished up with the handle when this guy ambles over, definitely a child of the islands, stout fella, what's called a *moke.*

"How long you gonna be?" he asked.

"Phone don work, brah," Cookie Boy announced flatly.

The barrel-chested moke looked to have been on the KFC diet for some time and had that 'don't fuck with me stare' down cold.

"So how com I jus seen you talk on dis phone if it no working, brah?"

There came the sound of hackles rising as he and Cookie Boy stared at one another; I paused the disinfecting and placed myself between these two hostile mountains of flesh.

"Hey, brah, he's just trying to help me out," I said cheerfully adopting the local pidgin dialect. "This here is Cookie Boy, my cuz. Name's Bert, I'm *kama'aina*, born on Oahu, but my family comes from Maui. Mostly I grew up in Texas, brah. Also spent some time in Tennessee—military school, brutal, you don't even want to know, brah—"

The moke shrugged, "... Just wan use da phone."

"I understand that, brah, but first of all, let me tell you ..." I said dangling the phone from its cord like an infected rat. "... This phone, when we first arrived—you would have caught hepatitis from it—all three kinds, brah."

Of course, I went on too long, but I had to keep the phone open until the call came in. So I babbled, not hard to do under the influence of the ice, and watched as the moke worked his jaw muscles until, about minute five of my monologue, he actually started to relax: his head tilted to accommodate the sheer mass of information that was spilling towards him. At one point, he adjusted his stance, crossed his arms and settled-in for the whole story which I delivered with numerous back-trackings and digressions with many compliments to himself and his proud island heritage, something all of us present *shared*.

"... So," I said beginning my third conclusion. "That's the only way you can know if you actually have this disease, by that I mean the only way that *I* can know—remember, it's genetic. And that's why we need to find her, our mother—our *birth*-mother."

The moke shook his head. "*Dood* can talk-story," he said regarding my narrative skills. Then asked, "Whas her name?"

"Nunnie Kukona," I said. The moke scratched his head.

"And she from Maui, brah?"

At this point two large women had ambled out of the KFC and joined us.

"Dis my wife and her sista from Lahaina town, brah," He turned to her and asked, "Do you know a Nunnie Kukona from Maui?"

The woman thought for a minute. Shook her head. These were Hawaiians or at least that sufficiently swarthy mix of Asian, Filipino, Portuguese and Hawaiian.

"*Dood* is trying to find his birthmother so he can see if he's dying or not," the moke said reducing my story for the sake of the others.

"Oh," the wife said. "You doing da genealogy thing? Dat's cool, like on TV, reunions and all."

"Yes, exactly," I said. "We're working on a reunion here."

Then I showed off my fresh tattoo and boorishly explained the significance of the fish hook in Hawaiian mythology to the Hawaiians who nodded politely and were probably just as relieved as we were when the phone finally rang. Everyone froze as Cookie Boy grabbed the receiver.

"Yeah, it's me cuz, uh huh …"

He motioned for a pen to write with, and every one began searching for a pen. The wife's sister mined one from the depths of her purse—handed it to Cookie. Digits were scrawled on his massive hand. "… Umm hmm … ummm hmm … got it, brah," He said and hung up the phone.

"She at dis number, cuz."

"Who is?" I ask.

"Your Auntie Syrilla. Nunnie's older sister, brah. And another ting,"

"What?"

"We all out of quarters, cuz."

I didn't have any more. The wife looked in her purse. The sister checked hers; even the moke dug in his pockets. They came up with four between them.

Cookie dialed.

"Syrilla?" Cookie Boy asked on the phone. With a nod of his head, he gave us the thumbs up over his shoulder. At this point, the kid from the counter had joined us out in the parking lot just to see what was going on. And we all listened intently as Cookie gave her the story: Johnny, the funeral, me—she had heard about it.

Cookie turned back to us and whispered, "She say she no come to the funeral because she thought your mother might be there, dey make beef."

"Okay," I said, "But does she have any idea where the woman might be?"

Cookie nodded his head and shushed me as he listened to the other end—grunts and nods. Then Cookie Boy hung-up the phone and turned to us assembled there waiting, heads tilted up, mouths opened expectantly as if for a feeding.

"… Last time she see Nunnie when she come here to visit, dat three years ago, but dey make beef. Da last she knows you muddah was living on da mainland."

"Did she say where?"

Cookie Boy nodded his head. "Butte, Montana, brah."

"Montana? What are you telling me?"

"Dats what I'm telling you, brah. Butte, Montana. And she

don't have no phone. You have to leave a message wid da police to get to her."

"What? The police? Is she in prison?"

"I tink she jus don't have da phone, brah. So people leaves da message wid police. Dat's de last anybody know 'bout her."

"Okay. Butte, the police, that's certainly something. Anything else?"

"Yeah, but it's not so nice, brah," Cookie said glancing awkwardly at the others assembled in the parking lot. To see this hulk of a man, this mountain of flesh and appetites demurely withhold saying something that might embarrass me was, well, how else do I put it—touching. Cookie had helped me, taken me by the hand, nearly gotten in a fight with the moke over the phone on my behalf and what had I done when Johnny wrecked his place? I stood by and watched. It was time to come clean.

"Cookie, I was there when Johnny tore your place up. He was acting crazy. I didn't know what to do, how to stop him. Didn't even know it was your place. I'm really sorry."

"Yeah, I figured all dat, brah."

"Oh … okay. Well, then go ahead. Everyone here has helped us. Tell me what else she said."

"She say, you mama, she was 'a lady of the night, brah'."

Chapter 32

Butte, Montana

FOR ANY FLIGHT OVER EIGHT HOURS, YOU should be put to sleep by professionals. There was no sleep for me; it had been chemically banished from my body. Then came the shaky scramble for a connecting flight, the carry-on bag forgotten as the brilliance of the 'ice' high melted down leaving me in puddles of doubt: *Would my birthmother even see me? Had I done absolutely everything in my life wrong? A lady of the night?*

It was a brutal crash: my body seemed three times its normal weight as the self-loathing compounded, piled up like boulders on my chest until I had to force myself to breathe. Not hard to see how an addiction could send you screaming off the Pali with a glass pipe in your hand.

Inside, the Butte Police Station was a wax works; no one was moving. They didn't seem to understand—I was so *close.* And so tired. Things take so much longer than you imagine they will when you're high—you forget to factor in the patience that reality requires.

The town of Butte was a collection of red brick buildings from another era that some people had neatly constructed, and then abandoned. It felt vacated, thinned-out like the mile-high air. On the way in, the taxi driver pointed out one particular building done in the Victorian style, "That there is the Dumas Brothel built in 1890, America's longest running house of prostitution, yes sir, she's still working."

As I took in the blunt exterior of the building, the cramped dimensions of its single front door, Cookie's words at the pay phone echoed back to me, "… She said your mama was a lady of the night …"

I couldn't help but wonder if this celebrated establishment

had influenced my birthmother's decision to settle here: a historic building with a long reputation, not much training required just a willingness to work closely with the community.

The good thoughts in my brain had been burnt black by the ice. Call it fairy dust—it was still meth, speed, a dirty, body ravaging killer. But it had gotten me all the way from a lava tube in Hawaii to the police station in Butte, Montana.

Officer Mangram folded his arms and cocked his head after I began my explanation. I may have gotten a little shrill waving the documents around like an attorney offering overwhelming evidence, "… It says here, I am her son. And since her sister, my aunt back in Hawaii, says she has no phone, I was told to contact the Butte police department to leave any messages …"

Officer Mangram suggested very slowly that I might wanna take a seat. I had walked in of my own free will, and no laws had been broken, though from the look in his eyes I could tell he was doing a cursory flip through his mental mug book. I had that kind of face—guilty.

Requesting the Montana police to lead you to an unlisted person with only a few obscure documents to prove you're related, required, if not humility on my part, then at least restraint. I'd been up for seventy-two hours; brain and all attached ganglia constricting with alternating waves of paranoia and hostility. I decided it best I head for the drug store for something calming from over the counter. When I asked if there was one nearby, one of the other cops chuckled and said, "What kind of drugs you looking for?" I amazed myself by saying absolutely nothing.

"Here's your papers back," Officer Mangram said and after what seemed like several long and difficult days, he passed me my sweat-stained manila envelope, but just before releasing it said, "First, we need to run a computer check on you."

Fine. No flies on me except maybe that missing tire iron from the rental car. There was nothing else—was there? The spasm of paranoia. I inquired as to the time factor on the computer check.

"When we get 'er done, pardner" he answered and lumbered away. Pardner? Wasn't that what you said to boys under ten, and then ruffled their hair? And there was my hostility.

Maybe I had always been paranoid and hostile and my current debilitated state just allowed me to see it. And that raised another question. Had I always been hostile because I was paranoid? And therefore, paranoid of what? What was the shape and source of my fear? My foot twitched as if to remind me—oh yes, the disease—the specter of untimely death. And that's why I was here, doing my darnedest to appear normal which is easier than you think. Focus on the externals: stay reasonably clean, keep your mouth shut and stare at something like a book or magazine. And so, in a tone scrubbed free of any authority issues, I quietly excused myself and headed around to the corner Seven Eleven.

I purchased a tube of Neosporin, a pack of scented moist towelettes, and a pint of Butte's own Open Pit Porter to wash down the six Advil. Back at the police station bathroom, I dabbed the Neosporin on my seeping tattoo and gave myself a good wiping down with the towelettes. I was in need of some fresh clothes—what happened to my clothes? Ah, the forgotten carry on. Never mind. Just stuff. First things first.

Wafting aloe and belching porter, I stepped out of the bathroom. The beer/Advil combo seemed to smooth the edginess, though later, when Officer Mangram cleared his throat and woke me slumped on the bench I jumped as if hit with a Taser. I was beyond tired. One minute my eyes were open and the next he was standing over me wiping the mustard out of his mustache with a paper napkin. Why did they all have mustaches? Would it help if I grew a mustache? No, it would somehow appear sinister on me. Guilty.

"I'll drive you over now if you want," Officer Mangram announced.

And the first thing that came to mind was, *Oh, you mean, drive me over to the Dumas Brothel to meet my mother who works there as a dick greeter?*

But once again, amazed by my restraint, I simply asked, "And where exactly are we going, officer?"

"Big Sky Trailer Ranch," came the answer as he strapped on his holster causing me to wonder if my birthmother was someone better met with a side arm handy.

Riding in a patrol car has never been comfortable for me. The associations are obvious. I found it similar to riding with my parents and so adopted the same strategy—silence. And officer Mangram appeared okay with that as we drove towards the outskirts of Butte and eventually, turned into the entrance of Big Sky Trailer Ranch. After winding around a collection of weathered mobile homes, we came to one with a scalloped yellow trim leached of all cheerfulness. An attached porch looked out over a tangled bed of white narcissus.

Officer Mangram heaved himself out of the car, adjusted his belted gear and waddled up to the door.

"Nunnie?" He called out with a rap that rattled the flimsy screen door.

The fact that the local police knew my birth mother by first name was not lost on me. Then came the outline of a short, dark figure shadowed on the screen door. While he talked the figure looked over at the car and nodded.

Officer Mangram made his way back and leaned into my window. "She says she'll talk with you. But I am an officer of the state, not a taxi service, so you'll have to find your way back to wherever it is you're going."

As he drove away I suddenly went dewy inside and wanted to shake his hand and thank him and the other good men on the force doing their part down at the station. But, he was gone and she was already on the move, screen door banging, barreling down the steps: thick-waisted, brown as teak, a dark helmet of wiry hair tamed with swipes of styling gel, dyed highlights glinting brass in the sun.

"Hi, I'm Bert," I said, and with those words all the moisture in my mouth evaporated. Suddenly, I wished for a solid twelve hours of sleep underneath me, wished that I was stronger and better prepared, or at least not alone for this encounter. I needed back-up, a pair of reassuring eyes to look into—Margery. I should have begged her to come just so I could anchor myself in her eyes. But she had her own life. A child. That's the most important thing to a mother, to most of them.

"Oh, Bertie," she gushed as her brown hands reached out, and before you could say cliché, there were my hands playing their part—reaching out and grasping hers, the reunion scene being played out: brown eyes welling, the outpouring of earnestness, the enmeshing of the hands.

"They told me you were dead ..." she said wringing moisture from my palms.

"That wasn't me," I said thinking she'd heard about Johnny.

"They told me you had all been killed in a car accident!"

She had intense eyes, the vigorous, effusive manner of a performer projecting to an audience.

"... When you were a little boy you always wanted cowboy boots. That's all you wanted. Cowboy boots. And they told me you were dead! They said you had all been killed in a terrible accident! Oh, it was a terrible time. Just terrible. But look at you—you're a handsome man!"

She beamed at me standing there in Butte, Montana, the long lost son—a living miracle—and then she turned, introduction over, and led me inside the trailer.

She guided me to a sofa, asked if I wanted a beer and picked-up a full ashtray on her way to the fridge. I assumed from the Budweiser lighted wall clock complete with Clydesdales that she liked beer. How a promotional item usually displayed in a tavern had found its way into her home I could only guess. A blue-colored can of beer was set before me. She lowered herself into a well-worn easy chair and took a comforting gulp. On closer inspection I could see her hair was thinning and some of the hair dye had colored her scalp. She was also doing some noticing of her own.

"You have the Kukona nose," she said as she gazed at me gazing at her and my hand instinctively went to my nose. She was right; her nose was shaped like mine. And my eyebrows, they were also dark and prominent like hers. The tree and the fallen apple tipped their beers and toasted one another.

With the short hair, she could have passed for a small squat man from Guatemala. And if not completely at ease, (who would be in those circumstances), neither did she seem like someone who would quail at the first sign of social conflict. There was vitality about her—a woman of strong urges as she shook out a Marlboro Light 100, fired it up and sucked back a deep thoracic hit allowing me room for a question.

"You were told we all died in a car accident? That must have been awful. Did you ask to see the bodies?"

"Yes, of course. But they said it was too horrible."

"Who said that?"

"The people who came to the house. The authorities."

"Oh. Was the driver killed too?"

"The driver?" she repeated and tapped the ash from her cigarette.

"We were all under six years of age at the time so I assume someone else was driving the car. Were they also killed in the accident?"

"Oh, yes. Yes, everything burned. The car caught fire …" she said summoning some grief from the yellow shag carpet. "… I don't even want to think about it."

That much I believed—the not wanting to think about it part. As for the rest, she was lying. Poor court room acting. And yet, I was the one who became uncomfortable. Uncomfortable for her, for her need to lie. Like back when I witnessed Ween lying to his wife and mother—I didn't dare look any of them in the eye for fear of either giving it away or being considered in on it. Of course, we all lie for any number of reasons: so we don't get hit, humiliated or fired. Or to keep something intact—usually a false image held by others about ourselves. We lie thinking it's easier to live with than the truth. Or because, much of the time, the other person, the one being lied to, doesn't really want to hear the truth. But Nunnie was lying because *she* didn't want to hear the truth. And I let her lie because it was too painful to expose her. Besides, there were other things I wanted from her.

"I'll get you another beer," she said and sprang to her sturdy legs though I was barely half-way through the one in my hand.

"Have you heard anything from Baine's people?" I asked.

"Oh, no. When we divorced that was it. Done with. You know he brought me to the mainland, to Texas where he was from, but his family didn't like me. They were racists. And they turned him against me."

"Was Baine sick then?"

"Sick? No, he wasn't sick. Why?"

"He died from Huntington's Disease. It's inherited, in the genes. But it takes a while, not a sudden death."

"Oh. I had no idea. But you got some uncles who are alcoholics. I hear that's in the genes too. Cancer, everything now they claim." She handed me a fresh beer.

"That's why I came to see you, Nunnie. I'm trying to locate any of Baine's kin."

"Oh, I wouldn't know anything about them. That was a long time ago and another place and ... when they told me you kids had been killed I was so upset I had to move on or just go crazy."

Refusing to be thrown off by her play for sympathy, I kept the questions coming. "I'm sure it must have been difficult for you. So did Johnny and I have the same father?"

"Yes, no—wait. Johnny was before you. Bert ..." her voice dropped to a confessional tone. "... I was sexually assaulted as young girl in high school. I became pregnant. That was Johnny."

"Oh," I said. "I'm sorry. I met Johnny just before he died."

"Johnny died?"

"Yes. He either fell or jumped off a cliff last week. I'm not sure which, but he was drunk if that means anything," I said emptying my first beer and reaching for the second.

"Oh, that's terrible."

"Yes, it was. But then you already thought he was dead—so it shouldn't be too much of a shock," I said knowing it was cruel, but unable to help myself.

"Still, poor little Johnny ..." she finished her sentence with a swig of beer and fired up another Marlboro.

Our eyes buzzed the room in search of a less loaded topic and lit simultaneously on the framed photograph of a dark-haired youth with almond eyes.

"That's Niki," she said brightening with the shift into the present. "Or Nicholas they call him at school." She rose and retrieved the photo.

"He just graduated," she said proudly and passed it to me.

Niki had a smooth effeminate look and could probably work as a model though probably not in Butte.

"Nice face," I said and handed it back to her.

"Oh, yes, he's a beautiful boy."

"So you're married now, Nunnie?"

"Yes, but not to Niki's father. His father passed away. I'm married to Alfred Cox now." She checked the Clydesdales for the time.

"How many children have you had, do you think, altogether now?"

"Let's see …" she said and took a meditative drag. "… With your father there was the three of you … "

"Three? I thought it was two, Johnny having a different father?"

"Oh, it was all so long ago. Another time. Let's not go back to all that please. I have spent so much of my time being a nanny and taking care of so many children."

"A nanny?" I sputtered, it generally being at the other end of the spectrum from '… a lady of the night …'

"Yes, I took care of other people's children—so many children—it gets all mixed up."

"I can imagine it would. So you've been married how many times?"

"Married four times. It took a while to get it right," she chuckled, stubbed out her Marlboro and fired-up another. Chain smoker.

"And you had children with each husband?"

"Oh, yes, I love children," she said beaming and puffing. Puffing and beaming.

"So you had maybe two or three children with each husband?"

"Well … yes," she said not liking this new direction.

"And Johnny too?" She nodded her head as I persisted. "So you've had at least twelve or thirteen children, maybe more?"

"It's difficult for me to think about all this right now."

"But they would all be my half-brothers and sisters," I pressed harder, my intensity building as if I might break through some wall with her and hit upon an actual truth.

"Why don't we talk again later. Give me some time to go over it. I have other people to think about," she said and stood up signaling an end to our discussion.

But I wasn't done. "I just have one thing to ask you, Nunnie. Was Baine Browford my father?"

"How can you ask me that? Of course he was your father."

"Because it's very important that I know that he was my father. Could there have been another man?"

"Now that hurts me, Bert," she said accusingly and I found myself standing up from my chair.

"I'm sorry. But I need to know exactly what happened?"

"What happened? What happened is things just didn't work out."

Face to face. Brown eyes locked on brown eyes. Nose to Kukona nose, but instead of defiance, when I looked into her eyes what I found was a lump climbing up in my throat; a constricting mass forming. I could neither swallow nor talk around it and it seemed to draw what strength was left in my body into itself rising like a gorge and leaving my arms limp, my hands hung useless like two boneless puppies. And, as if she sensed an opening, she reached out and grasped them in her own—my puppy hands. How dare she touch my puppy hands!

"Bert, you have to move on with your life," she said. Forget about the past. Find a nice girl. Get married."

I wanted to laugh at this simple-headed formula, one she herself had repeated numerous times and to what effect? But I couldn't. Not with the swelling in my throat, and then she put her arms around me; she hugged me. How could I allow this squat little woman who had abandoned me as a child to comfort me? It was obscene. And the lump rose higher, fizzed in my throat like a hot bubble risen from some ancient and long-protected place, loosed by my exhaustion, the volatile nature of this meeting, driven upwards until—the bubble burst—and one terrible, shameful sob belched out of me.

Like a drunk man, I reeled away from her; separated myself to stand apart. And unsteady, as if finding my legs, I began to pull my blasted parts together—there was my resentment, my anger, and the shame, that was mine; there was my twitch and the hunger and the burnt black hollow place.

And I said, without looking at her, said very slowly, "I am so … tired. Is there a hotel?"

The palpable sadness of the cut-rate motel room: the thin wafer of soap, the scratchy gray towel, the Rorschach of a rust stain under the tub spout—what face did I see in that brown stain? It kept changing like the characters I had emulated through my life; characters from books, TV or the movies. I would assume their charm or skill or courage until the illusion wore off or was found impractical for daily use, and then, deprived of this shield I would find myself naked again under the glare of self-loathing.

I wondered if I had hated myself even before my father told me about the disease. Had I hated myself even before the adoption? Was it born in some pre-verbal place—transferred in my birthmother's eyes, in Nunnie's eyes when she held me up and all she could see was a burden, a limitation, a life she didn't want; something she needed to get rid of?

The threat of the disease hardly mattered after that. She may as well have struck us all dead. Which is what she had done in her mind—killed us in a car accident.

Early the next morning, I was awakened by the phone.

"Hello, Bert? Did I wake you?" Nunnie calling from the neighbor's phone.

"No, no—been up for hours."

"Good. I had a great idea and was so excited I had to call. You know Niki, my youngest son—the one you saw in the picture?"

"Yes."

"Well, he wants to be an actor and I told him how you were from LA and all and we thought we might come out to visit you."

I sat up in bed and shook my head. "… Come to visit me?"

"Yes, out in LA. After you get back home and have time to settle in."

Had I heard her right? The woman, who had abandoned

my brothers and me as children, just asked if she could bring her latest issue out to LA and see if I could help him jump start his acting career? And, as a bonus, she was going to come along and stay with me? Even more disturbing was the high probability that she was arranging to dump her current son in my lap and return to Butte child-free once again! I was too gobsmacked to put together a coherent response.

"Uh, well … I'm not really sure exactly when I'll be back in LA …"

"Oh. Okay," she back-pedaled. "Well you think about it and when you want us to come out for a visit just let us know."

"Yes ... I will … think about it. And I'll call the Butte police and have them contact you."

"You could leave a message with our neighbors."

I was now standing beside the bed naked when, as if launched from a distance and accelerating as it neared, the incoming shriek of anger landed.

"Yes, of course. I'd be happy to help you and your son number? Well, I guess we don't really know what number he is—so many children, eh, Nunnie?"

"… You sound angry, Bert."

"Angry? They found us—me, Johnny, Brion—they found us, after you left us alone for god-knows how many days, eating from a garbage can. There wasn't any accident, Nunnie. Unless you had one and couldn't seem to get back home to feed us."

She hung up.

I wished I had gotten the number so I could call her up and say it all over again—louder. Blast it from loudspeakers around her trailer night and day. There is nothing like a good rest to put your rage back in order.

After toying with a plate of scrambled eggs and a heaping side of self-righteousness, I went back up to my room, and then again, as if coming from afar—more slowly but just as loud—the incoming shriek of remorse; I should never have said that to her. It could not be left this way.

A cab was dispatched.

Nunnie came to the door when she saw the cab pull up. She stepped out and closed the door behind her.

"Bert, all this has been very upsetting for me," she said with a quiet intensity. And I believed her.

"I know. I was exhausted. I'm sorry …"

With a quarter turn of her head back towards the trailer she said, "Well, I've talked with my family about it and they said I need to let all this go."

"All this?"

"Yes. This is all too upsetting for me."

"This? Oh, you mean me?"

"You need to move on, Bert. This all happened in the past. You are a young man. Go be happy."

And with that she turned and trundled back to her trailer. The dead bolt turned on the trailer door while I erupted in her front yard.

"Hey, the past found me! And I can't just walk away from it like you did. You go be happy Nunnie! Let somebody else worry about your children!"

Oh, how I hated it. Hated the sound of it. That old trumpet of blame and accusation. How could I really know what she had suffered? It was as Lani had promised when she inked the tattoo on my shoulder—my hook had caught and pulled my fish up from the bottom of the sea. And though few answers had been found and certainly no love, what was of even greater concern, standing there on the scabby lawn of the woman who had given birth to me thirty years earlier, I saw with piercing clarity into my own paltry heart—there was no love in me.

Chapter 33

Odessa, Texas

"SHE LOOKS WORRIED," ELLIE MURMURED, bent over Arlene's body arranged in a box, looking as artificial as the flowers that surrounded her. And then, as if following a clue, Ellie crooked her head up towards the ceiling to squint accusingly at the spot light that hung there.

"… It's that light," she pointed to the culprit. "It throws a shadow. Drag that chair over."

I had returned from Butte to find, that in my absence, Arlene, the woman who had adopted me, the one I called Mother, had died. Just like that. Aunt Ellie, my father's younger sister, had flown in and taken the reins. A practiced hand at funereal duties, she had buried her mother, her father, a husband, numerous friends, relatives and a multitude of pets. Ellie knew the ropes. Brisk in her choice of caskets, she waved aside the top of the line 'Buckingham' as too ostentatious for Mother's taste and pointed instead to the 'Smithfield': solid ash in a high gloss natural finish. Ellie remarked that in color and grain it resembled Mother's favorite bridge table.

Dad had no intention of ever seeing her body again so he did not concern himself with any details of the viewing.

Ellie smoothed the suede nap of Mother's turquoise bolero jacket and matching skirt with tenderness, "That was her favorite outfit." And strictly added, "I want the line of her lipstick adjusted. It should be fuller along her lip, see right there …" she indicated by extending her small finger. For a moment it looked as if she might put her finger to Mom's lip and get the job done herself.

Ellie was right, Mother did seem worried, but then she seemed to be worried most of her life. No matter; Ellie would not allow her to look worried for this her final social appearance—the viewing. I stood on the chair and adjusted the light.

"There, that's it, right there. Just the lipstick and she'll be ready," Ellie intoned and strode off in search of the make-up person. I stayed behind to survey the scene: the heated lights, the flowers posed on columns, a spray flowing over the lower part of the casket lid, split like Dutch doors and there was Mother's waxen face.

It was her.

And it was not her.

Wanting to touch her one last time, I slipped my hand just inside her suede jacket, pressed against the white blouse—it was soft, pliant. They had put her prosthesis in to fill out her blouse where the breast had been. Ellie had seen to it. I ran my hand down along her side; the feel of her rib cage, her waist was disturbingly solid and ungiving as if she'd been filled with concrete. Only the prosthetic remained familiar.

Funeral day was chapped and blustery; a tinge of moisture dampened the dry rustle of winter.

Dad and I had spoken little since my return. I had an urge to hug him when he told me the news, but I couldn't seem to find an entry point for the embrace. Like a man behind a Lucite pane, he made sounds at you from the other side, but I couldn't find the way in. I brought up the topic of Mother's marker and what it might say—an epitaph of some sort, but he seemed befuddled by my question.

"We could say something simple about who she was." I suggested.

He shrugged his shoulders, "Her name … wife."

I spent much of my time staring in the refrigerator contemplating how I might insert myself somewhere between the half-empty bag of salad and the last wedge of apple pie curled under plastic. The medicine cabinet repeatedly offered no surprises, no solutions. The dog refused to look at me.

When the car arrived from the funeral home, Dad pointed to the black limousine and declared, "I will not ride in that."

So it was Aunt Ellie and I in the back of the limo while Dad followed in his Bronco, both hands on the wheel, face rigid, riding above it all.

When I turned back from watching him out of the back window Ellie said, "People grieve their own way. Your father came to visit me once in Houston. He was on a break from medical school and dropped by. I opened the door and there he was standing with a grin on his face. He held out his hand and dropped something in mine, something small and I held it up trying to figure out what it was."

"That's the big toe bone of my cadaver," he said with a huge smile. He'd been a bad boy. Taken a forbidden trophy from the cadaver he was dissecting. He was so rarely like that—playful. When he left to go back to school I said to him, 'I love you, Hillard." He just nodded his head and said, 'Thank you'. That was about the best he could do in that department."

We sat in the front row, Aunt Ellie a buffer of warmth between Dad and me. A smattering of people; old friends of the family, men who had lost their wives, wives who had lost their husbands.

Dad and I let our eyes graze on the green skirt of Astroturf surrounding the hole where the casket would be lowered. Plastic grass, eternally cheerful like those baskets I'd found in my room on Easter mornings: stuffed with fake grass, the brightly colored candy eggs, and the long-eared chocolate bunnies. The mystery of Easter—Christ has arisen and I chewed off the ears of a chocolate bunny. I never really understood it: Jesus, the bunnies, the fake grass. I'd wear a new outfit to church on Easter Sundays, a white linen jacket blinding in the spring sun.

All the fertility stuff is obvious; the earth comes back to life after winter's dormancy. New life, new food to be eaten. We will survive. Have a chocolate bunny.

Craning my neck, I could see down through the Astroturf into the hole. There was a concrete slab down at the bottom. So it was not really a hole so much as it was a vault: they put the box in on the slab then filled it with dirt and collected rent for it. It was like burying her in a tiny condo. I would prefer her to lie in the earth so she would gradually become part of it; not lodged like a mannequin from a shop window. We weren't letting her go at all. We were leaving her stranded there for some future resurrection of real estate development or the apocalypse.

It was deeper than I thought. Six feet had been the standard since the plague decimated England. Six feet, they thought, would protect the living from being infected by the dead. But I doubt there are holes deep enough for that. Or enough Astro-turf to cover them all.

Reverend Glass spoke the closing words; his eyes somber, his comb-over lifted and lowered itself in the breeze, waving its own goodbye. He had baptized me as a three-year old, merry-eyed, hands smelling of cigarettes. And here I was, attending the burial of the woman who had been my mother—so calm, so unemotional. Dad should be proud. And then it was over.

Dad nodded to a few people as he moved towards his car; moved with the urgency of a man underwater who was running out of oxygen, trying to reach the surface before panic set in.

And then I heard my name and turned to find a woman very much like Margery only wearing a suit, hair freshly styled. It was Margery; dragging Andy who was clearly not interested in being there. We hadn't spoken since my return. I had stared at the phone a couple of times, but couldn't seem to pick it up.

She waved as she struggled with Andy, and, finally, stopped all forward progress to confront him directly.

Dad turned back from the Bronco, his hand on the door like a base he'd just stolen and was now safe.

"I'm done here," Dad called out, his voice on the verge of cracking, face straining against the emotion. But he bolstered himself, and climbed into the driver's seat.

Margery let go of Andy's hand and hugged me. "Bert, I'm so sorry about your mother."

"You know she's not even touching the earth? I just wish she was touching the earth. Something real you know … finally. Not fake grass. Real earth ..."

Margery gave me a considered look. "We should talk. After you've had some time. When you're ready."

She held out a card from a law firm. "I've got a work number now."

Andy did not look at me. Margery released me and was

all business, "There's been new information," Margery said. "When you're ready."

Andy shifted his eyes to me, and then away to the side. "She wasn't your real mother anyway," he said.

I was still trying to decipher his unexpected spitefulness when Margery slapped him across the face. I was stunned at the sound. Andy rebounded like a ball off a hard wall; took off running towards the cars.

"I've never struck him before," Margery said marveling at her own hand. "He's mad at me. I'm sorry …" And then she took off after him. I watched Andy open the door to a car and get in the driver's side. He started the engine as Margery ran towards the car.

She opened the door before he got it into gear and pulled him out. There was a physical struggle; he tore away and ran off down the street. She got in the car and followed.

It was me she should have slapped, slapped the numbness out of my face, my brain. And there was so much going on: Dad pulling away in the Bronco, Aunt Ellie instructing the workmen as they lowered the casket into the ground, Margery attempting to head her son off—I was unable to move towards any of them.

"… She's going in crooked," I heard Aunt Ellie say to the workers. "Get her straight ..."

Chapter 34

Quail Run

DAD WAS UPSTAIRS IN THEIR BEDROOM building a bulwark against grief with each pair of socks he took from the drawer and deposited in an orderly row on the bed.

"You left so abruptly," I said.

"The service was over."

On the mantel above the fireplace sat a white ceramic pitcher that she had painted. It was always my favorite. I broke it bouncing a tennis ball off the wall.

"Was I ten? Or older?" I asked dad.

"What?"

"That pitcher, when I broke it."

He looked at the pitcher as if he hadn't seen it in a long time, next to the china plates hand painted with ears of Indian corn, the sheaves of wheat—her strokes, her time, her effort to make something beautiful.

"You were doing something you weren't supposed to be doing."

That's right. I was old enough to know better, bouncing a tennis ball indoors. The cringe in my gut when the ball struck and I watched the pitcher totter on the shelf before it dropped, its fall partially broken by a cushion, a near miracle my heart hoped, but it bounced one more gritty, sickening time against the flagstones of the hearth and separated into three pieces.

The look on her face, her hands reaching out. It was punishment enough to watch her clutch the three pieces, not even acknowledging what I'd done, but quickly trying to fit them back together as if it were something alive and could be saved if she moved quickly enough, pressed at the right place.

"That morning at the hospital? The morning she died. Was that the morning they came to move her, take her to the nursing home?"

"Yes," he answered folding another pair of socks.

"And she knew they were coming that day to move her to the nursing home?"

"Yes, I had alerted her to the situation."

"And what did she say?"

"I can't say she was over-joyed at the prospect."

"And she was awake that morning?"

"Yes, the duty nurse had attended to her. She was a little weak, but seemed alright. But by the time the attendants arrived, prepared the gurney and went to move her she was gone."

"And she never said anything?"

"No."

"Are you sure she didn't have one of her hallucinations and was saying something, but it didn't make sense to you? Because I would like to know anything that she said, real or imagined."

"Nothing" he said with a shake of his head. "We didn't even know she was gone."

"Just slipped quietly away?"

"That's right."

"On the very same day they came to take her to the nursing home—sort of coincidence don't you think?"

"Well that's what happened. I see no further need to dwell on it."

"But she did not want to be moved, Dad. She wanted to come home."

"I could not care for her here. She's up half the night, wandering, not making sense."

"How long would it have taken? How long to let her die here instead of some nursing home?"

"I don't know. There is no way of knowing. And where were you, anyway? Off on some adventure in Hawaii?"

"That adventure started right

in this home when you told me I had a father dying from a genetic disease. That's what that adventure was about."

"Well, I did what I thought best at the time."

"I was fifteen years old! A kid for chrissakes. Telling me I was likely to die of some genetic disease? Don't have children? Do you have any idea what that did to my head?"

"I'm sure you have suffered."

"I didn't reach for anything. I didn't live! You crushed me. Dad, it was so unfeeling. Like you telling Mother that she was going to a nursing home when you knew she hated the idea. Why do you think she died the day they came to move her?"

"And were you going to take care of her?"

Unable to answer, I could only shake my head. I hadn't been there. Off looking for the other mother—lost in the riddle.

"It was a mistake," I said both to him and myself.

"We're done discussing it," he replied, anger darkening his face as he disappeared back into the closet.

He returned carrying shirts and Mother's valise, the one she had taken with her to the hospital, carry-on size in that ludicrous color—baboon-ass red. He sprung it open; her smell came out and walked the room, a ghost trailing a stale mix of the feminine apothecary: cosmetics and perfume, nail polish and sachet, bath powder and something else—something musty and female and gone.

"You're packing?" I realized as he laid the things inside the valise.

"Houston. For a few days."

"Houston? Now? "

"There is a class reunion."

"You are leaving for a class reunion?"

"Medical school."

"Oh. Why?" I asked unable to find the logic on my own.

"I want to."

"It's a little soon don't you think? Just after the funeral."

"There may not be another chance."

"When are you coming back?"

"A few days. This will all have to be sorted out," he said with an abbreviated motion that included all that surrounded us: the water colors hanging on the walls, the glazeless black pottery on the shelves, the wooden masks carved by some penniless tribe in Costa Rica. It was her sensibility that surrounded us; we just stood in the middle of it.

"You might start going through things, see what you want of your mother's. The rest goes to the church or Goodwill."

Ellie and I sat at the breakfast table. It was the morning of her departure. Dad had already made his escape. I wondered aloud why they had such a cheap yellow plastic napkin dispenser filled with those thin, practically useless paper napkin squares. Ellie interrupted my critical inventory.

"You think your father didn't love Arlene. But that's not true. He's fleeing. I've seen it before. Felt the urge myself."

Ellie placed her coffee spoon on the table, aligned it in a careful perpendicular to the yellow plastic place mat. "The fights were terrible."

"Hillard and Arlene?"

"No, no, the fights between our parents—your grandparents. When we were young," she continued. "Hillard and I could hear the two of them going at each other viciously, and we were just children. It was nigh-on to child abuse just to have to listen to that. And I think it was worse for him. He took it harder."

"She had come from a broken home," Ellie said referring to her mother Lydia. "Her mother was mentally ill and it carried a social stigma. She was ashamed of it. Of her own mother."

I recalled the sepia photograph of Lydia—a young woman when it was taken, a beauty with high cheek bones, aquiline nose, an abundance of hair elegantly coiffed; a Victorian collar rising up a slender neck and held with a cameo brooch. She gazed out with clear, determined eyes and the full curve of her lips withheld even the hint of a girlish smile.

Ellie added sugar and slowly stirred her coffee. "Mother was in her late teens when she was forced to move-in with a school friend and her family. Her own family and present condition were an embarrassment she endured, and as soon as she was old enough, she became a Harvey Girl."

"And papa was a conductor for the Katy line that ran

through Denison when he met her. He had to ask her twice to marry. She knew he was a railroad man, a solid job by the standards of the day. And he was a soft man, malleable enough to shake him of any bad habits. So they married, but it was as mis-matched a coupling as you're ever likely to see."

Ellie sipped her coffee. "First, your father was born, and then I came along, and then came the Depression, like a third thing that moved in with us. The railroad laid Papa off and he never really had a steady job after that. And oh, did she hound that man, persecuted him daily for it if not hourly: his laziness, his lack of gumption—we heard it all through those walls."

Ellie gazed out the window to the backyard as if hearing the voices again; she shook her head and continued.

"I'd go into Hillard's room, try to talk to him about it. But your father refused to discuss it. All he would talk about was the Boy Scouts, the merit badge he was working on. Mother would not let him play football even though he begged. She said he could join the scouts. But if he joined, he should excel. 'Be an Eagle Scout if you're going to join, son'. And that's what he did, methodically moved up the ranks, knocking off the merit badges until he was an Eagle. 'An Eagle Scout at fourteen' She was fond of saying. 'Not one of the other Eagles in the troop had achieved it so young'."

"She told him he would be a doctor, and whether he wanted it or not, that's what he did—Hillard became a doctor."

Again Ellie's gaze drifted out the window. "Oh, I almost forgot, there was a package delivered this morning before you were up."

Later that afternoon, after Aunt Ellie left, halfway through my third bourbon, I found my own gaze drifting out the window, staring out at the pool in the backyard when I noticed the stainless steel water bowl by the hose—the dog—was nowhere to be seen. He had gotten rid of the dog.

On the dining table, lay the package. It contained all the documents accumulated during the search: my Hawaiian birth certificate, Social Services court papers, adoption papers, Baine and Nunnie's marriage license and their divorce papers, birth certificates on both brothers, and a letter from Margery:

Dear Bert,

In my search for your biological father's death certificate I sent out a number of letters requesting information. Two days ago I received a call from Valentine, Texas—from a Baine Browford, the man listed as your biological father on all documents. Yes, he's alive! And apparently in good health. He has no symptoms of the disease. Not only has he never heard of it, he was a little miffed that he had been accused of having a disease of any kind. But he said he would be willing to talk to you. The number is attached. You should meet him.

Sorry about Andy, he's not mad at you, he's mad at me for going back to work. And the world in general it seems.

Sincerely,

Margery

PS <u>Finish it!</u>

Chapter 35

Marfa, Texas

THE CONCIERGE AT THE HOTEL PAISANO TOOK one look at me and reached for the key to the James Dean room. I was down to my Discover card and she actually took it.

The Hotel Paisano was the closest accommodation to Valentine, Texas; a dilapidated micro-town huddled against the train tracks a few miles south of Marfa. I'd come to meet my biological father or at least the man whose name appeared on the trail of legal documents that led to a gruff voice on the other end of the phone.

"*... I don't like people saying I got some disease,*" had been Baine's first words to me. And once again, I found myself playing the Ghost of Christmas Past knocking at a stranger's door.

James Dean had stayed at the hotel back in 1955 during the filming of "Giant". There was a display of memorabilia in glass cases that ringed the lobby. He hadn't been a star when he checked into the room; it was small, on the second floor and the door required a good slam. The one window was actually a skinny set of French doors that opened onto a wrought iron balcony the size of a lobster trap.

Dean's biography lay on the desk, the obligatory collection of black and white photos sandwiched towards the middle. No doubt about it, he was a beauty—squinting into the glare of his oncoming fame. The iconic image: the brooding American teenager, stranded between the big bad world and a clueless family—hair perfectly tousled. Died at twenty-four before he had to out-grow that image pound by pound like Brando and Elvis. The "Rebel Without a Cause" died alone in a car going too fast.

If Dean's life was on the desk, mine lay on the bed: a manila envelope stuffed with the documents Margery had amassed.

"Here—your biological parent's marriage certificate," she had said with the glow of a hunter hoisting a trophy. She read aloud the names, dates and locations. Then she handed it over and watched while I stuffed it back into the envelope without giving it a glance.

"Those are their signatures—their handwriting. Aren't you curious?"

But all I could see was the paper trail of a hapless passenger carried along by random events, victim of the poor choices made by those in charge.

"You were a child," Margery insisted. "You were responsible for none of this. All you are responsible for is how you deal with all this. You can either use this information to confirm your feelings of being born a victim or to get some insight into what happened—learn from it and move on."

"Move on," I said, "Like those boxes stacked in your garage?" I didn't realize how cruel it was until I saw it lodge somewhere in her chest and pull her chin down with a sigh.

In an effort to repair the moment, I began to mumble like a teenager, thanking her for her untiring work. And though I felt bad, I managed to leave the documents on her dining room table.

The Hi-Way Café had seen better days. Evidenced by the layers of paint, the previous incarnations of color that curled and flaked from its weathered exterior. Decades could be read there: a robin's egg blue period, a jazzy hot pink and a cheerful yellow era all sandwiched between dull strata of Navajo white.

"... Be stringing wire at the Hi-Way Café," Baine had answered when I asked to set-up a meeting. "Drop on by if you're in the area."

It had been a five and a half hour drive to put myself in the area, but I had to look him in the eye and ask the question. Like Margery said, I had to finish it.

Parked in front of the café was the old black panel truck he'd described on the phone, hand-painted on the side in flakey gold script: *You Phone Me, I'll Wire You!* The font done in squiggly lines like it was written in electricity. A sense of humor.

It appealed to me that he was an electrician. Back in grade school when the four elements were introduced, I always wondered why electricity hadn't made the grade. This mysterious 'thing' out there arcing across the sky; we would tap into it somehow, draw it into wires that could kill a man, tame it down, lure it into the walls of buildings, coax it into homes where it waited—snout flared and ready at the socket.

And here was a man skilled at moving that dangerous magic around, making the connections that beget all manner of light and action. *You Phone Me, I'll Wire You!* My bio dad. At least on paper.

Inside, the place was gutted. Conduit dangled. Fresh metal studs waited for the drywall stacked on pallets; a total renovation was in progress.

"Don't step on that," a voice apprehended me. When I looked down, there was a length of old wire snaking along the floor, insulation frayed.

"Never step on a wire. 'Specially with them city shoes." He was in the corner behind me bent over a coil of electrical conduit. Carefully, in my city shoes, I stepped towards him. His work boots were broken-in, worn soft as moccasins; crepe soles thin at the heels. He didn't look up.

"Is that your truck outside?" I asked.

"Afraid so," he replied still no look my way.

"We talked on the phone. Called you about maybe being … related."

"Well, I ain't got any money."

"That's not why I'm here."

He grabbed a wire coming out of an old plaster support wall and gave it a tug. A few feet slipped out then snagged. He jerked it, but it wasn't coming.

"Can I help?"

"Yeah, you can find the sumbitch that told me this was a three-day job."

He wrapped a couple of turns of the wire around his hand and leaned back leveraging with his weight. When it released all of a sudden, he stepped back to regain his balance and stumbled; my hands flew out and landed against his back to steady him.

"Damned old place, falling apart," he mumbled a little embarrassed. I realized my hands were still on him. He was nothing but sinew and bone under the flannel shirt; smaller and more fragile than he appeared. My hands dropped away as if I'd read a secret.

"Anyway ..." he stammered not knowing what else to do with our proximity, but offer me his hand, smallish like mine, but rough as if worn from use like his shoes.

For the first time he looked me full in the face. He had the raw look of fair-haired men out too long in the sun; the redness of the skin seemed to bleed up into the whites of his eyes—a sore, seen-too-much weariness. Parched camel-colored lashes blinked and the moment was done. He released my hand, reached around, tugged a bandana from a pocket, shook it out and wiped his hands.

"If I'd known they was taking you kids away I'd a come," he said studying his palms as if to glean something from the lines there. "By the time I found out, it was too late. Not a damn thing I could do to get you kids back."

Done with the bandana, he replaced it, scooped up the old wiring with one hand and began to loop it in lengths around his other hand and elbow, forming a spindle.

Encouraged by his words, I forged ahead.

"When you and Nunnie got married she was already pregnant with me?"

"Nunnie Quiipo Kukona," he said with a bemused shake of his head. "My grandmother is a Hawaiian chieftain's daughter!' I believe that was the first thing she said to me, something like that anyways perched on a stool at the Monkee Bar. Ever been to Hawaii?"

He looked over at me, and then in consideration of his own question added, "What the hell am I saying, you was born there."

I just nodded my head, less interested in sharing my recent experience than in listening to his.

"Well, I don't know about now, but it was one damn beautiful place back then. Something about the air, made your skin feel different. Probably made you crazy too. That and all the drinking."

"So you met in a bar?"

"That's what you did. If you were an airman you went to the Monkee Bar. The local girls lined up and we'd buy drinks. Nunnie was a talker. Always wanted to know where you were from. 'Tell me about New York' or 'Tell me about San Francisco'. She'd never been to the mainland, never been off the islands. Never seen snow," he paused as he wound the wire.

"One night she stood on the bar and did the hula to White Christmas playing on the juke box. And, buddy, there wasn't a dry eye in the room. It was like she took us all back home for a few minutes. Then she fell off the bar. What the hell, it was Hawaii like they say—we was all young, dumb and fulla cum, eh?"

He looked at me and grew self-conscious in the echo of his words: cum, sex, sperm equaled me—that awkward combination of offspring and stranger that stood before him. The smile faded; he renewed his looping of the wire.

"... It wasn't just that ..." he said. "Or I wouldn't have married her. Just so you know. And she already had a kid."

"Johnny?"

He nodded his head, "That's right. Little Johnny. Nunnie told me a sailor had forced himself on her. Then promised to take her to the mainland with him if she kept quiet. But he shipped out, left her with a bun in the oven. Anchors aweigh, that's your goddamn Navy."

"She caught hell from her family. Strict Mormons they were. Hard feelings all around. People got the wrong idea about Hawaiians—all that Aloha bullshit. They don't like white people. They like the dollar all right and they'll smile and put on a show, but underneath it they're angry people. Nunnie had that anger—fire in her eyes. Volcano people—everything's cool till they blow and you'd best get out the way."

"But you stayed with her."

"Well, she was pregnant. My tour was up. And I wasn't going to do like that Navy bastard done. And when things was good, we had fun. So we got hitched. Had a luau ..."

The light of a good memory flickered on his face, sputtered and went cold.

"... And then I took her home to meet the folks ..." He sighed and tossed the coiled wire on a pile of other coils; the bandana came out.

"You know I thought you were dead," I said with a lightheartedness that I hoped would give him a little breathing room.

"Some disease was it?"

"It's what killed Woody Guthrie, the folk singer. He wandered for years, not knowing what the hell was wrong with him—erratic behavior—in and out of mental institutions until they found out he had Huntington's. When he learned it was inherited, Woody realized that's why they had all thought his mother was so crazy."

"This Land Is Your Land."

"That's the guy. So I've been living my life thinking I've inherited this--"

"I told you I don't have any diseases."

"I can see that. But I was told by my father, rather my adopted father—he got a letter from an Air Force neurologist who was treating a patient dying from Huntington's, and being that it's a hereditary disease, they asked the patient if he had any children. My name came up. And he wrote that letter."

"But the patient's name was never stated in the letter. So there was no reason to assume the dying man was anyone other than the name found on my original birth certificate—your name. So in an effort to find any surviving family I began a search: letters, calls—and eventually I found you which is unusual being that you're supposed to be dead. Which also means, if you are not the guy that was dying of Huntington's that claimed to be my father—then who was he? And why did he think I was his son? Since he's dead, I'll never know. So I've come here to ask you, no strings attached, no judgments for whatever happened in the past—can you shed light on any of this? "

He shook his head in silence.

"That's one hell of a tangle. But I do believe that she, Nunnie, would have done anything to get off that island. Probably would have said anything to get away from her family. Must be hard growing up in paradise. Got to hanker for something else and for her it was the mainland."

He picked up a spool of wire, measured it by spreading his arms, then reached for a tool in his belt and snipped the length.

"What went wrong in Texas?" I asked knowing the marriage had ended after a year and nine months.

"You ever been married?"

I shook my head.

"Well, it involves more than two people I can tell you that. She got off on the wrong foot with my folks. They weren't charmed with the hula bit. Thought her a little brassy. It wasn't like she was putting on airs, she was just doing what she did. But this was Baptist Texas. I think it was too much for them to swallow at one go."

"Nunnie claimed they just didn't like her, called her names behind her back. Didn't approve of her parenting. No end to it. I tell you those Monkee Bar days was well behind us. It was all diapers, bottles and bills. And she'd be alone while I was out scrambling for work. And I was away more than I wanted to be ..."

"Anyway, I got a contract job in San Antone, had to be gone during the week. Come home every weekend. Then one week I come back a day early and there was some guy over there at the house. I had seen him before—from the base back in Honolulu—an airman, a sergeant. They was up in bed together. That broke it."

"Do you remember his name?"

"No, I don't. So I filed for divorce and stayed in San Antonio until it was finalized. The next thing I know is you kids had been taken by the county. Nunnie's no where to be found. And there's nothing I could do."

"Do you think you are my father?"

"Well, I think so, Bert."

Something shifted in me when he said my name, an involuntary movement in the organs. He had said my name before. I had heard him say it before. He must have held me as an infant, looked into my eyes, said my name.

"Yes, I think I am or I wouldn't have married her," he confirmed, and then seemed to drift off on another memory.

"But in the divorce papers you claimed none of the children were yours."

"Lawyers. I did what they told me to get it done and over with."

"Would you be willing to take a blood test?"

"I told you I don't have no disease."

"No, it's a test to see if you are my father."

"You doubt what I'm saying?"

"No, but it's a way of being sure. Of knowing for sure that I'm free of this thing."

"Well, I don't know. How much it cost?"

"Nothing. I'll pay for it," And I reached out my hand, grasped his to seal the deal and said, "Thanks, Dad."

Chapter 36

Marfa, Texas

NOT SURE HOW MANY TIMES THE STOP-light had changed when the milkshake exploded across the windshield. But I had been idling at Marfa's main intersection for some time, waiting for the road signs to speak to me.

The electrician never showed. I passed by the Hi Way Café a dozen times. No truck. A paint crew didn't know him. No answer at his number. Nothing. I never should have called him 'Dad', even if I was half-kidding; it had scared him off. And the blood test spooked him. Played that card too soon. Should have waited, let him warm up to me. Instead, I rushed it like every damn thing I do.

And when I told him about my adopted father being a doctor—something changed in him—a shift in skin color, tension in his body—as if I'd accused of him of being less than he could have been and he half-suspected it was true. And then his comment, "Well, I guess you done pretty good for yourself then."

"I didn't do anything. It's where I landed," I said. But that didn't seem to help matters. He went cold.

So there I was in Mother's car. The manila envelope stuffed with the documents from my search bulged on the passenger seat. The stoplight blinked through another sequence. And the road signs still pointed out different directions to get to nowhere. The street to my left dead-ended at the Marfa county courthouse. It was massively over-renovated and seemed loudly out of place, even self-conscious about its presence in such a small town. Like Arlene, the building seemed to be trying too hard, over-reacting—puffed up to compensate for insecurities. Had there been no wisdom for her in the end? Was she ever finally comfortable inside her own skin? And if I had been there that last morning would she have said something to me before she died? Something I could take forward with me? And what could that have possibly been? To childishly think that things might miraculously be transformed at the hour of death. That my mother would turn and say, 'I love you'? Is that what it comes down to in the end—we all want a Hallmark card? For my part, I just wanted to tell her she mattered. And to thank her. That's when the car honked behind me. Followed by the squeal of impatient tires as it pulled around, and then, as it passed, the thud of the milkshake exploding across the windshield.

Honking I understood. A raised finger, okay. But throwing a milkshake on my dead mother's car? Completely unacceptable.

My lack of direction evaporated under the heat of sudden purpose. Dispense with all the head noise, the mewling, and the questions. Always the questions. And get busy with vengeance! Catch the motherfuckers who had thrown that milkshake. On my mother's car!

Pedal to the metal; the animal thrill; the sluice of adrenalin opens and all considerations are washed aside in the heart-thundering chase. And though visibility was restricted by the smear of the milkshake, I kept it firmly on the floor. Flicked on the wipers, squeegeed the mess around; peeked through curved patches at the road, the car up ahead gaining distance. They were running, fleeing the scene. Coals on the fire!

I started to gain on them. Closing in, their tail lights swelled through the murky glass. Flashed the hi-beams. Honked the horn. Let the bastards know—I'm coming!

They sped up. If they wanted to drive fast, fine with me—I would drive faster. They think I give a fuck? I don't give a fuck. They think they can just do things to people and not expect some payback? And what was I going to do? Something. I didn't know yet. But I would punish them.

They were in my sights—a Lexus SUV. Some pudgy, golf-shirted rich prick sitting high in the saddle. Probably a doctor. I flashed my lights, laid on the horn. His brake lights flared. He slowed. I swerved around him into the passing lane. Riding alongside, I rolled down my window and yelled, "Hey, asshole, I want some fries with that shake!"

There was a woman in the front. He probably threw the milkshake to impress the bitch. What fun, throw a milkshake at the guy at the intersection. They continued to slow, dropping back. But I stayed right next to them in the other lane. Herded them like a dog, nipped at their heels with little swerves and feints until I convinced them to move off onto the shoulder.

As they slowed to a stop, I decided to block him off so they couldn't pull away. I skidded past them and turned sharp to the right. A little too fast—dodged the mesquite bush, but there, popping up like an old memory, was the telephone pole. The nose of the Mercury bit into the pole. I'd wrecked my mother's car. Again. And it was all their fault.

I'd bring that to their attention too. But first, I needed something in hand. Something threatening. In the back, on the floor were two blue dumb-bell looking things. Made of foam rubber. Some kind of a floatie-weight for swimming pool exercises. No matter. They didn't know that. They had their hazard blinkers on. Good idea as I rolled out of the crippled Mercury, a dark cloud of rage moving towards them wielding a blue floatie weight.

"That is my dead mother's car!" I gestured to the smeared windshield, steam rising from under the hood like a slow moving ghost taking its leave.

"Clean it right now! Or I will put a major fucking dent in your Lexus!"

The man behind the window was engaged in an animated discussion with the woman, who seemed to be talking to someone in the back—Holy Fuck! There was a kid in the back seat.

The man rolled the window half-down, said, "We had no idea he threw it. I don't think he meant to hit your car. I am very sorry."

The woman leaned towards me, across the driver, pleading, "He spilled the shake in the car. I just told him to get rid of it. I did not tell him to throw it out the window. He knows better—don't you!" She said with a turn back to the boy.

"Very sorry, very sorry," the man repeated. "Are you all right?"

"… My dead mother's car …" I tried to bellow, but the righteous anger was fizzing away like the steam from the car.

"… Tell the man you're sorry," the mother prompted the kid.

And down came the tinted rear window to reveal the flushed face of a chubby ten-year old.

"Sir, I'm sorry, sir."

Sir, he called me twice, like some cowering new guy back in military school. Then the kid clambered out, shirt marked with an oblong milkshake stain, head hung low as he shuffled towards the hissing car. His mother called him back to get a box of Kleenex. He turned and shuffled back flushed with humiliation; took the box of Kleenex.

"Wipe it good now," admonished dad.

"I can't believe he tossed it out the window," Mom said. "You know better!" she called out to him as he swabbed at the sticky goo, steam wafting around him.

"I don't know if that car is going to drive," dad said.

"It won't come off," the kid whined. Sheets of Kleenex had stuck to the windshield in fuzzy puffs. I walked over to him.

"That's okay. You just did a dumb thing. Believe me, what I did was much worse." The kid stood blinking, wondering what to do next. I resisted the impulse to hug him. "So forget about the windshield, that's fine. Really. "

"What's with the floatie weight?" the kid asked. There it was still gripped in my hand.

"Good question." I motioned the kid away from the car with the floatie weight. He slumped back to the Lexus and climbed in. Then they all looked at me in a frozen tableau: anxious family staring back at the nut who forced them off the road.

Inside the car the manila envelope of documents was on the floor where it had fallen. I reached in, grabbed it and left the floatie weight on the seat.

"Sorry," I muttered as I approached their car. "I overreacted, you know it's my mother's car, she just passed away. And ..."

"We are very sorry for your loss," the woman said wanting to help me along.

"Can we give you a ride to a service station?" The man offered. And the woman forced her head up and down in agreement with her husband.

"Hop in. It's the least we can do," he confirmed.

It was warm in that car. I had smelled it when the kid opened the door; he had been wrapped in it when he clambered out, exuded it like a forgotten perfume—human warmth. I knew what I wanted: to get in, climb into that warmth; be with them—a family. I sat in the back next to the kid. Things got quiet as we pulled onto the highway.

"What's that," the kid asked eyeballing the manila envelope.

"Never mind that, Noah," Dad said.

"And no milkshakes for a month." The mother added.

"No, please don't do that," I pleaded on the kid's behalf. In response to his question about the envelope. "It's my spoor," I replied.

"Spoor?"

"The trail left by a wild animal, foot prints, droppings … evidence."

"And what did we say about choices?" Mom continued to work on the boy. "Thinking before we act?" The kid shrugged his shoulders and stared out the window knowing as I had known at his age that the lecture would end sooner if you kept your mouth shut.

"Well, I made a pretty poor choice myself," I confessed out loud. "And I apologize for forcing you off the road. I thought I had been attacked or something and my mother's car …"

"Of course. Your recent loss. No need to explain. We understand completely." She was a dirty blonde with a cheerful bouffant puff that rose up behind a hedge of determined bangs.

"… But if I had caused a terrible accident. What if you'd flipped the car?"

"Oh, not this car. It's as stable as they come," Dad reassured us with a pat on the steering wheel. "Riding on a new set of Michelins."

"But, if I had hit you instead of the stupid telephone pole … your car rolls … the boy gets thrown from the back seat—the door flies open! He could have been killed. You see it on the news; ruined lives. The parents lose a child. They never recover. Grow apart. Divorce. Live lonely medicated lives. Maybe an eventual suicide. All because a thoughtless mistake, made by a child, gets blown out of proportion. A milkshake road rage perpetrated by a maniac looking to get even with a world he feels wronged by— classic!"

The car got quiet and I realized my voice had gotten a little loud. The mother seemed frozen in her seat as if waiting for a blow to fall.

"Well, fortunately, that was not the case," said Dad. "All safe and sound."

"This is not the first time I wrecked my mother's car," I turned to the boy. "This has all happened before. Years ago when I first got the news about my condition. Won't bore you with the details of a rotting brain except to say—it has haunted me. And here I am fifteen years later and the guy that's my father—the one that's supposed to be dead—surprise. He's alive! And he won't even take the test so I can stop obsessing about losing control of my body, dying—all that crap. And if he actually *was* my father and this whole thing has just been one huge fucking mistake, and then what am I supposed to feel—relieved? Ok. Well, what about all the wasted years? Buried alive under a piece of misinformation. I feel cheated is what I feel. Like that fifth button business that sent Johnny over the edge ..."

I knew this was not having the desired effect on my listeners. The father kept checking me in the rearview mirror. The mother stared straight ahead, her shoulders shaking almost imperceptibly.

"Please don't hurt us," she blurted with a shudder. The boy was staring at me eyes wide, sweat beaded on his face.

They had offered me assistance and not only had I succeeded in spilling my guts, I had completely terrified them. Time to leave before I left my mark on them. Immediately or something bad would happen.

My fingers through the door pull, "I'm really very sorry." And to the boy, "Tell her you love her, no matter how mad she makes you. One day she will be gone and you will miss her."

I opened the door—the thrum of asphalt under tires—the father said, "... Hold on ..."

He was slowing, but I was already out the door. Even though I found the softer ground off the shoulder, the impact was harder than expected; got a mouth full of grass and dirt for my trouble, but my front teeth survived the impact. However, when I hit, I let go of the manila envelope. It burst open spilling the contents; all the legal documents—the paper trail from hopeful beginning to disastrous ending blowing down the road like so much litter.

He managed to stop the car about forty yards past me. Huddled in the shell of their car, they stared out at the half-mad, feral thing I'd become there on the side of the road spitting grass and dirt; the scattered papers trailing in their back wash.

"Go on," I yelled. "I'm fine!" I waved at them, not just waving them off, but also in a benediction—blessing them as a family in their car traveling; good luck and good health, I wished them. And patience with each other. Good people. Go on. And be happy. Go on.

It was near dusk when I noticed most of the cars that passed me were pulling off the road up ahead and parking. A gathering. Wood smoke was in the air. The flames of a bonfire came into view. A sign stuck on the road side read: *MARFA LIGHTS VIEWING AREA*. Parked cars lined both sides of the road. A woman with a braided hank of gray hair walked by wearing a tee-shirt that said *Abduct Me Now*. Her weathered face crinkled into a smile "It's a clear night. They'll be coming in," she looked up at the sky.

"Who?" I asked.

"Them," she said and her eyes flared with a twinkle.

Chapter 37

The Gathering

"THEY ARE FAR ADVANCED BEYOND OUR way of being, beyond war. We are like children to them, just learning to read."

I nodded and kept walking through the organic collection of travelers that pulled off the road in their trucks and RVs. Bushy bearded and balding hippies; their fading youth gripped with rubber bands twined round meager remnants of pony tails. Snow bird couples grown plump in their RVs, driven south by winter, mingled with a cadre of squinty-eyed desert rats, drop-outs, misfits, true-believers and the just curious come to build a bonfire, spread blankets, sleeping bags and beach chairs; nurse thermoses and tend coolers, their gimme caps tilted against the dying sun.

"Marfa lights," cackled a half-naked man all elbows and body hair, a watch cap snugged to the gables of his wild eyes. He talked over-loud to anyone near. Cheerful and half-mad or off his meds—no one seemed to mind; a stitch in the human fabric that spread out in a semi-circle from the anchoring fire.

An evening breeze freshened, pushed the temperature down and drew me closer to the bonfire. My body opened like a sail, hoping to capture warmth. Nearby, a ruddy-faced couple, territory staked with camp chairs and cooler, swaddled in lap blankets, grinned at nothing. She glanced up at me and I thought I might be blocking her view of whatever it was they were expecting to see.

"Sorry," I mumbled and shifted away.

"Sorry for what?" she crowed through an absent incisor, the other teeth folding in as if to fill the gap. "Sorry is for might-a-beens and shoulda-dones. This is the right here stuck in the right now. Have some grape juice, re-fucking-lax."

I must have looked tense and was in fact concerned how much listening I'd have to pay in return for the cup being proffered.

"... Go on, one won't kill you unless it was meant to be your last."

"Believe me, I done the research," her man gave his belly a pat. She re-capped the jug. I took a sip as a white-haired woman sidled near; slim-legged in faded denims and dusty boots, a beaded leather bag slung across a worn buckskin coat, expensive once. The mellowed straw of a cowboy hat crimped and fitted around her face crinkled by desert sun. A saddle blanket rolled under her arm, she looked to be edging gracefully into her sixties. But a younger light shone out from blue eyes lively and amused as she unfurled the blanket and eased down upon it side-legged and settled as if posed for a painting.

Around me, the gathered faced westerly where the sun melted like a gold coin behind Chinati peak. The bonfire leapt with vigor at the sudden loss of competition.

"So what are the Marfa lights?" I mused to no one in particular.

"Different things according to different folks," answered the white haired woman on the blanket in a dreamy voice. "Conventional theory is UFOs," her left hand gestured as an alien craft might hover on the horizon and revealed a stump where her ring finger had once been. What had she suffered?

"Un-identified Freak Outs," burbled the grape-juice husband. His wife elbowed him with a hoarse chuckle.

"So no one really knows?"

"You know if they start following you down the road," said the husband. "You may not know what exactly, but you do know something's on your six."

"Yep, not like they are big explainers," nodded his wife. "But they do let you know they're around. That's what they're doing. Letting us know. 'You are not alone'," she added in a deepened voice and cackled until she coughed, and then oddly dainty, dabbed at her mouth with a clean handkerchief.

"Kind of nice knowing that," said the woman on the saddle blanket. She snugged her buckskin around her, gazed into the fire. "Whatever they are, people seem to like gathering here and doing this." She patted her blanket with the nonchalance of one long used to being alone. "Sit if you like. This ground gets cold."

But I felt myself held in check, waiting for some proselytizing: a leaflet announcing a meeting, or a petition making the rounds. But none came. The people just stared into the fire or up at the sky as night darkened around them. The gathered were anchored with a quiet expectation and whether they were true believers or just beautiful messes in need of diets and dental work, health plans and haircuts, even homes for some. Yes for some, I could not tell. And as to what they waited for—the aliens? The "them" up in the sky—who were they really, but the dream father, the missing mother, the family that will understand you when you finally find them. Your tribe at last.

There was a tap on my shoulder. The grape juice wife handed me a sandwich in a baggie. Didn't ask if I wanted it or not. Didn't know me from Adam and didn't seem to care. The hardest part of the receiving was not having anything to give back. Maybe my taking, accepting what was offered was my end of the bargain. Maybe the sight of my face as I bit into that sandwich, tasted the tuna and egg and came to know all at once how hungry I was. Thanked them through chews and sips of grape juice grateful for the gift of chewing and swallowing.

"Come down brothers!" cried the hairy man with the watch cap. And the others answered with howls and cups raised to the night sky.

This odd man separate and yet, in the middle of it all, welcomed by the others; a part of this whole. I gave half my sandwich to the white haired woman whose blanket I shared. She took a bite and thanked me. Nodded her head to those behind. And I loved her right then, loved her white hair and crinkled face, the sweet young blueness in her older eyes, wanted to kiss her stump of a ring finger.

Another communal yelp rose as a log was tossed onto the fire and a shower of sparks released upwards to spirited applause. Their crazy desperate hunger for something outside ourselves, something bigger than we are. Smarter. Better. The Other that can help us love ourselves again.

And then it became clear to me that the "them" they were waiting for had already arrived—it was themselves; the gathered ones warming one another, sharing a belief, a delusion, or maybe just a bonfire, a sandwich and the mystery of a night sky. It made them a community.

Them. And *who* am I? The sum of all the events of my childhood conspired upon me? Yes, I am all of that and more. I am all the people that passed through me and more. I am those gathered here: the woman with the missing finger, the round and ruddy-faced couple who pass me drink and food while they are in need of dental work, the hairy loud guy calling out to the night to hear his tribe's response ring in his ears. I am no better nor any worse than these strangers here. I am one of them.

I could not love in the past because of an inability to see beyond what I perceived as wrong with others: their doubts and deformities; the hopes misaligned with habits—the hapless delusions. Just as I was obsessed with all I thought was wrong with me; clutching at hedonism, a frightened child gorging on the jelly beans of drugs and alcohol to dampen the terror. And, at bottom, the worst addiction of all—hating yourself.

I am all of them gathered here. And none of them. Just as this gathering is but a unique part of a larger all-encompassing whole—a history that extends behind us in time and moves forwards into an unknown. It is more than I can ever know or ever name or store up in safety. It is an ancestry beyond blood, it is the human family—each limping, individually marked and beautiful. I surrender to it. And to my destiny. To the mystery we share—the hide and seek of love losing itself as we wander in terrible darkness, only to emerge surprised anew and surrender to its own self once again. Oh, my sweet soul, there it is—if you can call it anything, call it Love.

Chapter 38

Houston

"YOUR FATHER IS HAVING SOME DIFficulties," Dr. Lois Thayer said, an old flame of Hillard's from medical school and the real reason my father had fled to Houston after Mother's funeral. Perhaps not the reason he fled so much as she was the destination of his flight.

Though delighted to see Hillard and sympathetic to his recent loss, Lois did not join in his vision of a shared future which I think was mostly about her shopping and cooking meals for him. And, of course, she was 'the one that got away' back in those salad days before he could, in his own words, "afford" a wife.

"Visibly crestfallen." was the phrase she used over the phone to describe Hillard's initial reaction, and then, in a more professional tone she summarized, "No doubt he found himself thrown uncomfortably back onto the recent loss of his wife. And I believe he suffered some sort of a stroke that night."

Dr. Thayer had told him to relax; take it easy for a day or two before returning to Odessa. He agreed. She left to shop for dinner and returned to find Hillard in the guest room, pajamas on, back in bed. She entered the room and asked if he was feeling well. He opened his eyes and asked, "Is it time for breakfast?"

It required immediate action on my part, or at least a statement to Dr. Lois Thayer of what I intended to do about my father. All I could manage over the phone was, "Thank you very much, I'll check my schedule and get right back to you ... thank you."

She responded with an excruciating pause and said, "... We'll be waiting."

Petrified, I immediately called Aunt Ellie, explained events and asked her what I should do.

"Go see him," she said calmly.

"But I don't know what he needs or how to take care of him."

"He's your father. You will know what to do."

Dr. Thayer was a handsome woman with a bohemian flair; a colorful scarf wrapped around her head, gold hoop ear rings—just the type that would be bored to tears with Hillard.

"Hullo," he said surprised to see me. I wasn't sure if he couldn't remember my name or just wasn't interested in taking the conversation any further.

"I'll get his bag," Lois said and stepped away, polite but ready to get rid of him.

"Where have you been?" Dad asked while we waited for her return; the harshness of our last encounter apparently forgotten.

"Doesn't matter," I said. "I'm here now."

"Oh," he said. "Where did ..." And then he paused to find the word. "... the, uh..."

The word had snagged somewhere in his brain and could not complete the journey to his mouth, "Oh, hell," he said with a shake of his head. "... Never mind."

"Here it is," Lois entered carrying Mom's red valise. She handed it off to me and patted Dad on the back.

"You get to feeling better, Hillard," she said. "I want to see you at the next reunion."

"Okay," he said. "I'll see you there." He smiled cheerfully, but remained seated.

"Okay, Dad, let's go," I put my hand out. He looked at it and then took it. I pulled him up, took him by the elbow. Lois waited until the last moment to open the front door to the wall of humidity banked outside. He stared out the door, the pulse of the cicadas rose in the wavering heat.

"Where do we go from here?" he asked as if we were setting out on an expedition through uncharted lands.

"Home," I said.

"Okay," he nodded and we shuffled toward his Bronco. While I put his bag in the back, he opened the front door and got in the driver's seat. He was looking around for the keys, "I'm driving, Dad."

"That's all right. I'm fine. What did you do with … the uh …" Again he searched for the word, but it wouldn't come.

"I have the keys, Dad. I'm driving the car."

"This is my car, I paid for it and I'm going to drive it," he said in a blush of defiance.

"Not until you see a doctor and he says it's all right for you to drive."

"I am a …" The word wouldn't come.

"Doctor."

"Yes. And if I say it's … all right, now let's have the…."

"When another doctor besides yourself says it's all right you can drive. But until then I am driving."

"You don't know … where you're … going."

"That may be true, but we've got a map and I'll get us there. So if you would, please get into the passenger's seat and let's get this done."

"Who are you to tell me? I had a successful practice for…"

"For thirty years."

"… Performed …"

"… Many prostate surgeries."

"I served in the war..."

"You were a Major."

"What have … *you* done?"

"I pray I haven't hurt anyone."

Dad blew a razz berry at this—a childish, mocking gesture I had never seen him use before.

"Okay, Dad, let's cut the shit! I didn't come here to humiliate you. You've done a lot of great stuff, but this is *not* about that. Something has happened to you. A stroke or something. We don't know how extensive. But it has impaired you. And it is outside of your control. Mom's gone. It's just you and me now. We are all we've got. I'm your legal son and believe it or not, I am grateful for that, more than words can say. But I am driving us home in this car. After that, we will see. So please, humor me, Dad and let's get out of this poor woman's driveway."

He held the steering wheel in his hands, internally coming to some assessment, sorting himself like a horse before it takes a jump.

"Okay … but when we get home I want the … "

"Keys."

"My keys."

Aunt Ellie came to help settle him in. As wars make heroes, she was inspired by disability in others. And though I wrestled with all the questions about how I was supposed to take care of him or even if I could—all those questions seemed to dissolve around Ellie.

"One simply does what needs doing. When that's done, move on to the next thing."

She promised to return and give me time away when I needed a break. She also suggested that additional care could be provided for by his generous medical plan and that I should make full use of it.

"He's got plenty socked away. Don't worry."

Reassurance was her gift to me; a simple trust in my ability to do the right thing. He was my father. I was his son. He needed care. I would stay and help him.

Chapter 39
Home

I STAND IN THE LIVING ROOM OF MY FATHER'S house. A rectangle of sunlight falls through the window, slants across the coffee table and warms the beige carpet under foot. The National Geographics, Mother's double deck of playing cards and a heavy glass ashtray are at the ready. Having just awakened from a nap, I could be fifteen years old. Or three. It seems equally the same time in this domestic patch of sunlight; the same vague expectation, a hopefulness tempered with suburban tedium. A lawn mower drones somewhere in the neighborhood, testifying to the world of daily chores, of schedules and responsibilities. There are things to be done. And I am not a child anymore. I am, as much as any of us can be, in charge of this day, trusting as we must, that it will fold into the next.

Margery called out from the threshold of the open door. Andy at her side, they formed a single shape, a human skyline that lifted my heart. Friends. Andy stepped forward, cued by an unseen hand and hugged me in a limp kid-like way. I patted him on the back, too embarrassed by my sudden happiness to attempt speaking. It was the old way of thinking, as if I didn't deserve happiness—the giddy lightness of it—you must give up the shadow to wear it.

"A bargain Cabernet?" a bottle of wine in her large hands. The sway of her dress, a touch of color on the lips—she was a different woman from the armored cab driver, the lone mother bewildered by her loss.

She glanced around, "So how is he?"

"He keeps buying the same novel," I gestured to various locations about the room where copies of the same colorful book lay.

"Does he read it again?"

"Yes. We go to the store, get the ice cream, the pie, the meat and he picks out the same book. Maybe it's the color."

Margery picked one up, "... Or the thickness—lots of words—a good deal?"

At first, I had protested, "You've already read that one." I said to him when he picked it out a third time. But then why shouldn't he read the same book again and again? People listen to the same song; I've watched Clint Eastwood kick the same bully in the balls more times than I care to admit. As for buying it repeatedly, well, it's not like Dad couldn't afford it. If he likes buying that book, let him buy it. He so rarely treats himself.

"Is it any good?" Margery asked.

"I don't know. Take one home. Take two," I said grating nutmeg into the moussaka. It was the old recipe, written in Arlene's hand; well-shaped and consistent letters. Arlene, whose last companion may well have been the one that lived spitefully in her imagination—the Girl in the Blue Dress. I hoped not; hoped Arlene had passed peacefully, released from that feeling of never being enough. She whispers to us all, the Girl in the Blue Dress, at one time or another. Let her prattle, you'll never catch me buying her another drink.

"Maybe we should start a book club," Margery said with a wry grin and lay the book back on the table. That too was new. Margery had a sense of humor.

I placed the moussaka in the oven; got a soda for Andy while Margery opened the wine. She poured two glasses. A toast.

"To finishing," she said and raised her glass.

"And beginning," I added. We clinked and sipped.

"So what's the plan?"

I nearly cringed at the word "plan"; facing the future with some kind of organized visualization that did not include my early demise. In a sense, I actually had the disease, or at least addled myself with alcohol and drugs to the point where I may well have induced a brain disorder; conjured it up into my nerves—an outward and visible sign of an inward and spiritual break. It had left marks, but who can say they have really lived without getting a few?

And there are moments when I regret the squandered years.

But then I'll look at the way the wind moves through the leaves of a tree and forgive myself—forgive the world.

"What's his name?" Andy called out. The boy and the dog warily stared at one another waiting for the first move. The kennel employees seemed relieved to return the animal.

"Call him what you like. Dad, calls him 'dog' so I think it's wide open."

"How about Balthazar?"

"The wisest of the wise men? Why not. Tomorrow we get a tag, but you have to spell it."

I called out to the patio, "Dad, the dog's name is Balthazar."

My father sat in the wrought iron rocker, highball in hand, head cocked intently toward nothing.

"You better ask your mother," he replied automatically. "Oh, never mind ..." He took a sip, checked his watch. My father remained the man designed by his mother, the frugal doctor, rocking on the patio in Odessa, bourbon snug in his lap, wondering where he left himself behind. I assumed that he loved me and also accepted that he would never say it.

"Let me help," Margery said as if she could do anything other than help; it must be a gene thing—the urge to help.

"Music," I suggested, "Turn on some music."

The boy tried the name out. "Balthazar," he repeated. The dog barked and the boy grew bolder, reached a tentative hand out to the dog and scratched his chest. He took a risk and the unknown became known.

I reached out into the world to find my story, and in turn fling this story out to you as Maui cast his fishing line—this sinuous braid, this language of our ancestors that we throw back and forth to one another that binds and connects us; that makes us feel less alone. Maui's myth is for each of us. Be brave, cast your line, and pull from the depths the needed thing—it will be you found wriggling on the end of that hook. You, held alive in your own hands.

—The End—

Appendix of Lies

This is, for all intents and purposes a memoir. But facing one's own weaknesses, mistakes and out and out bad behavior is not easy—it is painful and humiliating: the astoundingly poor choices, the embarrassing incidents. So I changed my name. Then I changed the names of the people closest to me. And then I started to alter things because, well, you simply have to for narrative effect. It actually made it easier when *Bert* did it or said it. And watching from this imposed distance, I forgave Bert a little more than I would myself and therefore, I continued to write. When I got to the end, I realized that there was way more truth in these pages than not. You will see, and perhaps judge for yourself what really matters in the end.

Here then is a list of embellishments, exaggerations, a few stretchers and some flat out lies that adorn, inflate and concentrate this story:

Did I set myself on fire? Let's say I regularly got 'lit'. In fact, one night I was with a gathering of friends, one of those indulgent evenings that went on and on. One friend, an artist, I caught sketching me on the back of an envelope. It was in black ink, my face a frenzy of black strokes that flared off the edge of the paper. "You're on fire," he said, "Burning from the inside out—all heat and ash …" So setting myself on fire became a metaphor for a conflagration that was consuming me internally. I lied.

No one was immediately killed in the car accident at the military academy. One cadet did lose his hand and another died years later from hepatitis in the blood transfusion he received as a consequence of the accident; the third could not drive a car for many years. They never returned to the academy.

The demise of the military academy was a combination of things, but the final blow was delivered by the growing number of disgruntled cadets who fomented a general strike the year after I left. And, yes, I played an active role in shaping the stake they drove into the heart of that cruel and defunct system.

The brother I call Johnny did not jump from the Pali. But he did hurl himself into a whiskey bottle and has yet to emerge, therefore and unfortunately, he is lost to us. We do have his true story of the Fifth Button.

Johnny's funeral was, in reality, for a distant relative that had died while I happened to be in the islands. Since I did not know the relative, I took the occasion to mourn Johnny's broken state and my other siblings who suffered neglect and an early abandonment.

I did not meet my birth mother in Butte, Montana. I've never been to Butte. I wanted to go to Butte, but she beat me by practically showing up on my doorstep in Los Angeles. And yes, it was to help her current son break into show business.

I never got a tat in the lava tubes. I wish I had.

My biological father I never met face to face. We spoke over the phone. What I've written is based on the information that he imparted and the emotional footprint left from that conversation.

Margery is not one woman, but a composite. Among the kind and generous souls merged into one character, there is the very real and tenacious woman who assisted in my search and did some major hand holding. If you are interested in her services I will pass along her information.

I have a younger brother and an older sister from my adopted family. Out of respect for their privacy and in the interests of good relations, both have been spared an appearance in this book. They are loving and generous people. Though fate brought us together, they are my family beyond blood and in the truest sense of the word. I am blessed to have them.

In an effort to deliver a vivid experience of my emotional journey to the reader, the imagination was given free rein—events heightened and time compressed. For obvious reasons names have been changed, places relocated and scenes altered or invented. But the circumstances of my adoption, the history of my adopted parents along with the specter of Huntington's disease and the resulting search for my gene pool—all are true and verifiable. Cross my heart and hope to live a hundred years.

This book is dedicated to
Ronda Berkeley,
a player of the long game,
dispenser of humor, nourishment
and hard truths—an artist,
a loving friend, my wife,
my muse.

Acknowledgements:
Thanks to Dan Akst, Tom Bryant,
Charlie Peters and Leslie Ferreira—
fellow artists & colleagues in life.

Mel Green has written on such seminal television series as "Saturday Night Live" and SCTV. After leaving SNL, he developed his popular autobiographical one man show, "Back to the Big O," produced in Los Angeles where he lives with his wife, an English Bull Terrier and a conflicted parrot.

Made in the USA
Charleston, SC
14 July 2010